JOHN CAUDWELL

LOVE, PAIN & MONEY

MY AUTOBIOGRAPHY

In the spring of 2022, my mother passed away. She was 98 years old. She had suffered a major stroke when she was 80. During these final 18 years of her life, my brother Brian and I, as well as the rest of the family, had the most wonderful time with her. Despite her suffering, she showed phenomenal spirit, incredible joy of life and was a pure delight. We did not have a traditional funeral. Instead we celebrated her life in magnificent style, with music, speeches and fun. It was a true celebration. I dedicate this book to my mother, the most inspiring person I have ever known. She was so loved by us all. She will be so sadly missed.

John Caudwell

JOHN CAUDWELL

LOVE, PAIN & MONEY

MY AUTOBIOGRAPHY

m
B

MIRROR BOOKS

MIRROR BOOKS

First published in Great Britain and Ireland in 2022 by Mirror Books, a Reach PLC business, 5 St. Paul's Square, Liverpool, L3 9SJ.

www.mirrorbooks.co.uk
@TheMirrorBooks

Hardback ISBN: 9781915306227
eBook ISBN: 9781915306234

Photographic acknowledgements:
Alamy, John Caudwell personal collection

Written with Louise Gannon.
Editor: Chris Brereton
Cover design: Rick Cooke
Production: Michael McGuinness, Simon Monk

Printed and bound by CPI Group (UK) Ltd,
Croydon, CR0 4YY.

CONTENTS

FOREWORD

Over the last forty years many friends and associates have urged me to write a book. They had seen snapshots of my life that frightened, delighted or inspired them.

The idea of a book appealed to me for a number of reasons but, quite simply, I never had the time. There always seemed be so many more pressing priorities – huge business challenges, charity, family, ill health, or a friend in personal crisis. These had a real urgency and so the book, not a priority, was not written.

Then Covid-19 happened. Suddenly, I couldn't visit my businesses. I couldn't visit family. My charity work was thwarted and there were no weddings, birthday parties and charity events. Almost overnight I found myself with time to spare, something I had not experienced for fifty years. Actually I have to say it was a shock. To not have my day filled to the brim, from early morning until late at night, temporarily left a huge void. And so it was that I chatted to my prospective biographer, Louise Gannon.

That was in March 2020, as the world was in increasing chaos. It was crystal clear to me that, even in the best-case scenario, Covid-19 was going to wreak destruction on the economy, on people's mental state and, in general, on the health of the nation. I immediately started campaigning for the government to be financially supportive of all people and businesses negatively affected by their imposed lockdown. If the government failed to take these measures, I forecast three million unemployed, tens of thousands of businesses lost forever and huge emotional and mental health problems. I introduced a very clear recovery plan for the UK economy, and it was a plan that I encouraged the government to follow. I did this via social media and direct campaigning to cabinet ministers, including the then-Prime Minister Boris Johnson, with whom I already had a relationship.

At the same time, being locked down in my beautiful 30-acre estate allowed me to start managing the people, the house and the grounds in a way that I have never previously had time to. Like many, my life changed dramatically. However, the short-lived glut of spare time did get swallowed up rapidly as a consequence of my endless campaigning for the financial and physical health of the nation, and then this book project, of course, as well as all the jobs that I had put off doing for the last few decades.

I had hours of emotional turmoil as I delved into fifty years of memorabilia, organising memory boxes for all the important people in my life. But there was even more emotional turmoil, as I relayed my story to my wonderfully probing co-writer, Louise.

I have been incredibly honest in its writing. I have constantly corrected even the most minor detail, to be as truly representative of the facts as possible, while trying to minimise the hurt that anybody might experience as a result of my stories. I have also been very happy to take my own mistakes and follies on the chin, to take responsibility for them and to take the blame.

*****

THE PRESS OFTEN portrays me as a 'glamorous billionaire'. While that might be true, when you really know me you realise quickly that is one of the last descriptions you would use. My story is about fighting, about hardship, about challenge, about trauma. And yes, it is also about success, about wealth and about glamour. Above all else it is about love, friendship and trying to help people be the best that they can be.

I have never been into politics. In fact, there are many aspects of the politician that I despise. Yet because of my vision of Covid-19's effect on the economy, I found myself constantly campaigning in the media and directly with the government to encourage the right behaviour on their part, in supporting people and businesses throughout the pandemic. I wanted the government to think about building a much bigger, stronger and better post pandemic Britain by adopting my CPR (Caudwell Pandemic Recovery) plan.

The centrepiece of this concept is to build an enterprise zone, that would become the Silicon Valley of environmental technology. This would eventually become a huge industry exported all over the world, helping Britain's GDP, at the same time as helping to save the world from the impending environmental catastrophe. I write this with passionate hope that this will be the case, allowing Britain to prosper and, simultaneously, become a fairer society for all, looking after the poor, the aged and the infirm.

Towards the end of 2020 I also became painfully aware of the three million people who call themselves 'excluded' or 'forgotten'. So I found myself with yet another campaign, this time trying to persuade the government to support these people who had fallen through the cracks of the system.

At the time of writing the government is still insisting that these people are being appropriately helped. I really believe that is not the case and that the government, for whatever reason, is choosing to ignore their existence. There are many heart-breaking cases that I have become aware of and I find it very difficult, as a humanitarian, to accept what is happening. This seems to be a constantly repeated theme of mine, since I have been outraged many times in recent years by the neglect that Lyme Disease patients suffer through the NHS. It is the same story for children with PANS/PANDAS and autism. We can, of course, only do so much within our budget constraints, but often I feel that so much more should be done for certain categories of people.

There is a great deal about the world that I would love to change. I do believe in the capitalist model and low tax regimes, but I just wish I could influence more rich people to pay all their taxes, as appropriate, and to join The Giving Pledge and commit to donating at least 50 percent of their wealth to charitable causes during or after their lifetime. These two acts alone would start to address the rather disastrous rich-poor divide in terms of wealth and income.

For about 35 years now I have been talking about our toxic planet and the effects of fossil fuels. The world never seems to respond aggressively enough on these issues, probably for fear that it will cause a small reduction in people's standard of living. I do fear that we have left it too late, and I form this conclusion from many years of studying the loss of arable farm land, the reduction of available water supplies, the warming of the planet and the consequential loss of the polar ice caps, the rising of sea levels and the loss of further arable farm land from the result of flooding the low-lying areas. For instance, scientists don't tell us that the polar ice reflects most of the sun's rays and that sea water absorbs most of them, so causing an exponential rise in water temperature. In addition, we have increasingly toxic food, toxic air and enough plastic to build our own Mount Everest.

Many people, especially through social media, have called for me to be Prime Minister. While in many respects this would be my worst nightmare, I also know I would make decisions that were for the benefit of the people, for the country and the environment. At the same time I know that I would have to play the political game of doing what was required in order to win, rather than necessarily doing what I knew was right. So I feel that I am destined to stay on the sidelines, as a lobbyist trying to improve the world in whatever small way I can.

*****

SOCRATES SAID, 'A life unexamined is not worth living.' On this basis my life would be hugely worth living. I have constantly questioned myself every day of my 70 years, but never more so than throughout the pandemic – which created a time for all of us to reflect.

The greatest accolade for any human being, I have always felt, is the way that they bring up their children; raising them to be humanitarian adults, who make the world a better place. It seems that every year I feel more strongly about the contribution that my family makes to society. But, even more strongly, of my own personal contribution.

I find myself puzzling over rich people who won't join The Giving Pledge, over rich people who don't want to pay their reasonable share of taxes, of people that are generally selfish rather than considering others. I find myself preaching kindness, though I know at times I am unkind and definitely no angel, that is without doubt. Equally, without doubt, I do fight for the underdog, I do hate unfairness and I do want the world to be a better place.

I have just watched a Netflix series on the history of Hitler, which has caused me – yet again, for the thousandth time – to try to comprehend the cruelty that occurs regularly within history against humanity. How could the German regime cruelly and vilely murder six million Jews, men, women and children? And yet this sort of intense cruelty has been a feature of mankind since the beginning of history.

One of my greatest beliefs is that we should teach kindness in schools as a subject, and that could cover lots of illnesses or conditions or characteristics that cause children to bully other children from an early age. It could cover the many different characteristics of autism, PANS/PANDAS and other neurological problems, as well as ginger hair, freckles, and any one of the hundreds of characteristics that can cause somebody to be singled out for attack. Kindness needs to be endemic in our childhood. It should be practised by all, in order to become the go-to behaviour. That way, racism would disappear, along with all other prejudices that are held by ill-educated human beings. (At the time of writing, I have a Ukrainian family living with me. As you would expect, they have been left distraught by the events unfolding in their homeland. For my part, I need to do a lot more, and I remain incredibly frustrated and angry that one man can cause such devastation to innocent democratic people.)

The objectives of my book are manyfold. I want people to be inspired to believe in themselves and to realise that they can fight adversity and win. To achieve this I want people to see the real John Caudwell. I want the book to be successful, since all the proceeds will go to charity. I want people to see that my life has been a complete battle, from birth right through to present day. I want people to see that no matter how life conspires against you, if you have your health then you can fight against any bad luck that comes your way, and turn every negative into a positive. This I really want more than anything. If readers say they find the book helpful, inspiring and feel motivated then I will have achieved my most important desire.

John Caudwell, August 2022

Chapter 1

HOME – PITS AND POTS

'WHY DID YOU buy that blouse? There's no money for a new blouse in this house.' [Clang of metal pots being bashed together.]

'It's just a blouse!'

'Listen to my mother, will you? What do you need a new blouse for?' [Sound of crockery breaking.]

My routine was the same, every single night. At seven o'clock, I'd be sent up to bed. No-one would come with me to hold my hand on the climb up the dark, steep stairs. No-one would tuck me into the wooden single bed that stood on bare floorboards. So I would run up the stairs, tear past the yawning black hole in the ceiling that was the attic, then jump on my bed and hide under my blankets. Under the covers I'd shiver from the cold (there was no heating in our house) and strain every sense as I listened to the words and sounds of three people arguing in the kitchen directly beneath me while they washed the dishes.

My dad, Walter, my mum, Beryl, and my grandmother, my dad's mum, Mary. My world.

Mostly what I remember of those early childhood years is living in a state of bewilderment and anxiety. Those harsh words and worrying sounds were repeated in varying permutations every week but it's all I could remember.

I couldn't sleep, not because I wasn't tired – I was absolutely exhausted from days of running around the streets of Shelton, helping my grandma with chores, throwing myself into anything and everything I could find to entertain myself, and trying to avoid getting myself into trouble with Dad.

I couldn't sleep because I was scared. If I didn't stay up listening to those horrible rows, something bad might happen. Mum and Dad might split up; I might have to move away from Grandma. I'd be that boy in school who didn't have a mum and a dad. I'd be out on the streets with my mum. And then, more shameful still, if I did go to sleep that other terrible thing might happen: I might wet the bed again, and wake up with that horrible dampness on my sheets and pyjamas; the awful dark patch spreading across the mattress like the hot humiliation flushing through my body.

'Wee-wee,' my dad called me. If he caught a glimpse of my mother with my sheets bundled up in her arms in the morning he'd shout. 'Not again, Wee-wee!' Once I went with him to a car auction in Newcastle and a friend of his came over as Dad stood inspecting a potential bargain and I stood by his side feeling very grown up to be in this busy, fascinating place.

'Who is this little lad, then Walter?' called out his friend.

'Oh, he's called Wee-wee,' Dad answered. I stood there red-faced and silent as two grown-ups laughed at my discomfort and shame. Why would this man I loved who I desperately wanted to love me back do that to me? I was mortified but I refused to allow any tears to fall from my eyes. I might wet the bed but I was never going to be called a cry-baby.

So as a child, my enemy was sleep. I needed to stay awake, and I had to think hard of ways to stop these bad things happening. I had to be tough. I had to be invincible. It was down to me to make everything better for my family.

I was six years old.

*****

A CHILD'S ABILITY to love is both endless and complex. I loved my mother, I loved my father, and I loved and idolised my grandmother, who, in her own way, loved and worshipped me. But my grandmother could not stand my mother, and the feeling was mutual. My father, who was caught between the two of them, gave his mother his first loyalty over his wife, probably because it was her who was responsible for the roof over our heads in her once rather-distinguished and now – in 1956 – rather run-down, four-bedroom terraced house on the corner of Wellesley Street in Shelton, Stoke-on-Trent. That was just how it was.

Times were tough – for every working-class family in the country, not just me and my family. Hard times make people hard. Life becomes about survival, and there's little room for niceties or special treatment in the daily grind of getting through each day and making ends meet. I was a post-war baby, the first child of a man who had come back broken and mentally scarred from a bloody, vicious war against Nazi Germany, and of a woman who was having to cope with a battle-scarred, traumatised, angry husband, a small child and a mother-in-law who couldn't stand the sight of her.

My external landscape provided the perfect backdrop to this grim household because I was born into the grit and smoke of the filthiest city in England, Stoke-on-Trent. I close my eyes and almost see my childhood in black and white.

My life today is full of colour. I have made many things better. I look out of a window in the Grade I star listed Jacobean mansion in Eccleshall that I am privileged enough to call my home, and I see a vast, vibrant, green lawn and explosions of scarlet, purple and lilac flowers.

I have a 73-metre superyacht, Titania, which I sail into vistas of the deepest blue oceans and shining aquamarine surf, and I can sit on deck and see pink, yellow and orange sunsets under indigo skies dotted with silver stars. I've seen the red brown rock of Ayres Rock in Australia, the dazzling white slopes of the Alps and the yellow sands of the Arabian desert. I marvel at natural beauty. I cannot get enough of it; the infinite colours, the infinite splendours. It is part of the reason I am such a passionate campaigner for the environment and passionate about people making the best of their lives.

Perhaps it is because back then my world was grey, dark, cold and dirty in what was known as 'smoky old Stoke'. Back in 1888, six towns – Hanley, Burslem, Longton, Stoke, Tunstall and Fenton – were linked together to make up Stoke-on-Trent. It was less of a city, more an industrial patchwork peopled by factory workers and coal miners eking out a living in either the potteries, the steel works, the Michelin factory, or one of the many collieries that dotted the area.

There were around 2,000 bottle kilns that were still going strong when I was born, each of them requiring 15 tonnes of coal to heat up to the red-hot temperature of 1,250 Celsius that is required for just one firing of those precious Staffordshire pots. Those ugly kilns – which made beautiful, highly-desirable, dainty pieces of Wedgewood, Royal Doulton, Spode and Minton – endlessly pumped acrid black smoke into the atmosphere.

Alongside them were the tall, sooty chimneys from the Shelton Steel factory and the coal mines. The air was so thick at times with soot and sulphur that when it rained it would rapidly turn into a black smog where you couldn't see more than a foot in front of you.

In 1956 – four years after I was born – the government passed the Clean Air Act 'to make provision for abating the pollution of the air'. The factories were given seven years to comply with this act, and so began the decline of the area, even though the dark smoke continued to pour from those chimneys for most of my childhood. There were certain days of the week when women could not hang out their washing, and countless other days I'd be in the backyard with my mother or my grandmother, painstakingly passing the wet washing through our old mangle, and I'd see dark spots appear on the white linen as it went between the wooden rollers.

'Soot!' I'd yell, looking up at the sky in a panic, and there would be a mad scramble. My mum would leap up to rip the washing off the line and I'd start dragging the heavy, tin washtub into the lean-to by the house, trying to shield the soapy laundry with my skinny, sinewy body and at the same time minimise the amount of pearly-grey water sploshing over the sides and onto the lean-to floor.

Then I'd have to mop up any puddles of water that had escaped and help arrange the washing, still quite wet, over chairs. Of course, if it was my mum's turn for one of these washing disasters, Grandma would bustle into the kitchen and immediately start a row. 'Of all the days to pick to do the wash, Beryl!' she'd shrug. 'I said yesterday it was going to be a bad day, and now that wet washing is going to take the varnish off the back of my good wooden chairs.' I said nothing, even though me and Grandma always used the kitchen chairs when her wash days went wrong.

My poor mother could do nothing right. Grandma waged a daily war of attrition against her. 'You've burnt the potatoes again.' 'Who was the man you were talking to outside the butchers? The whole road is talking about it!' 'John's got a bad chest again. I told you to make sure he had his vest on.'

The list of my mother's sins was endless, though in reality all she did was spend hours trying to clean our dark, dusty, unforgiving house then cook, clean and start again. She didn't have a moment to herself. Dad never stuck up for Mum. He would either join in or side with his own mum, and then ten minutes later the two of them would be fighting. There was nothing I could do. If anything, I simply made things worse.

'You've got great big scuffs on those shoes,' my dad would yell, looking down at the hard black, leather lace-ups he insisted on buying me. I hated those shoes. They were not only incredibly uncomfortable to wear, but completely impractical for running, kicking balls, climbing walls, riding bikes and all the other things I spent half my little life doing.

'We can't afford more shoes for you,' he'd snap. 'Isn't it enough we've got to keep washing your sheets?' I'd put my head down, bite my lip to make sure I didn't cry or shout back. Wait for the rage to end. 'Sorry, Dad. It won't happen again.'

It did. The very next day, and the next and the next.

Despite my plans to fix everything between my mum, my dad and my grandma, and my nocturnal vows to fix myself – largely to stop myself wetting the bed – I often made the tensions in the house a lot worse. The state of my shoes was a constant bone of contention. And so was I.

If I ran up the stairs, I was 'too noisy'. If I played with toys I was 'messing up the place'. Then there was the fact that once I started at the local nursery school, the teachers would complain about my behaviour. 'He's a bright boy but he just won't do as he's told,' they would moan. 'And he won't go to sleep at nap time.'

It was all true. I wanted to do my own thing, not be told what to do. And no-one had naps in the afternoon at my house unless there was something seriously wrong. I didn't want to go to sleep, there were other things I could be doing. The teachers were all a bit too soft for me to worry about being told off. So I continued to do my own thing.

At home, as a kid, I knew I had to keep quiet and try to look penitent when it came to my dad's extreme rages about various misdemeanours. These misdemeanours could be anything from taking one of Dad's precious tools from his tool box (even if I put them back perfectly in the exact same way that I'd found them, he would somehow know I'd had them) to coming home ten minutes late.

But out on the streets, and at school, I was a different kid – tougher, harder, always on the lookout for a dare, a joke or a way to make a few pennies. I was – as a lot of kids were then – scared of my dad but the fear that existed inside my house made me braver and more fearless when I was outside it. Perhaps because I silently resented my father's iron rule and I had no automatic respect for authority. I knew all the rules but then I'd find a way to bend them, to make them suit myself. And if that wasn't enough, I'd just break them.

I had a strong sense of fending for myself in life. I wasn't going to be given hand-outs from my dad. I'd never dare ask him for sweets or a toy. By the age of four I was trading in old toys; mine and any I could buy or beg from my neighbours. A few years later, I discovered a trick of asking for change for a three-penny bit – that rather quirky, attractive 12-sided nickel and brass three-pence coin that existed before being wiped out by decimalisation in 1971.

First, I had to find someone who wasn't well known to my mum, my dad or my grandma. Ideally, they'd be a man or woman on their own with a kind-looking face. 'Can you change my thrupenny bit for three pennies, please?' I'd ask very politely. They'd pull out change from their pockets, one or two pennies, and say, 'Sorry, lad.' Quite often they'd give me a penny because I'd look so crushed. I'd spend my spoils on sweets and – believe it or not – cigarettes. At seven I was a regular smoker. I could buy a single cigarette from the newsagent (back then they didn't really bat an eyelid if they were selling cigarettes to a kid who could barely see over the top of the counter), or I would buy cigarette papers and collect fag ends from outside pubs or shops and unwrap any remaining shreds of tobacco until I had enough to make a full cigarette. It makes me feel ill now to think I did that, but I was a full-blown street urchin.

My younger brother Brian, who was born when I was seven, remembers me initiating him into all sorts of dubious ways of entertaining ourselves for free. Brian was the apple of Dad's eye, he was dark haired and good-looking like him with an easy going confidence which was all his own. I loved him right from the start and as soon as he was able to walk and talk he was my partner in crime. We got up to all sorts of innocent mischief. Most tricky – but the most fun – was sneaking into the local cinema where I'd found a small entrance that led right to the back of the seats, and was hidden by a long, velvet curtain and unmanned by any sharp-eyed usherettes.

As the other kids lined up with their tickets, I'd tell Brian, 'Run down to the curtain when they're not looking. If you get stopped, tell the lady you were trying to find the toilet.' He'd run down and hold the curtain up. I'd wait till the usherette was busy and then sneak down after him, duck under the curtain into the cinema, and watch whatever movie happened to be playing. Genius!

Then there were those tempting wooden boats floating on the lake in Hanley Park. I'd spend a few minutes watching, waiting for a quiet moment when the boat man was having a cigarette or eating a sandwich, then Brian and I would run – heads bent, bodies low, army-style – towards the lake. 'Jump in, Brian,' I'd command, as I scrambled to untie its rope in record time. Then I'd drop the rope, hop in after him and row as fast as I could to the middle of the water.

We'd both laugh our heads off, and pretend not to hear when the park keeper started shouting, 'Oi, you two… Get back here! You've not paid for that boat!' We never got caught because, once we'd finished, we'd just jump out on the far side, push the boat back into the pond and hare off into the distance.

Occasionally there was trouble when we got back home. 'Your dad's after you, John,' my mum would tell me, as I walked through the door. 'What've you done wrong now?' I'd shrug and say nothing. What hadn't I done wrong? I knew I was for it.

I had so many issues with my dad as a kid. I did love him but it was difficult to find that love after years of living with him, constantly feeling like I was a problem, an irritation and an inconvenience. If I hadn't been a child, if there had been more communication, I would have understood that his temper, his harshness and his coldness was because of what he had been through and what his life had become. I would have had compassion for him. I would have realised the anger he so often directed towards me was his anger at the world, at himself. I would never have allowed that love to be buried under layers of fear, resentment and hurt.

*****

WALTER CAUDWELL WAS an intelligent, physically active, hard-working and ingenious man who could have had a bright future. He came back from serving with the RAF in the Second World War. He'd seen combat in Africa, the Middle East and for several years he was based at the embattled Ta Kali airfield in Malta. He returned with two medals (a silver war medal and a gold star), and the sort of mental and emotional damage which would now have been recognised as PTSD.

He was 23 when he was conscripted and 29 when he returned home to Shelton. His father, John, had died in 1941 at the age of 59 when Walter was thousands of miles away. He came home to his widowed mother, Mary, and immediately assumed the role of the man of the house.

Whatever his ambitions had been, he stayed put in Stoke, getting himself a job locally as a rep for an engineering company, taking over any repairs that needed doing on the house and putting food on the table for himself and his mum. Three years later, in 1951, he married my mother, Beryl Walsh, in a small ceremony near her family home in Birmingham. She was 28, but despite the scarcity of young men in post war Britain, mum was an exceptionally smart, attractive and cultured young lady and she had several proposals of marriage. Walter, with his quiet charisma, was the only man she really fell for.

They met just after the war ended, when she was finishing her war duties working at the Air Ministry at RAF Defford in Worcester. My dad was strong, dark and handsome in his RAF uniform and, although they saw each other quite infrequently once the war ended, her family approved of the way he'd remained at home looking after his mother.

They rarely spoke about their courtship, but once when we were all on holiday years later my mother told my ex-wife Kate that she remembered being attracted to my dad because he was 'well-spoken compared to a lot of men I knew back then, and he didn't curse'. I think that my mother and father didn't really know each other at all when each of them said, 'I do'. But back then it was the same for a lot of young couples who often rushed into marriage believing their futures would be very different to the way they turned out.

Regardless of his issues, Walter – like mum – was definitely 'a catch'. In post-war Britain many women in their late twenties and early thirties were resigned to spending the rest of their lives as what were then called 'old maids', living out their years looking after their parents. My mother had already had a glimpse of this life. In between working for the Air Ministry, she had spent months in their small family house in College Road, Perry Barr, Birmingham caring for her mother, Beatrice, who had suffered a nervous breakdown during the war.

And although my mother was deeply attached to her fragile mother,

her disciplinarian father, Harry, and her brothers, Douglas, Malcolm and David, she was very much her own person. She loved classical music, she could sing and play the piano. She was intelligent, well-educated and doubtless excited to embark on married life with my father.

For the first six weeks of my life, we all lived together in Birmingham but my dad insisted we return to his widowed mother in Stoke. Mum's life, as she knew it, came to a shuddering halt. At 100 Wellesley Street in Shelton, Grandma ruled the roost. Dad put his energy into working, bottling up his wartime demons and keeping Grandma happy. Mum found herself stuck as a cook, cleaner and general dogsbody stuck in a permanent battle zone with grandma with no-one to take her side.

Despite outward appearances, money was tight and, once I was about eight, my mother contributed to the family purse by getting a job as a general assistant in one of the local potteries. She fast became a valued worker moving from the potteries to a local tool company and when I was 13, she was employed in the Post Room of one of the local potteries – the renowned Royal Doulton factory which was built on the side of the Caldon Canal in 1882. However badly she was treated at home, at Royal Doulton my mother was greatly valued and within a matter of years she was made manager of the Post Room – no mean feat for a woman of that time.

My memories of Mum are of her forever working. I see her back turned to me as she cooked at the stove or scrubbed the floor on her knees, or washed up at the big stone sink. She had a difficult life which is what I used to think of every week when I visited her before she passed away. At her cosy home, an hour or so from my house, I would cook for her, we would watch her favourite television shows together and we would listen to classical music. I brought her flowers, talked to her about her grandchildren and – even though she was unable to speak in the later years of her life – she never stopped smiling. And that will always be my memory of my mum now. Her beautiful smile.

*****

I TRY TO remember some father-and-son moments with my dad. Maybe him kicking a ball with me, or laughing with me on his knee. I don't have any of those memories. But I also have no idea what dreadful memories of war went through my father's head. I never saw his medals. He never talked about where he went, what he did or who his companions were.

My only knowledge of my father's war is being told he'd been to Africa and the Middle East, and once he said how he'd been in a plane when the engine failed and it crashed into a tree. To a seven-year-old, the horror and trauma of that experience is merely reduced to a comic book image of a plane stuck in the branches of a tree. I didn't understand why he couldn't bear my noise, my energy and my inability to keep the shoes he bought me from the Army & Navy store in perfect condition.

But I do remember his kindness to others. There's a poignancy to it because it relates to his role as an engineer in the air force, and his instinctive ability to understand the intricacies of any piece of machinery.

My dad's real love was cars. He loved to drive, and would stop and admire any car he thought was particularly well-made. Way back, long before I started haunting the car auctions, my dad would often go to an auction and buy up a bit of a wreck and lovingly restore it.

His greatest joy, however, was to spot someone parked up on the side of the road because their car had broken down. It didn't matter where we were going or what we were doing, my dad would immediately stop, leap out of our car shouting, 'Having a bit of trouble over there?' Then he'd pull out his tool kit and, at times, spend hours taking apart an engine until he'd got the car on the road again, waving away any thanks.

'Please, you must let us give you something. You've been a life-saver?' I'd hear as I sat in the back of our car, bored rigid after hours of waiting. 'No, no, no. It's no trouble,' I'd hear his response, in the sort of cheery tone that was never directed at me. At this point I'd pop my head up because I would often have a sixpence thrust into my hands by the grateful motorist. 'At least let us give the lad a few pennies for some sweets.' I'd smile. My dad would smile. Then once that was over, we'd resume our journey in silence, my dad scanning the roads for any other folk in need.

They were some of the few moments I recall my dad coming close to something called happiness.

Chapter 2

GRANDMA

OUR HOUSE IN Wellesley Street set me apart from a lot of the other kids at Shelton Church of England Primary School. Many of them lived in two up two down houses as sparse and run down as my own house. But I was aware from a very young age that we Caudwells were a little bit different.

Our house itself could have been quite grand. From the outside it was a large, brick built, three storey end-of-terrace. It was very definitely middle class territory and looked spacious and comfortable compared to the squashed-up little houses my friends went home to. But, on the inside, it was a different story. There was little comfort anywhere, from the hard-wooden floors to the tired, scuffed paintwork and dark rooms. When the atmosphere wasn't tense with on-going battles between the adults, an almost palpable feeling of disappointment hung in the air at that house.

'John, you know the Caudwell family were once very wealthy,' Grandma would tell me as I sat at the kitchen table listening, entranced. 'Your great, great, great, great grandfather owned a huge mill which he passed down through his family. They were very important people and they built a big bakery just up the road. It was meant to go to your grandad but there was a big row and he never got it...'

I would sit and listen to her tell the same story over and over again, these same stories she'd been telling me since I was a toddler. I was completely fascinated. 'There's a big mill in a place called Rowley in

20

Derbyshire,' she'd say. 'And that's the Caudwell Mill. And the man who built it was called John Caudwell – he had exactly the same name as you. He was a very, very successful man… An important man. So many of the Caudwells have made money.'

Then there would be a shake of the head. I'd go over to her and pat her hand, my head spinning, hoping to hear more about these incredible wealthy Caudwells, but that would be the end of it. Then I would wonder how I could make it all better, how I – with the great mill-owning John's blood in my veins – could bring the Caudwell fortune back to our family.

I adored my grandma. She was a tough, proud Northern woman and a natural leader. Physically, she was pretty formidable. Short, plump, always wearing a shin-length dress and often a scarf around her head, she looked rather like Ena Sharples (played by the wonderful, late actress Violet Carson) from Coronation Street and her tongue was just as sharp. She was a huge influence on me as a child and I was her companion from as soon as I could walk, digging with her on her allotment or helping in the kitchen and round the house.

Grandma never stopped. Whether she was rowing with my mum, showing me how to pick runner beans, cleaning, cooking or telling me stories.

There was always a huge element of drama to her stories and certain facts that were never quite explained but completely intrigued me. 'What was the row with grandad about?' I'd ask her, and she'd shake her head and say, 'You know… families, John.' I didn't know but I felt somehow that I was being let into a big secret.

She would tell me how, as a young girl – then called Mary Greenhalgh – she was so pretty that men would try to chase her, to have their way with her. 'But I always had an eight-inch hat pin in my hat, and I'd pull it out and jab them and run away.' Mouth open,

I'd wonder what 'their way' was, and would marvel at how fearless and smart she was.

She had grown up in Nottingham and I thought of her in Sherwood Forest being saved by Robin Hood. But men wanting their way with her seemed to happen all over the place. 'It happened once on Ilkley Moor,' she told me. 'On Ilkley Moor Baht' at,' she'd say, and start singing the Yorkshire folk song. I assumed it was written about her.

Many of the beliefs and motivations I have today are a direct result of what I learnt from my grandmother. From listening to her, watching her, trusting her. I am passionate about health and nutrition, but I do not automatically have faith in doctors or medical opinion.

My father died at age of 53, after breaking his hips in a fall and being told to stay in bed. There he got an infection, which went to his lungs, and then he died. Even as an 18-year-old, I knew that Dad should have been kept mobile in order to prevent infections. And when my own son, Rufus, became inexplicably and terrifyingly anxious and unwell at the age of ten, it took me another decade – with scores of doctors, medical experts and psychiatrists – to get a diagnosis of Lyme Disease and PANS/PANDAS. I know more now about these horrendous illnesses than most qualified physicians.

Grandma was, she told me, a white witch. She had a crystal ball that was kept covered with a black cloth. Every now and again she would bring out the precious crystal globe and tell me: 'Look deep into it, John, and you will see your future.' I would squeeze my eyes shut, concentrate furiously, then open them to stare as hard as I could into its mysterious depths really believing if I did it right, I would see my future. But all I saw was glass.

Other times she would take my hand, smooth it out, a slight frown furrowing her brow as she traced the tiny lines that criss-crossed my palms. Then she would sit back with a big smile on her time-worn face. 'You're going to have a long, good life, John,' she'd tell me. I have little faith in palm readers or crystal balls these days, but back then I drank in every word she said.

Grandma was known throughout Stoke for being able to cure certain skin complaints, such as ulcers and eczema, for which doctors were only able to prescribe ineffective creams. 'John, pass me the zinc oxide,' she'd say, and I'd haul up a large tub of white zinc from the cupboard which she would mix with liquid paraffin and the oil and roots of various plants that she grew on her allotment. I wish I had taken note of her formula – that may well have made our fortune. All I recall is that comfrey leaves and various roots from her allotment were involved.

Almost every day of the week there would be a knock at the back door. Sometimes two or three in one day. 'Get the door, John,' she'd say and I'd jump up. There would be someone who might have travelled miles to see her – that was a lot back then. I'd slide back into my seat in the kitchen knowing that if I was quiet, I would be able to stay and watch. The stories were all quite similar. 'The doctor told me this would go weeks ago, but it's still giving me trouble,' a woman would explain, lifting up her skirt to expose a large, livid ulcer.

My eyes would widen and sometimes I'd have to crane my neck to see the painful problem. Grandma would be very serious, she'd ask questions and turn the leg or arm this way and that, staring intently at the offensive boils and pustules. Then she would get to work with her creams.

There was one particular lady I distinctly remember because she had the worst ulceration, all the way up her calf. She'd been to her doctor and to hospital, but the injury wasn't healing under its bandages. Every evening the lady would turn up and my grandma would spend an hour massaging her leg, gently dabbing her cream over the area, and then re-dressing the wound. As the weeks went by the wound got smaller and smaller and then, finally, one evening my grandma took off the bandage. The skin underneath was perfect. 'I knew we could get rid of it,' Grandma said calmly but with great satisfaction.

She never took a penny for her services although often a basket of vegetables or bread would be left sitting on the doorstep. 'Very few have the skill, John,' she'd tell me. 'So if you have it, you have to use it. You have to help these poor folk. That's your duty.'

A few hours later, this same kind woman who would help anyone in need, would be savagely attempting to reduce Mum to tears over an infringement of one of her many kitchen rules. Then later at night, I'd hear Mum screaming at Dad about how she couldn't spend a day longer living with 'that woman'.

I didn't understand why the women I loved seemed so unhappy together. Somewhere something was wrong. In order to ward off sleep, I'd puzzle over everything, trying to put together all the pieces of my family life. I needed to make some sort of sense – the lost fortune, the mysterious 'family row', the powerful ancestors, Dad's anger, the bakery business, the miserable old house, Dad's love of cars, Grandma's medicines, Mum's suffering, and the way both Dad and Grandma smiled and seemed completely transformed when they helped complete strangers.

One night, at the age of seven, shortly after my little brother Brian was born, I was sitting in my room at the top of the house, preoccupied with these thoughts, along with other issues I was having with some bullies at school. I probably drifted off, but I had a dream so real that it woke me up, and I thought of it as a vision, a direct command of what my future must be.

I was in the back of a gleaming Rolls-Royce (a car my father spoke about with reverence) and being driven through the streets of Shelton by a chauffeur in a cap and suit. People – poor people – from the neighbourhood were looking at the car, their faces tense and worried, like the women who turned up on our back doorstep.

'Drive very slowly, please,' I instructed my chauffeur, and I wound down the back window holding out £5 notes for everyone to come and take from me. Their faces broke into smiles. 'We can pay for our daughter to get her leg treated,' one lady shouted gleefully. 'And I can pay for proper food for my kids,' another told me.

The car drove on, with me handing out more £5 notes from a huge bag of money at my side. People were holding the money, laughing and waving at me and I felt completely, unbelievably happy. It was an emotion of pure, spiritual joy, a feeling I'd never experienced in my life.

I immediately woke up, my heart pounding. The dream was still running in my head like a movie on a screen; me, the Rolls-Royce, the money, the smiling faces, the sense of satisfaction in that act of giving. In my dark, little room I felt someone, somewhere was telling me what my destiny had to be.

I had always had a sense it was my responsibility to make life better for my family. Now I felt I had been given a clear goal to achieve and it was far, far bigger than just helping my family. I had to make enough money to make things better for all these people.

As I sat in my bed thinking this over, that beatific sense of happiness I felt in my dream slowly turned into a far more familiar knot of emotions. Panic, anxiety and fear.

Some kids at school were mean to me; I was in trouble with my teacher for not doing what I was told, and my dad thought I was a waste of space. Yet it was, in my mind, a proper vision, my own glimpse into the future without the help of Grandma's crystal ball so I had to make it come true. How the hell was I going to do this? I couldn't tell anyone because they'd laugh their heads off. Me, John

Caudwell, in a Rolls-Royce. As if! I couldn't even let myself go to sleep again in case I wet the bed.

Now it felt my vision was more a curse than a blessing. But whatever it was, I had to make it happen.

*****

JOHN CAUDWELL WAS my great, great, great grandfather. He was born in Rowsley, Derbyshire, the third child and second son of a prosperous land owner called Joseph Caudwell. Joseph had a total of seventeen children with his wife, the very appropriately named Patience.

Joseph's eldest son – who was also called Joseph – was convicted of horse stealing and, in 1884, was sent along with his wife, Anne Lowe Caudwell, on a convict ship to Australia. After seven years he received a pardon and left for Tasmania.

Rebellious genes clearly run in the family. The second son John, however, then became the next head of the family and inherited the bulk of his father's property.

John had ten children with his wife Catherine Naylor, but it was his namesake and third son who was born not just with a sense of business but with vision. In 1874, he tore down his father's corn mill at Rowsley, on the banks of the River Wye, radicalising production of the former single mill by powering it with two water wheels which drove eight sets of millstones to grind flour, and a further three sets to grind animal feed.

Just as I did with all my enterprises in years to come, my 19th century namesake was constantly looking for ways to improve the business, and in 1885 – and remarkably for a Derbyshire mill owner – he travelled to Antwerp for the International Milling Exhibition. There, he witnessed the new invention of steel rollers which replaced the old stone mills, enabling a much finer grind of flour free from the bits of stone that often ended up in bread.

John was a powerhouse. I wish I could have met him. He expanded his business, investing in other mills around the area, and was father to ten children, including seven boys. So, even as I celebrated the birth of my own sixth child at the age of 68, I realise I am seriously flagging behind my ancestors with my comparatively modest-sized brood.

Theirs really was a family business empire. Two of John's sons, Charles and Edward, moved into the milling business, while my great grandfather, William, focused on farming, providing the grain for the operation. Charles opened a mill in Southwell and Congleton, earning prizes for his fine flour. Edward focused on technology to keep Rowsley at the top of its game.

Shortly before the outbreak of the First World War, Edward looked again to Europe for new improvements in technology. He upgraded his milling process once more, and employed 40 German men to fit their complex sifting machines, known as plansifters, into the mill. The German recruits were still at work in 1914 when war broke out. All but six of them returned home. Those men who remained finished the installation and were then interned as prisoners of war on the Isle of Man.

By the time Edward and Charles' father John died, there were five mills under Caudwell ownership: Amber Mill in Derbyshire; Kingsmill in Mansfield; Southwell Mill, near the poet Lord Byron's childhood home in Nottingham, which Charles ran along with a mill in Congleton. Charles had the idea to expand into bakeries and owned Caudwell's Victoria Bakery in Shelton, opposite Hanley Park, which was built in 1924 – five years before he died.

This was the bakery destined for my grandfather, John, who moved from the Caudwell base in Derbyshire first to Basford in

Staffordshire, and then to Shelton. The bakery was on Victoria Road – since renamed College Road – and his house in Wellesley Street practically ran along the back of the building, a perfectly convenient five-minute walk, door-to-door.

Despite all my extensive research, I'm still not sure of the precise reasons why the next chain of events happened. All I know is that my side of the family missed out on the fortune as the Caudwell business was expanding.

But after Charles' death, there was a row between the brothers. My grandma never told me the cause of the argument but it created a huge rift in this family that had worked together in unison for almost a century. That makes me very sad because family is everything to me.

It left my great grandfather William and his son, John, out of the business. My grandfather, who had married my grandmother in 1917 (a few years before the bakery was up and running) then became a travelling grocer, selling vegetables from a cart but still living in the house which had been destined for the proprietor of Caudwell's Victoria Bakery.

'There it is, John,' my grandma would say as we walked along College Road and there would be customers coming out of the low brick building, carrying cakes and loaves of bread. I never asked Grandma who was running it, but there it was, just a few minutes from our doorstep and opposite the park which was my childhood playground – the comfortable future my grandad should have had, a symbol of a lost family unity and one of the reasons for those sighs and that air of loss that hung in the house.

*****

I LOST GRANDMA twice when I was eleven years old. After years of daily tears, rows and recriminations between Grandma and Mum, my dad had finally had enough.

'We're moving out, John, you need to start packing your things. We're getting our own place,' my mum said to me one morning. I could barely take it all in. Turned out we were moving into a two-bedroom upstairs council flat on the huge, sprawling Bentilee estate that was built to house the coal and factory workers of Stoke. Not only would we be moving, but I'd be sharing a room with my four-year-old brother, and I'd be going to a new school, Berry Hill High. It was about seven miles from my old school, which meant I wouldn't know any of the other pupils. Grandma wouldn't be coming with us. And we were leaving in a couple of days.

I couldn't moan or pull a face because my mum was clearly so happy. 'Isn't it exciting, John? A whole new start,' she'd say, and then she'd start to sing as she rooted through cupboards and drawers, pulling out her crockery, her pots and her pans.

'What about Grandma?' I asked.

'Grandma will be fine,' she said, and the matter was closed. There was also another bit of 'good news'. The day after we moved, we'd be going on holiday to a caravan for a few days. 'Won't that be lovely?'

Grandma wasn't there the following day, when we loaded up the car and left for Bentilee. It didn't feel right. I hadn't even said goodbye to her. When we arrived at the tiny flat, I felt sad and underwhelmed. There was no space compared to those big, old rooms we'd lived in. I didn't know the rules here. In Wellesley Street I knew all the rules. Three pieces of coal for the fire. One kettle of hot water for my bath. Who came in the back way and who came in the front. And I knew all Grandma's idiosyncratic ways about what went where, and why.

I saw my bike being hauled off the roof of the car. 'I'm just going for a ride,' I muttered to Mum, who was busy carrying boxes. My dad was in the house so he couldn't stop me. I cycled the seven miles back to Wellesley Street. 'Grandma,' I shouted, pounding on the door an hour later. No reply. I went round the back and shouted. Silence. I climbed over the wall and into the house through the scullery window. Nothing. Everything looked eerily empty.

'The allotment,' I said to myself and, off I cycled to her allotment, shouting 'Grandma' as I peered through her plants. 'Have you seen my grandma?' I asked anyone I saw there.

'No lad, she's not been here today,' came the response.

I racked my brains for Grandma's daily routines. It was Friday, she must have gone shopping. I cycled back to Wellesley Street, parched and exhausted and sat on the wall waiting for her. We'd have a cup of tea when she got back. After an hour I saw her in the distance. Her bulky body perched on skinny legs was unmistakable. 'Grandma!' I yelled running towards her. But the closer I got I realised it wasn't her. 'Sorry, lady,' I said and ran back to my post. Two hours later, I saw her again and sprinted up the road towards her but I'd made a similar mistake.

I didn't know what to do. My backside was numb from sitting on the wall which had the uncomfortable stumps of old metal railings that were all taken away during the war to be melted down for iron for the armed forces. I was starving hungry and it was getting late so I'd be in for it with my dad. I took a last look at the house and set off back to Bentilee.

I can't remember if I got a hiding from my dad for disappearing back to Wellesley Street but the next day we went off in the car to the caravan. We'd been there for a day when there was a knock on the caravan door. My dad opened it and I saw a policeman.

'Walter Caudwell,' the policeman asked as I craned forward, mouth open wondering what on earth the police wanted with my dad. 'I'm afraid to tell you your mother has died.' I went white. My dad stood outside talking to the policeman and I tried to hear every word.

GRANDMA

She had gone to Eastwood in Nottinghamshire to see some relatives who still lived in the house she grew up in. She went up to her old bedroom, got into the bed she was born in and never woke up. It was 1964 and my grandma was 80 years old when she passed. My dad did not shed a tear. Nor did I. We were men.

I didn't think then how it must have been for Grandma to think she would be living in that great big house on her own. I didn't think how much I might have meant to her, or my dad and how hard it must have been for her to see us go which was probably the reason I never saw her on that day.

But in my head for years to come were two thoughts. I never got to say goodbye and I will never see my grandma again.

Chapter 3

BULLIES

'COURAGE IS FIRE and bullying is smoke.' So said Benjamin Disraeli. But, bent double in the middle of a rainy playground at the age of six, and terrified to open my eye in case it had been knocked out by an expertly-delivered punch, I would have told you the great 19th century Prime Minister was an idiot who didn't have a clue what he was talking about.

It was my eye that was on fire, burning in its socket with a jagged pain I can still remember today. The only smoke was my breath coming out in steaming gasps in the freezing cold air.

My baptism of bullying came on my first day of juniors at Shelton Church of England Primary School. All I'd done was joined a bunch of other – admittedly bigger – boys sheltering from the cold wind and rain under a little alcove and then – Bam! Out of nowhere, a fist hit me in the eye and I had ricocheted backwards, hands covering my face, into a crumpled heap – exposed in front of all the sniggering kids as that boy who was, from then onwards, the target for everyone else.

'Oi, Ginger!' Slam. 'Come on then, Carrot.' Crack. 'Look at his freckles… Urgh. Disgusting. They're everywhere.' Too many times it happened. Bruises and cuts decorated my body with red, purple, yellow and black marks. No-one seemed to notice or comment. One day I had half a brick (or a 'half-ender' as we called them) thrown at my head. It knocked me out for a few seconds. When I came to, I realised my head was split, blood gushing red onto the black asphalt.

I don't remember any teachers taking me aside with a comforting word. I don't remember the bullies being taken to task. After the brick incident one thing changed. Every afternoon in class the teacher would read us a story. The next day she would say, 'John, can you tell me where I left off yesterday?' And proudly I would quote the very last line she had read the day before. It was my star turn, the moment I shined and the teacher smiled at me.

In the afternoon of the day after the brick, the teacher looked at me: 'John, can you remember where we finished off the story.' I drew a blank. For the life of me I couldn't remember. 'No, Miss.' It was the same the next day and the next. The teacher gave up asking. My memory was never the same and has not recovered to this day.

Being bullied became a familiar part of my life. I accepted it in the same way I accepted rubbery liver and lumpy yellow custard in the school dinners and my father's black moods at home. It was just part of my day, something I had to deal with. I didn't tell my mum or my dad, they had their own worries. And anyway, it was my problem to solve.

'How was school?' Mum would sometimes ask when she came back from work.

'Good,' I'd mumble, head down.

She'd give me a look. 'Why is the back of your shirt covered in dirt?'

'Playing,' I'd say, giving nothing away.

She'd sigh. 'Your dad's not going to be happy, John.' More trouble.

I am not, however, going to complain about the bullying. For a long time, I chose to think of it as the making of me, but that was a choice. Bullying doesn't really make anyone. In my case it hardened me. I created a tough layer to cover the damage that had been done. It made me mistrustful of people. It made me determined to prove myself and to be accepted, but it also made me aware that I was never going to be the sort of person who was instantly accepted. So I'd do my own thing and show them what I could do. The older I got, the more I understood Disraeli's words – although I interpreted them very differently. To me, it was the bullying smoke that gave me the courageous fire.

Bullying also makes you an outsider. The advantage of being an outsider is that it gives you perspective. I was born with a very analytical, logical brain which is the perfect accompaniment to perspective. Even at the age of six, I would treat my abysmal playground situation as a puzzle that I needed to solve. I didn't sit and cry. Instead, I sat and thought about it logically.

'This is because I'm smaller, I'm ginger and I have freckles,' I would think to myself as I ran home, head down, hoping to get to my road before any trouble started. These were things the kids saw on the outside and I couldn't do anything about that. But just because I clearly looked ugly on the outside, I knew I had things inside me which I could turn to my advantage.

Thanks to being constantly picked on and verbally ripped apart by my dad, I never committed the mortal sin of bursting into tears like some of the other lads at school. I wasn't scared of being in fights with bigger kids – everyone I wanted to play with was bigger than me. And I was used to being jumped on by four or five at a time. So being outnumbered did not faze me, either. I was also very agile and athletic with an extremely high pain threshold.

My six-year-old brain worked out that if I was as fast, strong and brave as I possibly could be, then the other kids at school might like me or, at the very least, they might respect me. I needed to come up with a way to make them realise that. But how could I let them know that's who I was, and not just small, skinny, freckly and ginger? That was the challenge.

The more I thought about it, the answer to that was obvious. It was all in that word 'challenge'. I would challenge them – dare them – to do things. Then this daily hell I went through might eventually stop.

I didn't care so much about the physical bullying. I'd been hit by bricks, pushed down steep banks, beaten up by five kids at once, dangled over the murky canal – and I was still in one piece. But the name calling, being pushed out of a group in the playground, the girls laughing at me, and even the occasional sympathetic, weary look from a teacher, made me feel even more pathetic. That was harder to deal with. It lingered in my head. It was there at night when I was worrying about the rows at home. It wasn't who I wanted to be. So I had to change that. And no-one else could do it except me.

Nowadays I am passionate about training, especially if there's a cycling race coming up. I push myself hard, I don't stint on the hours I put in. I pay attention to nutrition, hydration, stretching and focus on being the best that I can be. I am highly competitive by nature and I know that in order to get the best results, you have to put in the work. I am exactly the same in business. I am logical, I think every situation through, I analyse my competition, see how I can beat them or join forces with them. I always play to win.

Back then, I was constantly preparing myself. I spent a lot of time on my own so I could practise running, jumping down steeper and steeper drops. I did a lot of lifting and carrying for my dad and my grandma. I was exceptionally strong for my age and size. At the allotments, I'd pick up huge sacks of soil, stacks of planks of wood. At home I'd drag that tin bath full of water and wet washing around the back yard.

I could feel my muscles growing, my determination focusing me every single day. Kids in the road would watch as I'd climb any wall, leap off any roof, tear down a slope on my bike and abruptly navigate a sharp turn without once falling off. Outside our house, I'd harness all the anger I felt at my dad, all the unfairness I felt about being picked on, and I'd channel it into a cold, calm rage that I could switch on and off at will. Already I was getting a reputation with the kids in my street, and I would never, ever back down from any dare.

*****

'LOOK OUT! IT'S that ginger kid.' I was at the gates of Hanley Park with my little gang from home and we were spotted by some bigger kids from the neighbourhood. The group included a pretty girl called Francesca who was three years older than me (I was eight at the time) but I was desperate to impress her. So I walked towards the bigger kids who grinned at us all, obviously hoping to have a laugh at our expense.

My mission was to win over both Francesca and these big boys. 'Race you round the park,' I shouted to the biggest boy in the pack. He burst out laughing. Hanley Park is huge. One hell of a lap on a tiny old bike with no gears! 'Have you lost your marbles?' he said. I stood my ground, poker faced. The other lads pushed and shoved him. 'You can beat him easy. He's a wimp.' He sneered, 'Get ready to lose, Ginger.' And we were off.

It was easier than I thought. Within the first half mile I'd lost him. I carried on, not dropping my speed even though after a while my lungs felt they were about to burst. As our little crowd came back into view on the finishing line my legs were starting to turn to jelly and a stitch was digging into my sides. But I didn't care because I was winning.

Francesca was jumping up and down, and clapping, and one of the rival boys slapped me on the back. I stood and waited with them for their leader to arrive back – a good 60 seconds after me – puce in the face, and panting like he was about to die. His mates gave him a slow clap and jeered as he dropped to the floor. Next time I saw them, they nodded. 'All right, Caudwell.' Casual acceptance of my presence. That was all I needed.

I used this strategy again and again. If someone came at me, I'd be ready. 'Dare you to jump off the roof of that building,' I'd say, and often before they could answer, I'd be scrambling up the side of a wall and jumping two storeys onto scrubland. Frequently my dares went unchallenged or, at the last minute, my opponent would bottle out. What was important was that fact that whether or not they took me up on it, I would always complete the dare. 'Bet you can't jump this ditch,' I'd shout, taking a run at it before they'd even paused for breath. I got a few injuries but even then, I'd get up, not even so much as a tiny wince, however much blood was pouring from me. I never got to be the popular one but I was accepted. My reputation grew.

By my early teens the name-calling had stopped, but the dares didn't. That was fine by me; dares just brought more opportunities for me to prove myself. The older I got, it became all about gangs – the Shelton Gang, the Gas Works Gang, the Canal Lock Gang and the notorious Teddy Boys Gang. Gangs then weren't what they are now. 'Four o'clock, Saturday. Fight in Albion Street – the Gas Works,' would be shouted at you as you rode past a bunch of your boys on your bike. Then you'd turn up for a pre-organised road ruck, where a line of your gang would stand in the middle, opposite a line of the other gang. The aim was to push through your opposing gang to get to the other side punching, kicking, swearing and screaming insults as you went. It was rough – and pretty stupid – but skinny as I was, I excelled at these fights. My chance to show how fearless I was. My chance to show my fire.

*****

BEING A VICTIM of bullying definitely had an effect on my character, but I will never say I am grateful for it because that is to condone something that causes so much misery to so many, especially with the advent of social media. Things happen to you when you are bullied. It changes you as a person and you can use your experience for good – but also for bad.

Now I had proved myself, my peers at school moved on to other boys they deemed misfits. I'm ashamed to admit I got involved in the bullying of a boy – let's call him Thomas – who wore glasses, had freckles and was small. Those incidents made me feel sick. I silently willed him to hit back but he never did. The kickings he got were more traumatic to me than any of the ones I ever received. I didn't help him but I walked away, haunted by his face, haunted by the fact I had failed to stand up for him. I wanted to find a way to be a champion for people like that but, at the age of eight or nine, I had no idea how I could do that. All I knew was that I had worked out how to survive the dog-eat-dog world of the school playground.

Bullies exist everywhere. Not just in playgrounds but in the workplace, in politics, in business and in pretty much every walk of life. Having been bullied as a child, you can spot a bully a mile off, even if he or she happens to be very polite, nicely dressed and seems to be doing you a favour.

In business I am – as I learn to be at school – pretty fearless and tough, because you have to be, but I am also fair. My sense of justice is born out of the sense of injustice I felt as a child. With my company, Phones 4u, I built up the biggest mobile phone company in Britain. But in the early days we were a tiny operation, just a handful of us working out of a tiny office in Stoke.

There were lots of little companies like ours trying to make a go of things in this brave new world of mobile phones but it was a very new business and there were few rules. It was a bit like the Wild

West. At one point, the big manufacturers companies tried to tie all us distributors into contracts that would enable them to have an unfair control over our activities. You were made to feel you had no choice because there were so few suppliers. It's called being put between a rock and a hard place.

Now, as a kid, I more often felt bewildered as to why I was bullied. I accepted it as a fact and I worked out my way of dealing with it. As an adult, all the rage I felt about Thomas, all the frustration about the way I was treated surfaced into a cold, hard, brittle determination not to be pushed around.

There has been just one occasion where I resorted to the lessons that I learnt in my old Shelton Gang. In the late 70s, I got involved with a guy who initially seemed unbelievably charming and helpful, and who turned out to be a sociopath who tried to bully and threaten me for a period of two years.

He was a builder who told me about a beautiful split-level bungalow he had built, and how there was a plot of land right next door to his own house in Meir Park which would be perfect for such a build. We met several times and he seemed like a great guy. Turned out he was a cowboy and a dangerous man who had a history of trouble with the police and involvement with some very shady people.

Months in and my dream bungalow was a badly-built, half-built mess. I dealt with it quickly. I fired him and brought another team in to finish the job. For the next two years this man – who I will call Oliver – made my life hell with endless threats, obscene calls in the middle of the night and endless promises of violence. 'You're gonna get what's coming to you, Caudwell. Something is going to happen to you,' he'd growl down the phone at 2am. It was not pleasant.

One day I was in the garden with my daughter Rebekah, who was about four at the time. She was my first child. I absolutely adored her and all I ever wanted to do was look after her, protect her and

39

be a good dad. I was fixing the steps towards the house and had a hammer in my hand when Oliver leant over the wall. 'Caudwell you f***ing b******d, you're dead!' he yelled and continued screaming and swearing. I saw my daughter look up. Her face was frozen in shock and fear and that was it. I snapped. I ran towards him, cleared the wall in one leap and gave chase, hammer in hand. I felt positively murderous.

He managed to outrun me, which is lucky because I dread to think what would have happened if I'd caught him. But he never came near me or my family again. Those harsh lessons I'd learnt as a child held fast in my adulthood. Stand up to a bully and in the face of your fire they will turn to smoke.

Chapter 4

DAD

I STOOD IN the driveway of our new house in Dividy Road, Bucknall, and stared. My dad's car was standing on the tarmac in front of the garage. It had been parked just very slightly askew. Something was wrong. I could feel it.

I looked up at the nice, neat, three-bedroomed, semi-detached house which my dad had bought with the three-and-a-half-thousand pounds my grandma had left him in her will. It was an astronomical sum (the equivalent of about £65,000 in 2022) and money that none of us ever guessed she possessed.

To the average passer-by everything looked very suburban and normal but I knew the picture wasn't right. The car wasn't right. The position was wrong. The time was wrong. It was four in the afternoon and my dad was never home at this time.

'Dad,' I said hesitantly, as I pushed the door to the small conservatory extension on the back of the house and walked inside. No answer. Then I heard a clatter of china and the unmistakable sound of our kettle boiling. He was definitely home. Tentatively, I went through to the kitchen and then stopped. My father was standing by the kettle with his back towards me. But his stance – usually ramrod straight – was slumped and his left arm was hanging, lifeless.

'Dad,' I repeated, my voice catching in my throat with a note of fear. He turned and stared back at me. His face was grey and his eyes completely glazed. This man of steel that I loved and feared in equal measure, was just looking at me, his mouth half-open. Helpless.

'What's happened, Dad?' I could feel the panic rising in my body as I watched him struggling to speak. I couldn't move, my body was leaden as my brain worked overtime trying to comprehend this alien version of my father.

'I was driving the car... Something happened... I didn't know where I was... I think I might have crashed it.'

Broken sentences slowly tumbled from of his mouth, each one momentarily freezing the blood in my veins until a matter of seconds passed and, finally, I jumped in to action. 'Sit down, Dad,' I said, taking him by the arm and leading him to a chair. It felt awkwardly intimate and, at 14, I found it hard to comprehend the idea of this man being physically vulnerable. But I knew I had to take charge. I glanced at his arm, which was still limp.

'This isn't good, Dad,' I said quietly, and then, trying to behave with a new authority, I continued, my tone of voice sounding strong and decisive: 'I'm going to call Mum because you need to go to hospital. And don't worry, I'll check the car. I didn't see any dents so I think it's OK.'

I half expected him to brusquely tell me to leave him alone, but incredibly my dad just nodded, obediently. 'I don't feel good, John.' Pushing down my anxiety, I left him at the table and went to the newly-installed telephone in the hallway and I called my mum who was at the time working at a building company called Seddons.

'Mum, something's wrong with Dad.' I spoke as quickly and as calmly as I could. 'We need to get him to a doctor. Can you come home? Mum, can you come home now?'

Within the hour we were waiting in the emergency room corridor as a doctor walked towards us. 'Your husband has had a stroke, Mrs Caudwell,' he said. I stood up, hanging on every one of his words. 'The good news is you reacted very quickly and the damage has been limited. He should fully recover but he needs a few weeks full and complete rest. No exerting himself for some time. No strenuous exercise whatsoever.' My mum nodded.

I looked at her and looked at the doctor. The words running through my head were: 'That's never going to happen.'

*****

WALTER GREENHALGH CAUDWELL was a man who did not sit still. He would never dream of sitting and reading a book, lazing in front of the television or, even worse, lying in bed all day long. He was up with the sun every morning, dressed, shaved and working his way through a list of jobs around the house before he started work. When he came home in the evening, he would be out working on the car, clearing gutters, cleaning his tools. He could fix bikes, paint walls, mend fences, strip down car engines and put them back together again. He'd move from one task to the next, rarely taking a break in between. The man crackled with energy.

But every now and again in the midst of doing all these things, he would stop and clutch at his chest. And I would stop, frozen for a split second in my father's big shadow, watching, waiting, holding my breath. The moment would pass and I would watch his face set firm, resolute; a flicker of defiance igniting his steely-blue eyes, and he would carry on with the log-chopping or the uphill walk and I would breathe out. He rarely said a word about these incidents when they happened, he never complained, never fussed.

But I knew, because both Mum and Dad had told me on various occasions that he suffered from hardening of the arteries, or atherosclerosis. Deposits of plaque lodged themselves in the walls of his arteries and slowly narrowed them, weakening the supply of blood to his heart. Often I would go out with him, picking nettles – not the easiest of jobs – and the nettles were boiled up by Mum or

Grandma to make a tea, drunk by Dad to soothe his condition.

Whenever I picked the stinging nettles, I'd take my time to look for the biggest and, what I believed were the best, greenest, healthiest looking plants. I hoped they would be the ones holding the magical juice inside their leaves which would cure him, killing off that plaque in his arteries which made him unwell. Perhaps then we would all live happily ever after. I'm not sure that nettle tea had very much effect at all. Nothing ever changed. Those chest clutching moments continued throughout my childhood and I knew the problem remained.

It was an ironic situation really when I think about it. I spent so much of my childhood longing for his affection. Dad's heart may have been weakened by the condition of his arteries, but it was not soft and I only recall how inexplicably hard his heart was towards me.

I wish my recollection of Dad was not so coloured by unhappy memories.

I was a difficult child, I know that. I was always up to some mischief, whether it was trouble at school, setting piles of wood on fire in Hanley Park, doing reckless dares to impress other kids, or jumping free rides on the electric milk carts that were left (with the keys still in the ignition) outside the creamery, a few doors from our house.

The older I got, the more obstreperous I became towards my father. I was never going to win a special place in his heart. I didn't understand why he had such a problem with me. Why he so obviously favoured my little brother Brian, praising him as the 'good, handsome' boy and me as the 'bad, ugly one'. At school I'd worked out a way to deal with bullies and turn them into my friends. At home, however, there was nothing I could do to change Dad's opinion of me. So I did nothing except grow more and more rebellious.

Those hard, unforgiving Army & Navy shoes I was forced to wear became the symbol of my paternal mutiny. They were the main source of our regular battles. Every day they got scuffed and battered because every day I was outside, running about, making rafts to float on the canal, climbing up buildings and generally getting up to all sorts of adrenaline-fuelled adventures – despite being physically hampered by a pair of over-tight, excruciatingly-painful, black leather clodhoppers. For years I'd done my best to cover up marks, hide them from eyesight or just stand silent and penitent as my father ranted at me for being wasteful and negligent.

By the age of seven I was consumed with a sense of injustice about those shoes. Why on earth couldn't he get me a cheap pair of pumps like the ones worn by every other kid I played with? Why did I have to be singled out by my embarrassing stiff, black, leather lace-ups that 'cost a lot of money', were totally unsuitable for playing outdoors and crippling me? And why did my life have to be made so miserable in every way over the ridiculously unsuitable shoes I was being made to wear?

'Good God, John, these shoes are sodden and absolutely filthy.' I was standing in the kitchen at Wellesley Street when he loomed in front of me, holding the offensive shoes. I said nothing. 'What are you playing at? How many times have I told you to look after them? They cost good money, you know. You've got to be more careful and look after them. I'd better not see them like this again.'

Still I said nothing. I could feel the tension rising. My dad glared at me, I stuck my hands in my pockets and glared back. My poor mum turned round from the stove and tried to calm things down. 'Tell your dad you're sorry, John,' she said, trying to keep the peace as she always did. I thought about it for a split second. Why should I? How many times had I said sorry over those dreadful shoes, and how many times had the whole fight started over again and again?

'No,' I said. I saw my dad's eyes narrow and the colour rise in his face.

'Say sorry, John,' he said. 'Last chance.' I shook my head.

Bang. Immediately his fist came down on the table clattering a cup in its saucer and causing Mum to stiffen with anxiety. He grabbed hold of me by my arm and pulled me out of the kitchen, through the back yard where he picked up a length of wood.

'Are you going to apologise?' he said, holding it in his outstretched arm, giving me yet another chance to say sorry. I clamped my mouth together. 'No chance,' I thought.

We stood for a moment in silence. Both of us knew there was no going back. Dad drew back his stick and started to whack at my backside and the tops of my legs. The pain didn't mean anything. I screwed my eyes together as the wood cracked against my legs and gritted my teeth to stop from crying out. 'Still not sorry?' he said after a few minutes. 'No.' I said.

He looked at me and I looked straight back at him. No tears, just a defiant glare right back at him. 'Right, let's see if this makes you sorry,' he muttered. I was pushed into the coal shed which was right next to the old scullery. 'Stand up straight and don't move till I come and get you,' he barked slamming the door shut. There were rats in that cold shed and an unpleasant, musty, earthy smell. I don't know how long I stood in that dark, little room but I still remember I never said sorry for those shoes again.

*****

IN A LOT of ways, I am similar to my dad. I like to be busy. I like a long list of things to do and I'll keep going, adding more and more chores to my list, pushing myself to get through every task. I am fortunate to be wealthy enough to employ good people to work around my house and garden but, as they can themselves attest, there are plenty of times when I'll be out there with them, asking questions, checking on procedures and more often than not piling in myself. Like my dad, I'm methodical with the same logical engineer's brain, and able to easily grasp an understanding of everything, from electrics to plumbing to machinery. And as Dad always did, I try to keep things in good order and restore something that is broken rather than chuck it away and buy a new replacement.

From an early age, I'd helped Dad enough around the house to know what needed doing, so it was my idea to creosote the garden shed just a few weeks after his stroke. It needed doing and I could do it on my own. But even though I could already handle a car, I was still only 14 so Dad would have to drive me the five miles to Grandma's allotment where we kept the big tins of that tar-like liquid.

Looking back, I didn't think much about it. Dad hadn't – as I had predicted – taken heed of the doctor's advice. There had been the bare minimum bed rest, then he had gone back to work as usual and, as was often the case in our house, the subject of his stroke was never really raised again. But in my mind, it would be all right because he only needed to drive me to Wellesley Street and back and I'd do the rest.

The creosote was in five-gallon drums, more than enough for the shed and the fence. They weighed a ton. 'I'll go and carry them to the car,' I said as we pulled up in our old road. He shook his head. Maybe he didn't like to see me acting like the man, or maybe it was force of habit; either way, I couldn't stop him from helping me. I didn't dare hint at 'doctor's orders', so we both got out of the car and walked towards the allotment.

'I'm fine, John,' he said testily, catching me glancing at him warily as he went to lift the heavy creosote in its metal drum. He picked it up without so much as a flicker of pain and I felt a small twinge or relief. I knew I couldn't tell him to let me do it all myself. We were a good twenty minutes lugging the barrels back and forth to the car. I tried not to notice the occasional grimace across his face as we carried our loads.

We drove back home barely exchanging more than a few words. He didn't look any different, he wasn't clutching at his heart or breathing heavily so I forgot about those little grimaces and stopped worrying. I had no idea it would be the last time dad and I would be together side-by-side in a car, him driving, and me in the passenger seat. All I was thinking about was creosoting the shed. I wanted to do a good job for him and Mum. When we got back, I went into the garden and he went into the house with some jobs of his own to do. It was just any other average weekend.

There was however, a calamitous repercussion from those drums of creosote. A few days later Dad had a stroke so severe that it took away the use of his arm, his leg and much of his speech. When he came back from the hospital, he had a new place in the house – an old armchair. It was actually the most comfortable chair we possessed, the seat worn into a dip from years of use, but that armchair was a living hell for this proud man who defined himself by his physical strength and ability, and whose great passions in life existed beyond four walls – motorcars and hours spent in the outside air tinkering with his precious engines.

*****

'DAD, TRY PRESSING this ball with your hand,' I'd say, hovering by his armchair. 'The physiotherapist says if you keep moving it you might get some movement back.' He had no interest in even trying. He'd given up and the ball that I was pushing into his hand bounced uselessly to the floor.

With my father an invalid, I also had a new place in the house. I was the man of the house, and God, how much my dad must have resented me taking over his position including his car and his precious tool box. I wanted him to fight back against his stroke but he was a defeated man. He became increasingly bitter and resentful and his focus turned on completely controlling Mum.

As his speech improved, he spent most of his time questioning my beleaguered mother, trying as hard as he could to stop her from seeing her friends or staying late at work, making her feel guilty for time that she spent away from him. It was as if he was determined to make her feel as trapped inside the house as he was.

'Where have you been all day?' he'd ask her as soon as she walked through the door, even though he knew she'd had to increase her hours to make up for the money lost from his earnings.

'You don't need to go to the shops. John can go,' he'd say. Or, 'Why do you want to go and to see your friends, you spend enough time with them at work? And I'm here on my own.' My mum would sigh and stay home. It infuriated me. I could see he was making her life as difficult as possible.

As always I was witness to everything. I'd watch and I'd listen to them row, except Mum rarely answered back. She just wanted to make him feel better. So it was more just hearing him grinding her down day in day out. I found the situation desperate. I could feel myself losing any love and respect I'd ever had for Dad. I could see how unhappy he was. Just weeks before this cataclysmic stroke he'd bought a caravan and a brand-new Hillman Minx. He'd been talking about travelling around Europe. He'd had a vision of a different life opening up for himself and Mum. But now that was slammed shut, and his only travel was in a wheelchair or on the four-pronged stick he occasionally used when making the effort to move about downstairs.

I did feel sorry for him but I could not bear what he was doing to Mum. I could see how unhappy she was and how he was controlling her more and more, intent on keeping her in the house with him.

There was very little I could do – I was only 14 years old and I had other things that were bothering me. I worried girls would never find me attractive, I felt frustrated and desperate to do something with my life and did anything I could to earn money to fund my own passion for engines in the form of motorbikes.

The years ticked by, all of us lost in our own unhappy worlds. Once I hit 16, I passed my motorbike test. A few months later I passed my car test. My world suddenly expanded and I vowed to try to do something which might make life better for them too. I persuaded Mum to get Dad's blessing to exchange his Hillman for a second-hand white 1968 Jaguar 3.4S, which was better able to tow the caravan. She did.

Brian and I manhandled Dad into the car and I drove them to campsites in Malvern and Devon a few times in those years. It must have been strange for Dad to be in a car with me at the wheel. We both felt it and he'd often be very snappy with me as a result. But I refused to get into arguments and ruin the atmosphere because really I was doing these trips for Mum.

I was getting her out of that house and letting her have some happiness in her life too. And, even if I didn't show it then, I did really want Dad to be happy too and maybe a little grateful that his son was doing this for both of them.

I look back now and realise I should have had more sympathy towards his situation. I was a teenage boy and, as such, my world revolved around my own self, my own desires and my own problems. I did try to do what I could for Dad. I still took an interest in what the doctors had to say during his various hospital visits but even as he grew older and weaker his heart was still as hard towards me as it had always been. The difference was I cared less. My life was becoming my own. And that was the way I wanted it.

*****

'JOHN, CAN YOU come to the office please?' It was 1971 and I was 19 years old. I was at work at Michelin at the end of my first year as an apprentice, and immediately I knew something was up. It wasn't unusual for me to be called in to see the bosses at work, but generally I had an idea what the complaint would be – a practical joke that had gone too far, let's say, or some other tomfoolery. But it was the 'John' that got me. Usually it was just: 'Caudwell. Office. Now.'

What happened next is a blur. I remember standing there with one of my bosses but I can't even remember who that was. I recall a look of sadness on their face and that when I heard the words, 'Sit down, John,' I already knew what was going to come next. 'I'm really sorry to tell you, son. Your dad has passed away.' I remember a feeling of numbness mixed with a strong sense of inevitability and I remember that it happened late in the afternoon. I don't think I said anything. I got up and went back to my work station and slowly packed my things together. Then I went home to Mum.

I have buried my emotions too deep within my psyche. I don't remember Dad's funeral. I don't recall anything that happened next except for a feeling of relief. Not just for myself and Mum – who would no longer have to put up with her husband's endless demands, his depression and his horribly controlling ways – but a sense of relief for Dad himself.

He could not have had a crueller end to his pretty miserable life. He was angry. He was frustrated. He was powerless and impotent in his prison of an armchair. A week or so before he died – aged just 52 – he'd fallen down the stairs and broken his hip. He'd been advised to stay in bed where he got an infection then a cold and then pneumonia.

I do think about my dad. My brother Brian does not share my grim memories. His son-father relationship had softer, kinder edges. He was just twelve years old when Dad died, and he remembers a far nicer version of the man I describe. But what I do know is that without my dad in my life, I would not be the man I am – and the father I am – today.

Just like Grandma, my father influenced me in many, many ways. When I was a child, Dad would let me come to work with him during school holidays. As a rep for an engineering company, he spent a lot of his time in his car driving to old factories in Wolverhampton and the Black Country. As I sat next to him in the car, he'd point out various little businesses – just fruit and veg shops, or small independent mechanics – and he'd say, 'They wanted me to go in with that business.' And occasionally we'd stop and I'd look at this small, industrious hub across the road, thinking: 'That looks exciting.' Then he'd shake his head and say, 'I didn't want to get involved – too much of a risk.' We'd drive away and I'd look back over my shoulder, wondering if he regretted losing the chance to share in that busy place.

This in itself gave me my own philosophy towards risk. Some would say I have taken huge risks in my life. I bought a stock of mobile phones when hardly anyone wanted to buy them and built a business which threatened to fall to pieces a hundred times. But I would tell you I've never taken a risk – or to my mind a significant risk. I never go into anything without weighing up every possibility – be it loss of my house, loss of millions – whatever. Every decision I make is based on every single factor involved, good and bad. If the good outweighs the bad, then the risk/reward ratio is in your favour and you take that option. As a kid I knew that if I jumped off a roof I could break or twist my ankle, but if that jump raised my reputation with the local gang to a level far greater than I was currently at, then to me it wasn't a risk, it was the right decision.

My ability with engines comes from my dad, as does my love of cars, motorbikes and even bikes. Brian is the same. That ability, and that passion reminds me that he remains in our blood, along with the burning physicality which we both possess. I use that physicality to challenge myself in daily sessions in my gym where my partner Modesta, who is 32 years my junior and a former Olympic cyclist, will shake her head at me and tell me she's had enough and I will carry on. I will compete in bike races, car races and on black ski runs in order to push my body to the limits of fitness. A fitness and health that I crave in order to ward off the ill-health and disability that crucified my dad.

I know Dad was not the man he wanted to be. I am not always the man I want to be and I am not always the father I want to be. I have worked insane hours all my life but my children are – and always will be – my greatest treasure. My dad is the reason why I made sure I took Rebekah to school every morning, watched *Coronation Street* with Libby at night and sat for hours listening to Rufus play his musical instruments. Dad is the reason I hug and kiss all of them – Scarlett, Jacobi and Leo – all the time, and tell them that I love them more than words can say. I love my children equally. I never compare them and I have no favourites. I know my dad was a different generation. I know he did the best he could by me and had so many of his own demons. I know I think differently about him now and have let go of all that resentment because I'm old enough to understand what he went through himself. There was so much that he could never say to me and I can never say to him.

But if I could I'd say, 'Thank you, Dad, for every life lesson you taught me. You made me a better man. I just wish you could have loved me more.'

Chapter 5

OUT OF MY LEAGUE

I WATCHED her dancing with her friends in the bar of my local, The Thurston. I knew her name was Kate McFarlane. I'd spoken to her twice, and a few weeks earlier I'd even given her a ride around the block on the back on my BSA 650 motorbike.

'Is this yours?' she'd said, nodding towards the bike as I stood, smoking a cigarette outside the pub. I could see that she was entranced by my pride and joy which was in fact, a thing of beauty, a classic, and not just British-made but manufactured up the road in Birmingham. 'Want a go on it?' I'd asked and she'd laughed, jumped on the back and we'd roared through the streets for a couple of minutes. Then she'd climbed off, said 'Bye', and ran off in the direction of her parents' house in Bentilee. That was as close to Kate McFarlane as I'd got.

And now she was dancing a few yards away from me. I can't remember the song she was dancing to, but I can remember everything about her. Long dark hair, long legs, hour-glass figure, big blue eyes and a huge smile that showed off her imperfect teeth. She was hands down, the most beautiful girl in the whole area and, even at fifteen, she had the sort of easy confidence that eluded me.

At seventeen, I was two years older than her, but still, I thought, she was completely out of my league. She probably had no clue what I was called. I wasn't one of the cool ones in any way, shape or form. It was the '70s, and The Thurston was the hang out for bikers and rockers, or 'greasers' as we used to call them in Stoke. Lemmy from

Motorhead was a local hero because he was our boy, born in Burslem. Deep Purple, Black Sabbath (Brummie lads) and Led Zeppelin were the sort of band names you'd see painted on the backs of the leather jackets that crowded the bar.

I had the leather jacket and I had the motorbike, but that's where it all ended for me. Underneath the jacket was a scruffy tee-shirt paired with my old school trousers. As far as I was concerned, apart from being permanently broke, there was no point in me even trying to make an effort because I would never be able to get it right. I could never be cool.

The look back then – for the girls but particularly for the guys – was really all about the hair. It had to be long, and thick and artfully tangled; ideally jet black or a Californian dirty-blond colour. Mine was none of these. It was thin, wispy and ginger, and the bane of my life. I couldn't bear to look in the mirror at myself back then because I hated everything about the face that looked back at me. 'You're ugly,' I told myself. 'You'll never be anything else but ugly.' It makes me sad now, to think back on how low my self-esteem was and I hate to think of all the kids out there who beat themselves up because they don't feel they fit in. But as painful as those feelings were, I do believe they also pushed me on, pushed me to prove myself as a success in other ways.

There had been just one time in my early life when I had loved how I looked. I was seven and, on the radio, had heard The Beatles for the first time. I was hooked. I saw them on television, studied photos of them in magazines on the newsagent's shelves. I begged my classical music-loving parents to buy me a Beatles album, and I asked for a Beatles jacket for my birthday present.

'The Beatles are a load of rubbish,' my dad snapped. 'They can't sing, it's not proper music. They're a disgrace.' But still I loved them. All those beautiful early songs about holding girls' hands and seeing them standing there, it was magical to me. I didn't get an album or a jacket so I did the only thing I could do – I grew my hair and after a few months I had a perfect Beatles mop top. I was so happy, combing my hair in front of the mirror, singing the words to the songs. That happiness did not last long.

'John, sit down here.' My dad was standing in the kitchen, behind a chair and holding a pair of scissors in his hand. My stomach dropped. I knew what he was about to do. I also knew that there was nothing I could do or say to stop him. I walked to the chair and sat down. 'We are not having The Beatles in this house,' he said. Then he yanked back my head and – snip, snip, snip – began to chop off my hair. I was never able to grow it again. It simply wouldn't grow and it got thinner until I hit the age of fourteen, and then it started to fall out in little clumps, the early signs of male pattern baldness.

'Stop kidding yourself. She's not interested in you,' I thought as I watched her dance. But she was looking at me and smiling, which was extremely confusing. I had zero experience of girls. It wasn't just the fact that I hadn't had sex. I'd never so much as flirted with a girl or kissed a girl, other than one thwarted attempt in a tent on one of the communal spaces in the middle of Bentilee. I had never heard those words, 'My mate fancies you,' which every other bloke I knew seemed pretty familiar with. But Kate from the estate was definitely – very definitely – smiling at me. I took a couple of sips of my beer as my mind went into overdrive trying to work out what was going on. She was moving closer to where I was standing, laughing with her mates and every few minutes throwing her dazzling smile in my direction. She was less than a couple of feet away from me. I had to say something before it was too late.

'Do you want to go swimming at Cheadle baths tomorrow?' The words came out of my mouth before I really had time to think. Looking back, I guess it was the worst chat up line ever; the sort of thing a twelve-year-old would ask a girl. And then, just as I was expecting her to burst into laughter and walk away, Kate grinned. 'Yes,' she said, and she asked for my phone number. I couldn't begin to describe how I felt as I headed towards home that night because I was in a whole new emotional landscape. A girl… Not merely any girl, but the most beautiful girl in Bentilee, was going on a date with me. All I knew was that I couldn't blow it.

*****

'I CAN'T COME swimming.' It was Kate, calling me first thing Sunday morning from a phone box in her road. You'd think that my heart would sink at the words, but it didn't. The good thing about having no experience with girls was that I didn't take this to be any sort of brush-off. 'Why not?' I said bluntly. There was silence. 'Well,' she answered and there was more silence. 'It's my time of the month.'

I had no idea how I was supposed to respond to that. I was completely out of my depth but I didn't want to miss my one chance with this girl. I left a long pause and then asked, 'What do you want to do instead?' Another pause.

'I could come and watch you swim.'

'OK,' I said. 'I'll come and pick you up at your house.' Beep, beep, beep. The pips on the phone went, and then the line went dead. I took the keys to my dad's precious old Jaguar and put on my best jumper; an Aran knit that just happened to match the car's white paintwork. Then I drove from our house to Bentilee. Now, people talk about Bentilee estate as a really rough place. It's the biggest housing estate in Britain and became notorious in the 1980s when it did get pretty out of control. Back in the early '70s, however, it was full of hard-working families who took pride in keeping their houses and gardens neat and tidy. The women would even check out each other's washing on the lines, vying to see whose hanging techniques were the best and whose laundry was the most spotless.

Everybody knew everyone else and their business was your business, so a fair few curtains were twitching as I drove up in the Jaguar. Kate was ready, standing on the doorstep with her mother, Jean, right behind her and looking stunned at the arrival of this fancy white car which had come to whisk her daughter away. 'You've made a big impression,' Kate told me as she got in the car. And then she laughed. That was the thing with Kate, she was always laughing. And she was always completely straight. 'I was lying when I said it was my period,' she told me as we drove along. 'I can't swim and I was too embarrassed to tell you. I didn't want you to think I was an idiot.'

Actually, all I was thinking was: 'How on earth is this girl even sitting next to me and talking to me?' It was hard enough for me to manage to keep my eyes on the road. We drove to the swimming baths which was the only Olympic-sized pool in the area, and she sat up in the viewing gallery watching me swim. Then we walked and talked, nursing cups of tea in cafes and getting to know each other. Talking to Kate came easy. She listened, she nodded and incredibly she was interested in everything I had to say. In one afternoon she seemed to instinctively understand me and look beyond my bad hair, bad clothes and terrible features for who I actually was. I could not believe I'd been so lucky, and within a matter of hours I knew that this girl was going to change my life.

Incredibly, Kate thought I was really something. She even thought I was good-looking, in a quiet, brooding Cool-Hand-Luke sort of way. But what she liked about me most, she told me later, was that she could tell I was different from all the other guys she knew in Stoke. I wasn't flirty or cocky. I didn't play games. I was serious, telling her my plans to become a successful businessman even though I could barely scrape together enough coppers to buy us our tea. I liked to talk and she liked to listen. She thought I was someone she could trust. Someone who was going to at least try to do something with his life. She also had a sense of the absolute ridiculous, and we quickly developed a series of private jokes about silly things people said or silly things we did. No-one could crack me up like Kate.

But she was different, too. The eldest of two girls from a staunch Catholic family, her dad, Denis, also worked at the Michelin factory. Her mum, meanwhile, was one of the many talented artists who hand-painted figurines at the potteries. Kate, like me, had her own obsession. While I tortured myself night and day about how I was going to turn myself into a huge financial success, rich enough to be able to support my family and give bundles of money to people who needed it, Kate was happily fulfilling her passion every single day. Kate loved to read. By the age of nine she had read all the books in the Bentilee junior library and was given a special ticket to choose books from the adult section where she worked her way through literary classics, from Charles Dickens to Jane Austen and Thomas Hardy.

There's an expression that perfectly suited Kate: never judge a book by its cover. Beneath those model-girl looks was one of the smartest, most naturally intellectual brains I've ever come across. And that's saying something because I've met a hell of a lot of smart people in my life. In different times, and under different circumstances, she would have studied English Literature at university and gone on to be a writer or an academic, but Kate had other issues. She had a sister, Claire, who was eleven years her junior, and who had been diagnosed with diabetes at the age of six. Claire had been kept in hospital until she had learnt to inject herself with insulin. Kate did a lot of the caring for Claire as their parents worked full-time, but she didn't begrudge getting up in the middle of the night or cooking the dinners. Didn't begrudge it one bit because she loved her family.

John became John 'n' Kate. We'd call each other at 6pm every evening (Kate can still remember my old number, 22408, and she remembers the name of the song that was playing the night I asked her out, Alright Now by Free). Her parents were less impressed when they discovered that the white Jaguar wasn't actually mine, and I would arrive on my noisy motorbike, a penniless biker on an apprenticeship at the 'Mitch'. Kate bought a leather jacket to match mine but she'd have to hide it in the coal shed outside the house and run out in a little top and short skirt with her mum shouting, 'You can't go out in that.' Both of us were speed freaks, we loved riding as fast as the bike would go.

Her ambition was to be a librarian. We could not have been more different but we were perfectly suited. Her head was in the esoteric clouds with the novelists and the poets and my feet were firmly on the grubby ground, trying to find that elusive path to success. Kate was a complete romantic and I couldn't see the point of bunches of flowers or love sonnets. She could be so engrossed in her book she'd miss her bus stop. The only book I can remember reading was a biography of Margaret Thatcher, my idol – and I didn't even finish that.

*****

'JOHN, I'M NOT sure we can keep seeing each other, my mum and dad aren't happy.'

Of our nightly 6pm phone calls, it was the shortest one ever. 'I'm off round to Kate's,' I muttered to my mum. I didn't even get changed out of my work boiler suit. I got on my motorbike and zoomed over to her house. Kate answered the door looking uncharacteristically anxious.

'They think we aren't right for each other,' she said. 'And maybe we are too young, John.' It was true she was just 16 and I was barely 19 but I knew Kate was the only girl I ever wanted to be with. I didn't want to call things off, I wanted her mum and dad to know how serious I was.

'Are they in?' I said. Kate nodded. 'Can I talk to them?' She looked worried but pointed to the front room.

Denis and Jean were sitting on the sofa together, neither of them looked pleased to see me. Kate was their eldest daughter. She was bright, she was beautiful and she was also part of a strict Roman Catholic family who took religion very seriously. I didn't go to any church, I rode around on a motorbike and Kate had been spotted by various friends of the family, on the back of my bike in short skirts and the contraband leather jacket.

I made my point about being very serious about Kate. Dennis wasn't having it. 'This is ridic-lous, ridic-lous,' he kept on repeating. Jean (who years later became a second mother to me) said nothing and just looked like she wanted me to leave. I could feel Kate, next to me, squirming with embarrassment, but still I felt that everyone was over-reacting. We were old enough to know what we wanted, we were in love and I couldn't believe my religion – or lack of it – could even be an issue.

Kate was torn. She didn't like going against her parents. There was a bad atmosphere at home and they disapproved of me as her boyfriend. I was 'the wrong sort' in their eyes. I couldn't see why she was so upset about what they thought, which made things worse. She couldn't understand why I couldn't understand her and how important her parents' opinion was. For the first time ever we rowed.

'It's over,' she told me after our fifth fight on the phone. The line went dead. 'I'll call her tomorrow', I thought but when six o'clock came the phone box just rang out. I called her again the next day and the next. I went round to her house when I knew she'd be in and her parents' would still be at work but she wouldn't even open the door.

I didn't know how it had all fallen apart so fast. All I knew was I had to get her back. Nothing was right without her.

Bang. The first stone hit her bedroom window which was luckily for me on the street side. Bang, the second one hit and the curtain pulled back. It was 5am and Kate's rather bleary morning face was peering down at me. She opened the window and hissed: 'Stop it, you're going to wake the whole street up.' 'Not until you come down and talk to me,' I answered, taking aim with another chunk of stone. Five minutes later we were standing in the little alley that separated her house from next door. 'Marry me,' I said. She looked at me in total disbelief then threw her arms round me. 'I've missed you so much,' she cried.

We were engaged. We went to a pawn shop called Rosina Ward and Kate picked out a little sapphire ring which set me back £20. The engagement changed things in the McFarlane household. I might not be a Catholic – and I still rode a motorbike – but an engagement showed my intentions were good and it was a step towards real respectability. The freeze thawed. Denis, Jean, my mum and the two of us went out to celebrate at a swish nightclub called Jollees. Kate wore a long black dress with a silver bodice from C&A – the first dress she'd ever bought from a proper shop – and spent the whole night smiling and looking at her ring. Everybody was happy including me, even though I never imagined myself getting married. I had no money and no house. The little business schemes I was doing on the side of my day job at Michelin (respraying cars and selling door-to-door insurance investment packages) were not exactly fulfilling my dreams of financial success. They were barely filling the holes in my pockets.

Denis and Jean, God bless them, offered to pay for the wedding, and so a room was booked upstairs at The Dunrobin pub in Longton. And then Kate broke the news. 'John, You know we have to get married at our church so Mum says you need to go and see the priest. He knows you're not a Catholic but you have to talk to him before we can do anything.'

This was the first I'd heard about a church wedding. I'd been thinking we'd just go to the local register office and keep things simple. I shook my head. 'Sorry Kate, I can't go and see your priest. I don't believe in God and I don't want to get married in a church, especially a Catholic one. It's not something I can do.'

My stance – which, to this day, remains unchanged – was a bombshell. Kate cried. Her mum cried. Denis was cold and hurt. We were at a stalemate. Eventually I saw there was no other way but for me to go along to the church, to try it out. I am not a religious man. Every experience I've had of going to church – Catholic or otherwise – has left me cold with the feeling that organised religion encourages a sort of hypocrisy which I can't abide. 'It's not spiritual. It's just women in big hats looking at each other's hats,' I moaned to Kate.

In the end, I had to go through several weeks of religious instruction with the priest, Father Ryall at St Maria Goretti, the Catholic church in Bentilee. I listened to everything he said. I asked questions although I never got answers that would change my views and opinions. Kate, however, was impressed and the family was happy. We'd sit outside the pub, and she would smile as I'd moan about what the priest had said. 'I know you hate it, John,' she'd say. 'And I know you never do anything you don't want to do. So I know you must really want to marry me.' To Kate, it was probably my most romantic gesture.

*****

'JOHN, HELP! MY veil's blowing off!' We were standing outside the church, Mr and Mrs Caudwell. We were both in fits of laughter. Kate's veil was streaming like a thin, white flag across other people's faces in the official line-up, whilst I was still trying to hold my hair piece on without anybody realising. We had five bridesmaids dressed in calamine pink outfits, and Kate was wearing a long dress with a Swiss lace bodice that could have been designed by a nun – the neck was high, the hem was long and the sleeves were full and it had been lovingly made by Jean. Kate thought it was a bit too plain and prim but to me, she looked like a queen.

It was a great day. I remember it so clearly even now. We all trooped over to the pub after church for a hot meal. Not Denis's favourite dish of pork pie and pickle, but a proper dinner (or 'lunch', as I've learnt to call it). Come the late afternoon, our friends and neighbours rolled up, bringing plates of cheese and ham sandwiches. That was the way things were back then; everyone pitched in, no one worried about matching plates or tableware and little cards with place names on were unheard of. We all stood or perched on the pub seats. My mum and my little brother Brian were happy, and now I could tell Kate we had our own small place to live. Mum had said we could have my dad's old touring caravan, which was in the garden next to the house. That caravan was a space smaller than one of the utility rooms in the house I live in today. But we were both thrilled to have any place of our own.

'I'm going to carry you over the threshold,' I shouted when we finally got back home after many pints, lots of dancing and several slices of wedding cake. We fell into the caravan, laughing. Then we stood up, jumped onto the bed and the whole thing tipped over because my mates thought it would be hilarious to wind up all the jacks which kept the caravan stable. If anything, it made us laugh even more. We were in love.

She was seventeen and I was twenty, and there we were, just a couple of kids – but we were Mrs and Mrs Caudwell.

Chapter 6

BACK TO BLACK (INTO THE RED)

'ARE YOU CRAZY, Caudwell?'

My manager, Roger, was staring at me in disbelief, the beginnings of an incredulous grin playing about his mouth.

Minutes earlier I had gone into his tiny office at the Michelin Tyre Plant and stood in front of him in my green jacket which designated me as apprentice technical engineer.

As far as the managers at Michelin were concerned I was a bit of a problem. On the one hand, I'd been top of my class on many occasions throughout my apprenticeship, working in every department faster, more accurately and more productively than most of the other apprentices at the vast, sprawling Stoke-on-Trent factory site, from hydraulics to pneumatics, electrics, welding, bench tools and every machine tool known to man.

But the problem was my attitude. I didn't slot in with the other workers, nice and neatly like a cog in a wheel. I was a bit of a rebel. I complained that we could not get a cup of tea out of the machine in time, because the queue took up most of the 10-minute break. It was the same for the 30-minute lunch break when all of us had to dash to queue up at the works canteen and throw the food down as fast as you could. If there was trouble on the floor, odds on I'd be at the centre of it – setting off fire hoses for a water fight or putting araldite into the lock of a fellow trainee's work-bench so they had to break

65

through the rock solid glue, swearing under their breath as I laughed my head off.

When I look back, I know I was difficult but I loved a good laugh and a practical joke. In some ways I knew I was not quite like the rest. I was a non-conformist. I wasn't a sheep. My ambitions weren't to become a senior manager and die happy. I wanted more. I wanted to burst out of my green jacket like some sort of business superhero and run my own empire. I just needed to get my foot on the first rung of the ladder out of that factory. But whilst I searched for my destiny, I still had to clock in, clock out; still had to say 'yes sir, no sir', and so my frustrations built. I think a combination of this frustration, and my natural, mischievous character, made me a constant challenge for my bosses. They probably thought I was bored and needed to be kept occupied and stimulated.

That was no doubt how I'd been selected for a stint in 'tyre testing': basically, a Boy's Own dream of driving cars up and down the motorway, and on a skid pan at Hixon Airfield, to test those famous rubber tyres bearing the tubby white Michelin man logo. You could put your foot right down on the test track and pretend to be James Hunt or Jackie Stewart, the greatest racing car drivers of the day, and go as fast as you could. Of course you weren't supposed to but it was a blast and I loved it!

But a few months in, a low level panic began to kick in. I felt I was driving fast on a road to nowhere. I'd made it off the shop floor and I was having fun but I was still in my green jacket, still an employee, still hadn't found something that was going to get me out. That desperation to make real money, to make a success of myself took the edge off any enjoyment I was having. I had to get serious. I had to make more money. I racked my brains, looked around my area and started to put together a plan which would involve me and my teenage wife, Kate. But it would mean getting Roger to put me back in the toughest, filthiest, most-dreaded department in the whole of Michelin.

'Roger, can I come and see you this afternoon?' I asked. He nodded. 'I've got a few minutes after 2pm,' he answered. My plan to go from one of the most enjoyable positions at Michelin to the most appalling was about to begin.

The department, nicknamed 'the Black' was where the rubber for the tyres was made and mixed with a horrible sticky goo that contained, among other things, sulphur, carbon, black soot and oil. The conditions in the Black were awful. It was the most physically-demanding work on the whole site. The room was boiling hot and the visibility hazy, due to the semi-molten rubber and the clouds of carbon black that filled the atmosphere and turned the natural rubber into tyre rubber. It was like working in a filthy sauna with the stench of industrial chemicals that were added to the rubber mixture to achieve that perfect strength and flexibility needed for a Michelin tread.

There were huge mixers, called Banburys, like a giant mincemeat machine, into which we fed all of these obnoxious substances, mixing them round until they formed a gooey, rubbery, hot mix. Our job was to keep these machines operating which often involved working under the machine whilst this huge, hot fuming mix dripped onto our skin and hair.

It was deafeningly loud and, thanks to the dust and fumes, our eyes were permanently streaming. Many working in the Black developed what was known as 'the Black cough'. And there was no thought given to wearing masks back then, you just put up with it.

Few wanted to work in that hellhole, even though the money was good. As a trainee you had to do a stint in the Black but you got pulled out within a matter of weeks – unless you had upset the boss. It was viewed as a punishment for the kids who never made the grade, or as the home of the truly desperate workers. For the trainees who were condemned to the appalling conditions of the Black, Michelin had to add a bonus to the princely wage of £15 a week. There were always extra shifts going begging, and for me – along with the extra danger money – that was the only way I was going to bump up my pay. I didn't care how hard I had to work; for my plan to work, I needed as much cash as I could get. At 2pm precisely I walked into my manager's office with my request.

'You're not going in the Black, Caudwell,' Roger said, shaking his head and looking rather bemused. 'You'd be wasted. Sorry, but you're not going back there.' He nodded his head towards the door. My time was up. I refused to budge. I had to get him to put me in the Black, so I thought I would tell him my big plan, the idea that was going to turn my life around.

'There's going to be a massive property boom,' I explained, calmly and authoritatively. 'I've found a detached house in Ash Bank that's on the market for £18,000. It's a good area – a smart area. And it will really go up in value.' He was staring at me which I took as a good sign so I pushed on. 'But I need to earn more so I can get sufficient mortgage to buy it. When prices go up, I'll have a huge increase in equity.' Now he was starting to smile which I took as a positive sign. 'So if I work in the Black,' I said. 'I can make more and get extra shifts. That's why I need to be moved.'

As erudite and well-educated as he was, Roger could not grasp the concept that equity in a property was nearly as valuable as cash in the bank. Neither could he believe that someone like me would want to put myself in that position, saddled with a big mortgage. Although he was a young man he had that lack of visionary attitude like my dad to whom debt was an absolute anathema.

He shook his head and his voice took on an unmistakable edge of condescension. 'You haven't thought it through properly. House prices might go up a bit, but you won't have any equity because you'll be living in it so it just doesn't make sense John.' There was a slight pause as he let his words sink in, then he continued again with a rather patronising tone. 'And there might not be a property boom so then what are you going to do?' Before I could respond, he added, 'I couldn't afford a house in Ash Bank. No-one here has a house worth £18,000. You've got a good future in engineering but it's always best to live within your means.'

He smiled at me then looked down at his desk signalling the conversation was over. I had been told. But I stayed put. I knew that he was wrong and I was right. There WAS going to be a property boom, the house was in a smart area. All house prices were going to rocket but especially this one. I didn't care if he thought I was an idiot, I didn't care that he didn't understand about debt and equity, it wasn't important because I knew exactly what I was doing.

Key attributes of success are passion, drive and ambition and using those attributes to never let anyone stand in your way, no matter what they think. I didn't waver, I was going to make him move me because it had to happen to complete my plan. I knew if I kept insisting, I had every right to work in that department and I knew they needed people in there. If I stuck to my guns Roger would have to cave. The way I saw it then – the way I still see it – is that in business the word 'no' is just the first step on the road to 'yes'.

Five minutes later, I walked out of his office as the new recruit for the Black. I had a lot of respect for Roger but I knew exactly what I was doing. He was wrong. I knew in my bones that property was going to take off and this house was going to turn my life around.

*****

MONTHS LATER, KATE sat in our clapped-out, 15-year-old

banger of a Fiat 600D, her mouth wide open as she stared at the brand new, detached four-bedroom house in Ash Bank. 'Wow, John,' she laughed. 'I can't believe we are actually going to live here. This doesn't seem real.'

She was right. We weren't exactly the usual Ash Bank sort. We had both grown up in and around the Bentilee estate where most people either worked at the potteries, the Michelin factory, Shelton Iron and Steel factory or one of the many collieries which were dotted through the six small towns that together made up the city of Stoke-on-Trent.

Our first house was a tiny place in Weston Coyney to which I'd made several 'improvements', including knocking down a wall when Kate was out – she woke up to find a hole in the kitchen and plaster in the butter! This new house on a nice modern estate was the kind of place that a young doctor or lawyer would be moving into. Not one of the nine thousand blue collar employees of the Mitch, who was permanently covered in a layer of dirt, and whose fingernails remained stubbornly black no matter how viciously they were scrubbed. But this was where we were going to live. It all made sense to me. In order to make the most of the property boom I could see coming, I had to buy the most expensive house I could possibly afford in the best neighbourhood I could find. Ash Bank was it.

Kate stood by in stunned disbelief as I marshalled my plan into action, sacrificing whatever it took. Our meals were more frugal than ever and nights at the pub were a thing of the past. I'd sold my beloved Kawasaki motorbike, worked sixteen-hour double shifts in the Black, borrowed as much money as I could from the bank, and did a deal with the developer who'd built the house, as well as landing myself with a colossal mortgage to put my name on the deeds. I'd done it.

We moved in on a Saturday. It took less than a day to pack up all our belongings.

BACK TO BLACK (INTO THE RED)

'Talk about arriving in style,' Kate grinned as she jumped out of the car. All that we had to unpack were a few boxes of pots and pans, a couple of orange crates for us to sit on and Kate's beloved coffee table that we'd got free by collecting the coupons from packets of Embassy cigarettes. Our 'stuff' barely filled the corner of the sitting room. But we were in. It was our house and that was all that counted – even if the bed we had to sleep on was 30 years old and had totally collapsed in the middle.

Ash Bank really was my first little break into becoming the businessman I am today. Roger, as I said, was wrong and my forecast proved right. It was 1975, a year after Edward Heath ended his four-year term as Conservative Prime Minister to be succeeded by Labour's Harold Wilson. During Heath's prime ministership, he had appointed Anthony Barber as Chancellor of the Exchequer. And Barber would be the man who indirectly changed my fortunes.

In his first budget, Barber's plan was to encourage growth in the economy by easing credit conditions within the Bank of England. This, in turn, led to Britain's first experience of a housing bubble and it became known as the 'Barber boom' of 1973. It didn't last long – only a few years – but within that short period house price inflation peaked at 36 percent. Between 1950 and 1970, the average price of a home had risen from £2,000 to £5,000. However, during the Barber boom, house prices doubled.

Sure, I didn't have any cash to buy a posh sofa for me and Kate to sit on. But I did have, as I had predicted, precious equity to build an empire. And this house in Ash Bank, Stoke-on-Trent, meant that we were on our way.

Chapter 7

CORNER SHOPS, MAGGOTS AND OTHER CATASTROPHES

MINDFUL OF HER stiletto heels, Kate carefully picks her way through the rather battered doorway of a terraced house in Porthill on the outskirts of Stoke. She's come to see my latest big idea which I hope will be the start of creating my business empire. It's a twelve-foot by twelve-foot front room of a terraced house in Stoke, converted into a lock-up grocery shop complete with shelving, fridges and freezers. The owner, Mrs Shemilt, lived at the back of the property.

I wave my hands around the space, picturing in my head a cornucopia of cheap but tasty goods – mounds of cheeses, bacon, hams and the staple stocks of baked beans, bread, butter and own-brand soups and sauces. I can almost hear the ding, ding, ding of the till, busily opening and shutting, one swift transaction after another filling it up with cash. Completing the image in my head is Kate, smiling winningly at the queue of customers as she efficiently and carefully cuts and wraps a half pound of Cheddar for the first in line. I can visualise her looking glamorously beautiful behind the counter, charming customers with her witty one liners and charismatic personality.

'So we'd move the counter here,' I say enthusiastically, trying not to notice that the light had suddenly disappeared from her blue eyes and she was looking rather mournfully at the bleak metal walls. 'There'll be people in and out all day, never a dull moment. You'll love it Kate. It'll be way busier than the boring, old library.' She gave me a weak smile and nodded.

I look back now and cannot believe what I was thinking. Kate was eighteen, gorgeous, lively, smart, and had loved books all her life. At school she dreamt of becoming a librarian, and for the past year she'd been working at Hanley Library, loving every minute of her job. She got a buzz from being surrounded by literature and other literary enthusiasts. Nothing gave her greater pleasure than encouraging young readers to find books that they would fall in love with, or introducing hardened thriller readers to Daphne du Maurier or the Brontes. And there I was, trying to get her excited about the fact I'd found a deal on Spam at the Cash and Carry, enabling us to make an extra two-pence profit on every tin sold. 'And we can make great flyers, pin them up around the shop and post them through everybody's letterbox, with the bargain of the week,' I added. Another small nod.

Now, most people know me as a very successful businessman. I turned a failing mobile business into a £1.46 billion international empire in the space of 18 years, and came from nothing to seeing my name regularly listed in the *The Sunday Times* Rich List and *Forbes* magazine. I can look at any business and identify how it can be improved. I know – in forensic detail – what skills are needed to be successful. I understand exactly how the economy works, how shifts and falls in other countries affect the man on the street in Manchester and Tottenham. I can talk for hours about every intricate detail of business structure and logistics. But I have had 50 years of life and work experience, and I also know that the road to phenomenal success is paved with the bumps of failure. You can only be a winner if you learn tough lessons from very painful mistakes, and learn them rapidly. Back then, back in that front room in 1972, I didn't have a bloody clue what I was getting us into.

Anyone who has sat through the most rudimentary business studies lesson will have learnt the mantra that in order to succeed, you need to know your customer. This is absolutely true. But equally as important is the fact that you also need to know your staff. Back to front and inside out. You need to know what makes them tick. Find out what drives them, as well as their skills and their weaknesses. Do they need pushing and rewarding? Do they need to be given space and responsibility or regular guidance? When I interview a candidate who wants to work for me, their CV is a mere canapé. I want to know everything about them, from their childhood onwards, because to get the best from your staff you need to know you are always putting the right man or woman in the right job where they will be happiest and most productive, to help your business flourish.

And so, aged 20 and blissfully ignorant of this fundamental rule, I had decided to make the woman I knew best in the world, the first great love of my life, run our corner shop. It was an unmitigated disaster and I can now only laugh at my own foolishness and apologise to Kate for putting her through months of hell.

*****

'CALL FOR YOU in the office.' I was in the 'Black'. I looked up from the tar covered Banbury mixer, where I was tightening up the last bolt on the giant rubber mixing machine, to see my manager hovering over me, his lips pursed in evident disapproval. The Michelin did not allow us to take personal phone calls at work, unless it was an emergency. 'It's your wife,' he hissed. 'Hurry up. She's in a phone box.'

My heart sank as I looked at my watch. It was 11am which meant Kate should be in the shop. Something bad must have happened, I dreaded to think what. 'John,' I could hear Kate at the end of the line gulping back sobs. 'I've cut part of my hand off.'

'What?'

'The meat slicer. I forgot to put the guard on it. There's blood everywhere. I don't know what to do.'

I wasn't exactly up on health and safety back then, and I also had a unique attitude to injuries given my own ability to withstand pain. I was also aware of the manager pointedly looking over at me, clocking every minute I was taking up on the phone. 'Can't you just put a bandage on it?' I said, rather unsympathetically. 'It'll be fine.'

'OK.' I could hear another gulp.

'Kate,' I said, 'You did lock up before you came to the phone box, didn't you?' The pips on the phone went and I walked back to check on the Banbury, avoiding my manager's eye, wondering if she'd left the shop door wide open with all our stock just sitting there.

When I got home that night I did feel a twinge of guilt when I saw her hand. It was now wrapped in a massive bandage. 'It just wouldn't stop,' she said. 'So I got a bus to the hospital and had a tetanus.' She paused and looked at me. 'But I can't help thinking about the bit I sliced off which went into this old lady's ham. The blade was so sharp I didn't feel it when I did it. I only realised after I put the money in the till and there was blood everywhere. Part of my hand would be in with the slices of ham. She must have taken it home with her. What if she put it in a sandwich, John?' And we both burst out laughing.

'Maybe she asked for a quarter of boiled hand,' I chuckled. She burst into a fit of giggles. We'd laugh again and again about the 'boiled hand' incident. That was the thing with Kate and I, we always ended up seeing the funny side of all our disasters.

It took nearly a year for me to realise the shop was never going to work. I think I knew it all along but I just kept refusing to see all the problems. Kate never made a single one of those flyers. I had to make them secretly at work, and they'd often be still lying at the back of the counter several days later because she'd forgotten to pin them up.

To be fair, she did have a lot on her plate. Kate's mornings would consist of getting out of bed, cramming down a quick breakfast and every now and again helping to push my car to get it started. Then she'd get dressed, catch three different buses from Weston Coyney to Porthill and her first job was to check a lock-up I was also renting from Mrs Shemilt, to check on the batches of mushrooms I had growing as another side operation to earn extra cash. The mushrooms had to be treated like little queens of darkness. 'Open the garage door just a crack and squeeze in,' I'd instruct Kate. 'They do not like sunlight.' We shared the tasks of perfecting the compost in twenty or so boxes, sewing the mushroom spawn, covering it with plastic to keep it warm and propagate the spawn, and then carefully removing the covers and adding peat.

After six weeks, Kate sorrowfully delivered the news: 'Only 12 mushrooms have come up.' We ate them on toast for our tea that night. We tried again but we never got it right – there were either too few or too many. When there were too many we also ended up eating them – or rather the ones that had gone past the point of being able to sell so then we suffered withered mushrooms for breakfast, lunch and dinner until I finally called time on the mushroom operation.

To add to Kate's duties at the shop, I decided to include a free delivery service for our customers – largely old ladies with cauliflower perms who immediately realised this was the way to get their heavier food stuffs, such as cans and potatoes, without having to strain through the streets with unwieldy shopping bags. So, after catching her buses, checking on the mushrooms, Kate would open the shop and start on the deliveries. The only problem was that she – in her mini-skirt and stiletto heels – then had to cart heavy boxes through the streets. There were an awful lot of hills around Porthill, we weren't making any money on the deliveries and each delivery meant the shop was temporarily shut, so we started doing the deliveries on a Friday evening after the shop was shut, and after I had finished at Michelin.

I spent a great deal of time at work worrying about the shop. Had Kate remembered to put up the 'Back in ten minutes' sign when she went out on deliveries? Was she covering up the ham, the bacon and the cheese after each sale? Were the flyers up? Every time I turned up, it was all still left out, the cheese going hard around the edges, the ham and bacon curling unappetisingly. 'Kate, can't you see this is costing us money?' I'd say, slicing off the spoiled bits of the cheese and ham, and sorting the bad slices of bacon from the good. I'd add all these ruined goods to any others that were past their sell-by date products. We'd take them home to eat ourselves (it was all we could afford to eat) but at least it provided variety from the withered mushrooms. I simply could not understand why Kate, one of the most intelligent people I knew, never remembered to protect our fresh produce, and how she didn't seem to realise that it was costing us money.

The thing is, it was really my fault. I was hammering a square peg in a round hole. I was forcing a free, creative spirit into a soulless world of absolute drudgery. And of course, she knew she should put up the notices and cover the cheese, the ham and the bacon. She just couldn't be bothered. As she'd tell me years later, it was her small rebellion for those three buses she had to catch there and back, for having to give up the job she loved, for carrying the boxes and being confined to squabbling over the price of potatoes or a loaf of bread with a bunch of pensioners.

It also turned out later that she managed to get though reading the complete works of Charles Dickens in that corner shop. The run on deliveries – which involved shutting the shop (without putting the sign up!) – meant the daily footfall dropped enough for her to spend most of her time sitting in a chair behind the till reading. If I turned up, she'd quickly hide the book in a narrow shelf under the till. All that time I never realised she was just sitting, reading. And I thought no-one could be more vigilant than me. By the time she'd got through Dickens – and that's a lot of books – we were in so much debt, I had to give up the grocery dream and Kate was welcomed to Stoke Library with open arms. Although dreadful at the time, what it cost me in money, it taught me a valuable lesson in business. Learn to be a good manager and always find the right woman – or man – for the job.

*****

GOD BLESS POOR Kate. She lived through so many of my early ventures and, despite the corner shop debacle, she would always go along with anything. She believed that one day I'd get it right and strike gold although there must have been many times when she wondered what on earth she'd got herself into. A lot of my ideas weren't exactly the sort of things that would appeal to a young girl.

'I think I could do well with maggots,' I'd told her one night soon after we'd got married and were living in the caravan next to mum's house in Dividy Road. Kate's face dropped.

'Maggots!' she howled.

'Well, not quite maggots. I didn't mean maggots exactly. More like white worms.' I answered quickly, hoping to corral her into the idea. 'They use them to feed fish in pet shops and home aquariums. White worms are very easy and after you get one worm batch it keeps on multiplying, so you can also sell the worm cultures.' I made sure I stressed the word worm each time, as clearly the word maggot was a no-go. She was now looking at me patiently, which I took as a good sign.

'So, I'm going to order them. All I have to do is let the worm culture multiply. You just have boxes filled with soil to put the worms in. And then you put a small scoop of oats on top of the soil, cover it with a piece of glass. Overnight the worms will come to the top and stick to the glass. You scoop them into plastic bags and send them off to buyers. You can help if you like. I'll put ads out, and we can get an easy little income going.'

'OK John,' Kate answered, patient as ever while no doubt cringing inwardly at the prospect of dealing with squirming white worms.

The worms sadly went the way of the mushrooms, felled by an unexpected frost which decimated my little wriggling army within a month. Clearly I wasn't cut out to deal with plants, insects or animals. But soon after the mushroom experiment, I'd got my teeth into a venture that was right up my street – appealed to my wife – and which was proving to be a success.

As a motorcycling fanatic, I'd spotted in *Motor Cycling News* that the sought-after Belstaff waterproof jackets and trousers were all being sold in small independent ads for £20 – a 10 percent discount.

Now that I was in my early twenties, I felt a desperate pressure to fulfil this vision I'd had since I was a child, to turn the Caudwell name into something great and good, and to build a business that would give me enough money to make the world a better place. But here I was, still working at the Michelin, married, with a failing corner shop, and every scheme I tried to make work was going down the swanny and costing me money I simply didn't have.

Belstaff was a great name. It was a brand with strong roots in Stoke-on-Trent, having been founded there in 1924 by Eli Belovitch and Harry Grosberg and so it all seemed to fit. My plan was to negotiate with Belstaff and then sell the same items for a 20 percent discount in the same magazines and, as I confidently told the Account Manager at Belstaff a few hours later, 'I'd also like to sell them in my shop in Porthill so I'm talking retail as well as mail order.' Belstaff bought the idea of their gear being sold in an actual shop rather than only motorcycling magazines.

I have to admit that even though I did hang a few up in the shop, not a single customer bought one. 'I can't see one of my old ladies in one of them, John,' Kate laughed as I made space on a wall for the bikers' jackets and trousers, above the tins of baked beans and tomato soup.

I was onto a winner. Belstaff offered me a trade discount of 40 percent. This meant that even with a 20 percent discount to the customer, I would still be making a profit of 20 percent. Although not one item moved in the shop, I was getting dozens of orders through the magazines. I increased the size of my ads and after a few months I was selling hundreds of pieces every week. Our living space at home was stuffed with suits and packaging, and every night after work, we'd be folding jackets and trousers into brown paper wrapping, filling in address labels, and Kate or I would be dispatched down to the Post Office to make the deliveries.

It was exciting. The shop was failing but the Belstaff business was booming, and I was working out ways to expand, taking on new suppliers, increasing the range and looking into selling the gear in Europe through French, Spanish and Italian bike magazines. 'Kate, look at all these,' I'd yell every morning as I'd run to see the order letters piled up in the doorway. And then I had a call from the Account Manager at Belstaff, asking me to go to their office. 'I think we have a problem,' he said.

My heart sank. What was he talking about? I wanted to know there and then. In between work, the shop and doing the Belstaff orders I had no time to visit their offices. 'What is it?' I asked, racking my brains to think what he could possibly mean.

'We've had complaints.'

'From whom?' I wondered whether we were talking postal delays or wrong orders, and why this meant I was being called to task.

'Well, it's our regular suppliers. You're undercutting them. They're not happy about it.'

'But I explained to you right at the beginning, I'd be selling at a discount in my retail shop and through mail order.'

'Well,' he said, his tone changing. 'The thing is John, we didn't realise you'd be this successful. And it's not fair on our more established customers who are losing trade to you, so I'm afraid we won't be doing business with you anymore.' I fought back, but nothing I said made any difference. 'I'm sorry, but a decision has been made.'

The line went dead. I couldn't believe what I was hearing. The problem was I was too successful and in a heart sinking split second I realised this was going to leave me with a calamitous problem. Not only had I spent more money on ads for the next few weeks but I had pre-paid customers who I couldn't pay back, since the money had been committed to advertising. Meanwhile orders were flooding in every day and I wouldn't be able to fulfil them.

Whilst I was trying to work out what to do, the customers started ringing in and I came up with a strategy, which was actually just about telling the customers the truth. I spoke to every one of them explaining that Belstaff would not supply my orders, because they did not want the customers getting such a fantastic discount, and that there was no way I could refund their money if Belstaff did not supply the products. I explained business was booming and that my business was cut off in its prime by my supplier's ruthless and unethical behaviour. The blame was firmly at the feet of Belstaff. Every single one of them, hundreds of irate, worried customers, bombarded the factory office with screaming complaints.

A couple of days later the phone rang. 'John, we need to meet up.' It was Belstaff on the phone. This time I went to their four-storey offices in Caroline Street, Longton. It was like entering another world. There I was, a 20-year-old kid, a would-be entrepreneur who had pulled off something none of their other retailers had ever dreamed of, yet they wanted to crush the life out of the business I had built up.

Like a lamb to the slaughter, I was ushered into a boardroom dominated by a large highly polished, dark-wood table and high-backed chairs covered in rich leather. Cabinets ran along one wall, filled with silver trinkets and medals and above them hung large, heavy Victorian framed oil paintings of the Belstaff family. Around the table sat the entire Belstaff board, middle-aged men in perfectly-pressed pinstripe suits, one or two with old fashioned handlebar moustaches. I wasn't wearing a suit, I wasn't wearing a tie and I could sense they thought this was going to be easy.

It wasn't. I wasn't intimidated, I was in war mode. I had nothing to lose. As they prepared to flatten me with some well-prepared speeches about me being a 'little problem', I let them have it. To me, these guys were just bullies. Belstaff had deliberately left me in a massive financial mess, they had pulled the rug from under my feet as I was in the process of making a massively successful business.

They left me with outstanding orders I couldn't fulfil, hundreds of unhappy customers, debts for adverts which would impact on my meagre finances for months to come and more devastatingly they had ripped apart something that was flourishing for all of us for the stupidest of reasons.

I was furious. With a steady voice I began. 'You've betrayed me, you've betrayed your customers and I will make sure every one of them knows exactly what you've done. Your name will stink and I will do you as much damage to you as I possibly can.'

The handlebar moustache twitched, displaying a clear sense of concern. They knew I didn't have any money to resort to a legal battle but they did clearly see the amount of damage I could and would inflict on their reputation. Condescendingly, and reluctantly, they offered to supply all the stock required for my outstanding orders. I played hard ball and insisted that they not only supplied the current orders, but also those that would arrive daily over the next few weeks. They agreed and I was able to trade out of trouble, to break even and not a single person was any worse off, except me.

It was a bitter pill. It left me seriously demoralised. I had really believed that this was the start of my destiny, and actually to this day, believe that other than for Belstaff, I would be one of the biggest online suppliers in the world by now, but they cut me off right at the start and I did not have the power to fight or recover.

I realised that business can be the bloodiest of battlefields, that corporations could be utterly ruthless and to be way more cynical about everyone and everything in the future.

I sold the corner shop, cleared the decks, cleared my debts, licked my wounds and tried to work out how I was going to fulfil my destiny. I had to simplify my life and make sure I could rely on those I chose as business partner. But I also knew I had it in me to take on whatever was thrown at me and that unlike those maggots – sorry, those worms – I wasn't ever going to curl up and die after one bad frost.

Chapter 8

HERCULES

IT IS FINALLY happening. I am 26 years old and have found my empire. It is nothing fancy. Just a litter-strewn, playground-sized car sales lot near my childhood stamping ground of Shelton, and it is where I am going to sell cars with Brian.

In reality I've paid over the odds for this car lot. I handed over £10,000 to its owner Lenny Shenton, who kept telling me he 'couldn't part with it', and had me in knots over whether the sale was on or off. He kept me so focused on having to persuade him to sell, I didn't once challenge the price. Later, to my eternal embarrassment, I hear that he'd been desperate to shift that land for years – yet another lesson learned!

It is at the bottom of a steep hill, and its entrance is a few yards short of a perilous curve in the road, so an impulsive turn into my site to look at a car is a pretty difficult move. This is another short, sharp lesson in thinking things through but it wasn't going to get me down because it all added to the challenge. And there's nothing like a tough challenge to get me firing on all cylinders.

I am completely focused on making this work. It will work. I will make it work I have no doubt. I've used the equity from my house in Ash Bank, and my saint of a mother has agreed to mortgage her house in Dividy Road to raise the £30,000 we need from the bank to get everything we need up and running, from stock to supplies. I did initially call it JDC Car Sales, but I had made enough rookie mistakes. My business brain quickly kicked in. Stoke-on-Trent is a poor area really badly hit by the demise of the coal industry, the steel works and the potteries, where customers will haggle over a single pound let alone a few hundred. So I changed the name to The Wholesale Car Centre, which sounds like we're selling at factory prices. In any business, a name can be an influential part of the marketing formula.

Brian is my perfect partner – as committed, driven and passionate as I am to make this venture a success. (Eventually, once we were turning over fifty to sixty cars a month, Brian would hand in his notice as a Michelin trainee engineer to run the place day-to-day, and he would handle the lion's share of the sales.) I am now working two jobs. For the time being I'll be staying at Michelin, working six days a week on shifts, whilst dashing off to the car auctions whenever I can, then on car sales with every minute I could muster. I pushed myself harder than I could ever imagine, on average 20 hours each day, because I knew this was it. It all makes sense to me. I was going to make, not break.

I know we cannot fail because we are the dream team. Young, hungry, resourceful and ambitious. We even have Fred, a real character, an employee who we've inherited with the land sale. With his eyes glinting behind his thick, pebble glasses, he's a dab hand at valeting cars and an expert at telling tall tales. And he is always cheerful, which will be great. He will make customers feel at ease, they can crack jokes with him and have a laugh. Then me or Brian will do the serious business of selling.

'First we make it look good,' I say to Brian. He nods. In the far-left corner are the remains of an old shed attached to a derelict end-of-terrace house which is right next to a cabin that I had ear-marked for a special purpose. 'That's going to be the workshop,' I say. 'So we can fix cars on site. But we have to build it ourselves. We can't afford to pay anyone else.' He nods again. It's back-breaking work and often because of my shifts, I spend hours up there on my own. Painfully and slowly – actually, quite quickly – it comes together...

*****

MY DREAM TOOK shape. Over the next few weeks we spent every spare hour smashing through rubble, hauling concrete slabs that I bought from a mate, hoisting an RSJ onto the roof which I welded into place with a kit borrowed from work. I was on my own that day using every ounce of strength I had in me to push, pull and levy that unwieldy heavy metal into place. Even now when I think of it I can't quite believe I actually managed it on my own. I recall how hell-bent I was on getting things finished because that particular job would have challenged Hercules himself. But other days Brian was around which was great. We were totally united, brothers in arms turning this wasteland into our vision of a professional car sales outfit.

I felt real pride as we polished up a couple of second-hand desks, one for Brian, the other for me. These would go into the office cabin. We scrubbed out the interior, painted it and, on the walls, we put a massive calendar and a sales chart. We had copies of car manuals, *Auto Express* and *Auto Trader* lined up on a shelf, along with box files and accounts books. There was a rattly little blower heater in the cabin, which barely kept the frost off the inside of the windows, a bucket to catch the drips from the leaky roof and no toilet, but it was our first real office.

The whole place is still standing today. I drive past it and think of those times. Sometimes I will pop in and have a cup of tea with Jeff Rawlings who is running it today. It's not even changed very much on the inside so it's quite a strange, rather emotional feeling, like walking into the Tardis and going back in time to those days. Brian and I took everything so seriously, cleaning the floors, the walls, the windows, straightening the calendars so everything looked shipshape. We'd check the lines of the cars, we installed floodlights (essential for dark days), and we worked out where we'd put the price tags, and which cars we needed to move first. We took every detail seriously because we took ourselves seriously, and we wanted to be taken seriously. This time failure was not an option.

The day before we opened for business, we both stood in front of the cabin, exhausted but pumped with adrenaline, scanning the area for final improvements. I could almost feel my heart beating faster. 'Nearly ready, Brian,' I said, and grinned at him. The first lines of cars – carefully picked out of thousands, that I had inspected, from all the best car auctions, were put in perfect order, polished to a high shine by Fred, smelling fresh on the inside (in those days people smoked like chimneys in their cars) and presented in the most attractive possible way to look as appealing as possible. Only the best cars at the best value could be sold by us. Brian had red, white and blue bunting to put up around the perimeter but before he did that there was a problem I needed to fix.

'I'm going to get rid of those weeds,' I told him. I grabbed a strimmer that I'd bought to fix the thick tangle of brush wood, rosebay willow, thistles and thorny, twisting bind weeds that sprung out messily from behind the new office, bunching scratchily all over the far-left-hand corner of the plot. I marched towards them, strimmer buzzing sharply, ready for the assault. Two minutes into the clearing operation, as I was neatly attacking the border of the dilapidated end of terrace, I leapt back in horror as a hail of brown, stinking filth flew up from the jaws of the strimmer, and splattered my face, my arms and my clothes. Brian raced over as I ran towards the outside tap, retching violently.

'Bloody dog shit!' I yelled.

It wasn't exactly an auspicious start.

*****

IN MANY WAYS, being sprayed with dog shit just as you are thinking everything is going brilliantly is the ultimate metaphor for the life of an entrepreneur. You may have the vision; you may have done everything you possibly can to make that vision a reality but be prepared because all sorts of unexpected crap will fly in your face. So, make a decision early on whether you can handle this and either wipe yourself down and get back to the job, or walk away now.

When I think back, buying Ash Bank and then opening that used-car sales lot was definitely the right move for me. I was working on pure instinct and logic and finally playing to my strengths. I hadn't read a single book on how to succeed in business but I had learnt lessons the hard way, and partnering up with Brian, who I trust with my life and who I knew was just as determined as me, made it possible to make everything work.

I'd done so many things over the years to make cash – from selling door-to-door toiletries and growing those blasted mushrooms – but I knew everything there was to know about cars, how to do them up and turn them around. Thanks to Dad, cars had been in the Caudwell boys' blood since the day we were born.

At Ash Bank I'd been making a steady income, buying cars and beautifully presenting them, and correcting faults in the little garage before selling them on. I'd been doing this on an off since I was 17 years old. Being around cars was as familiar to me as being around family. As a youngster, I'd spent hours at Newcastle Motor Auctions with Dad. It was a fascinating experience watching the old bangers come through and the shenanigans of the motor traders, although at that tender age of seven, I often did not understand what was going on. I did feel an excitement though and it always felt special being there with Dad.

HERCULES

A lot of our time together was spent in silence, me trailing Dad as he walked slowly through the mass of cars to be auctioned.

'What about this one, Dad?' I'd say, as we approached some big, shiny-looking car. He'd say nothing. He'd carry on walking without so much as a backward glance. Then he'd stop dead in front of another car, as if there was a huge neon sign flashing, visible only to him. He'd peer through the driver's door, study the dashboard, and check the rather rudimentary catalogue. 'What's so good about it, Dad?' I'd ask, looking intently at what he was looking at to find a clue. I was eager to know what had managed to catch his attention. As a response, I'd get just a few words. Over the years, however, I garnered enough information to be able to spot a worthy bargain for myself.

If Dad stopped and looked at a car that I pointed out, it meant I'd scored. He might not say anything, maybe just a grunt of acknowledgement. But that to me was a huge deal because, like every little lad, I wanted approval from my father. So, I did my homework, I studied the catalogues, read his car magazines, picked up tips from the other enthusiasts. Like a sponge, I absorbed; amassing knowledge about engines, car makes and models, gear glitches, fuel consumption. I loved it. The older I got, the more I'd watch Dad as he worked.

A car engine wasn't just a motor to him, it was an orchestra. He'd turn the ignition, listen carefully to every sound – or gasp – and bury his head under the bonnet, return to the ignition, listen and repeat until he'd sorted whatever problem he'd found. I too would listen out for wrong notes, training my ears to tune into the sounds of the engine. Often it was my job to turn the ignition key and gently press the accelerator, finally, Dad's symphony of a perfectly-running machine.

Years later, I would do the same with Brian. From knee high he was my assistant. He'd be the one who was helping me to repair a car that I'd bought to sell, coming along with me to see my next bargain, and listening to me explain the ins and outs of engines, models and carburettors. By the age of ten he was able to flat panels and spray paint like a professional. 'Good job, Brian,' I always made sure I told him with every car he worked on, and any question he asked I took time to explain, passing on to him all my magazines. Cars and Caudwells were inextricably linked.

*****

A FEW WEEKS in, and business was motoring along, if you'll pardon the pun. A couple of years in and we were selling sixty cars a month. We employed another salesman, and Brian left Michelin. There were a few splutters and misfires but it was obvious from the start that we had a good chance of success – even if at times we had a cold wind of despair.

Brian and I learnt so much about customer preferences from model variations, to colour.

'Anything in red?' Brian would regularly ask me when I rang in from the auction. We had discovered red cars pretty much sell straight away. Or if I'd seen a great bargain at the auctions and ended my call to Brian with the words: 'But it's green' he'd groan and say. 'Leave it.' Green cars, it turned out, were the kiss of death.

In 1977, if you spotted a Vauxhall Cavalier GLS or even better a Vauxhall CD at an auction you were on to a winner. These were our best sellers in Stoke, customers loved them. We learnt all this through trial and error, making many mistakes on colour and models and sometimes on condition. But, with our passion to succeed, we were desperate to learn, desperate to get the most desirable cars and desperate to give the customer the best possible value.

Sometimes a car would 'stick' inexplicably. It could be the right model, the right colour and the right price and yet it just would not sell. Brian and I would puzzle this conundrum over, changing the position of the car, getting Fred to give it an extra polish, knocking a little money off the price. Still it would remain unsold. 'I'm going to put it back in the auction,' I told Brian realising that there's just no point flogging a dead horse. We soon had a rule that any stale car on the lot that had not sold within a few weeks had to go back to the auction even if – on occasion – it meant we lost money. Cars that didn't sell cost our reputation more as people would think we were not successful with the same cars still on the lot. We needed to keep everything switching up, which kept the site exciting, ever-changing and vibrant.

There were few other limits I had in life then. The problem with wanting to succeed at all costs is that it can cost you more than just money. In order to get the car business going, I had to keep working at Michelin. I had a mortgage to pay as well as interest to the bank – plus a wife and a house – and we were about to start a family. Kate had been desperate to have a baby for years and our first child was due in November. The time had never been quite right but now my future seemed to be more solid.

A few years earlier and a baby would have been out of the question, as far as I was concerned. Kate was, as always, totally understanding. Our version of married life was pretty chaotic, with all my plans and schemes being juggled in the air, along with debts incurred from the disastrous corner shop and the fall-out from Belstaff's duplicitous treatment of me.

Not many young wives could have put up with me. Other young couples were content to have a job and a little place to live. We had friends who'd come home from work, go out to the pub together, sit in front of the television, or invite their mates around for a night in.

Kate had married a man who was fanatical about making something of himself. In those early years it must have seemed to her that I was always running into brick walls at breakneck speed. Yet, corner shop aside, Kate continued to be my cheerleader for every new venture. We did truly love each other and she believed in me. But she wanted a family, as did I, and now I felt that I was in a place where my vision of our future was starting to crystallise.

There was a problem though. And that problem was me. Or more accurately being me. I did not stop. I did not rest. It was as if there was a switch in my head that could not be turned off until I had satisfied everything I wanted to accomplish, but the goal posts kept moving further forward and I was never satisfied. By the time Brian and I were up and running, I was sleeping two or three hours every night. I was doing double shifts at Michelin, getting home at 8am, and then I'd be up two hours later to drive to a BCA Auction, to scout for bargains. At weekends, most of my time was spent on site – we opened early and closed at 10pm. Adrenaline was constantly pumping through me. My mind was so focused on the future, building the business, getting from one job to another and not dropping any of my spinning plates, that a normal married life was not even an option. There must have been times Kate wondered what she'd let herself in for. 'I'm doing this for us,' I'd tell her if she ever questioned me or told me to slow down. 'Kate, this is all for us.' Although just maybe it was more for me?

Chapter 9

USED CAR SALESMEN

'JOHN... WHAT'S THE matter?' It was Kate, banging on the bathroom door. I'd been in there for almost 20 minutes, bent over the toilet, my forehead pouring with sweat, vomiting continually.

Unbeknown to Kate, this had been going on for months. She was the one who was pregnant but it was me who was constantly throwing up. I'd have to pull over on the motorway, run to the toilet at work, sometimes crouch down between cars at the auctions and start retching. It was awful and embarrassing, especially as I was now becoming the bone-fide businessman I had always dreamed of being. I didn't want anyone staring at me as I retched uncontrollably like a hung-over teenager. I kept telling myself it wouldn't happen tomorrow because I didn't have time to deal with it. But when tomorrow came, so did the vomiting.

'I think something's wrong,' I spluttered. 'I keep being sick. But I don't think it's anything serious. I don't know why it's happening, but don't worry – it'll pass.'

'John,' she said calmly. 'You've got to see a doctor. This can't carry on. It's not right.'

The same afternoon I sat in my doctor's surgery, fretting about wasting time and worrying about the pile of things I needed to do. I listened as he told me I was suffering from a combination of overwork, stress and anxiety.

'You need to rest, John,' the doctor told me. 'Get a proper night's sleep. You're overdoing it. Would it help to take a few days off work?'

I opened my mouth to say something, and then stopped myself and shut it. I couldn't begin to tell him every single reason why there was no way I could take any time off work, and that every second I was sitting in his surgery was costing me money. 'What can you give me to stop the vomiting?' I said bluntly. I just wanted the problem dealt with.

He shook his head and wrote out a prescription for a nerve tranquiliser called Librium. I took them and they helped, but I tried to take them as infrequently as possible because even back then I didn't like pills or medication. As always, I applied logic to the situation. I reasoned that there was no other way than for me to carry on like this for at least a year or 18 months. This would be enough time to get the business established, and then I could start to ease off. I figured my body would just get used to being pushed to the extreme, another challenge I had to complete.

In truth, there was another layer behind my thinking. I can't call it fear because it didn't scare me, but it was something that did affect my thought patterns and was deeply embedded in my psyche. As a Caudwell man, I felt that as I was in my late twenties I was in a race against time. My father, Walter, had died young, as had my grandfather, John. And I knew I pushed myself physically harder and faster than either of them had ever done. Somewhere in my head, I firmly believed that I would die by the time I was 40. I had no time to waste and the clock was ticking. There was a baby on the way and an empire in its fragile infancy. I could sleep, I told myself, when I was dead. Until then, I had to get back to business.

*****

BRIAN AND I made a great team. I loved working with my brother. It was the dawn of the '80s and, even though at the time we thought we had class and style, we were the archetypal pair of used-car salesmen.

We had the Used-Car Salesman uniform. This was seasonal because, like all outdoor workers, used-car salesmen are slaves to the weather. Much of the year, we'd wear a well-cut Crombie over a pin-striped suit. Come the winter months, we wore a sheepskin coat over our suits, and a pair of pigskin gloves. It's the look made famous by George Cole as Arthur Daley in the brilliant ITV series, Minder, but there's a good reason for those coats.

Maybe it's just my memory, but I don't recall a lot of sunshine. What I do remember is the rain and the bitter cold. Standing in an exposed car lot on a dark November day – as frost is beginning to form on your fingers because you've been scraping ice off windscreens and lifting up freezing metal bonnets to check engines haven't frozen – you need every layer of clothing you can possibly get on your body. And nothing, believe me, nothing is warmer or more windproof than a thick, sheepskin coat.

Times could be tough. Although we knew all about cars, we were on a steep learning curve with our customers. Both of us understood the principles of selling, and Brian and I have always been messianic about being as honest and transparent as possible with the customer.

If there's a hidden problem, that customer will come straight back, and if you don't deal with that your name will become mud in the area. A good business is reliant on your reputation or your brand. That was a lesson I carried with me throughout every other business. Just think to yourself what type of beans you prefer – the reason you may reach for a tin of Heinz is all to do with your trust in that brand.

But we didn't know how much the car trade depended on the calendar. And Stoke – like a lot of cities – had its own idiosyncratic quirks in the calendar months. In late May, all of a sudden, the yard would be empty. No-one came anywhere near us.

'I'm going to paint the perimeter and put up new bunting. The old stuff is looking tatty,' Brian told me one spring afternoon, as we tried to fend off any waves of panic and see if there was anything we could do to attract trade. I checked through the books, made some adjustments and focused on pushing a couple of real bargains. Fred was sent out to re-polish and valet the cars. We then moved all the cars around so – from the road at least – we looked like an active, busy outfit. Still, it was just us salesmen pacing the lot. It was the same two weeks later.

We fretted about the lack of buyers, which equaled a lack of profit. Then Paula came to do our accounts. Paula was Brian's pretty girlfriend, and he'd fallen in love with her as she walked past the lot on her way to work every day. She looked up from our most recent accounts, and shrugged. 'It's Potter's Fortnight,' she said. 'Everyone's saving their money to go away.'

Of course we knew all about Potter's Fortnight. We'd grown up with it. For two weeks in June every single pottery closed and the whole of Stoke seemed to up and go in one movement to Rhyl or Blackpool. It was a tradition dating back to the 1950s, and Rhyl itself was actually known as Stoke-on-Sea. But we didn't quite realise how badly it would affect our trade.

For a month before Potter's Fortnight, people were saving up. For a month after the holiday fortnight, belts were tightened to compensate for the costs of bed and breakfasts, fish and chips, donkey rides, and two weeks of eating, drinking and merry-making. The same happened in November, in the run-up to Christmas, and then, after the festive season, dragged on until February. One minute we'd be turning cars over like hot cakes, and the next we'd be lucky to see a couple of sales in a week.

Paula, who Brian went on to marry, and still remains happily married four decades later, proved her weight in gold. After a few weeks of chatting to her as she walked past, Brian had asked her out and almost immediately it was clear he'd found 'the one'. She was – and still is – a wonderful woman. Even better, she was a grafter. Not only did she do our accounts, but she'd sit in that tiny cabin with Brian till we closed at 10pm.

Life was precarious. There was just about enough to make Mum's mortgage payment and pay the staff but if things didn't turn around quite fast, the business could be in real trouble. To keep in profit, we had to make around 12 sales a week and we were lucky if we were selling two cars. After months of good trade, we'd hit a desperate few weeks. Customers were umming and ahing over our cheapest deals and no sales.

We were haemorrhaging money but there was no way we could ever let the business collapse and not keep up payments on Mum's house. That was non-negotiable. On the table was a £20 note, which a guy had put down as a deposit for the car. It must have felt to Paula back then that if he didn't come back we might not have made it through. However, as Brian put the note in the safe he shrugged and said, 'Right, let's not go home, let's go to the pub. I think we need a drink. And we certainly deserve one.'

What Brian realised was that there are times when it's just about holding your nerve, being fearless and having confidence in who you are. Brian had faith that the two of us would turn things around, confidence that the buyers would return and we'd be able to tighten our belts and push through until things picked up.

Luckily, the guy did come back the next day and we learnt one of the most important lessons about being used car salesmen – financial survival.

*****

WE WERE TIED to a wheel of fortune. When the good folk of Stoke had money in their pockets they bought. When times were tight, they stayed away. We went up and we came down but we always hung on in there, pushed ourselves harder and got through. We grew our reputation, and I started to think about getting another site, a few more salesmen. Our offices were still humble, a ten-foot square with no toilet, and our two second-hand desks rammed front to front, taking up most of the space. But I got a buzz out of working with Brian, and my confidence in myself was building. I liked working in a suit and tie rather than a Michelin boiler suit. Inspiring staff, coming up with ideas, growing the business, solving problems, all of these things I relished and I was good at them. Regardless of the exhaustive schedule, regardless of lack of sleep and endless issues with money, I was having fun.

'Not digestive biscuits again, Brian,' I'd say, as I returned from the auctions and spotted the red tube of the world's most boring biscuits propped up against the tea mugs.

'I like them, John.' And he'd demolish a couple with each cuppa.

'But I don't,' I'd say. Then I'd find myself eating them, crunching my way through half a pack and then berating myself for stuffing down so much sugar, which made Brian laugh. Plain and boring they might be, but digestive biscuits are highly addictive. Years later, when we had a company worth millions, and a boardroom with a polished, oak table heaving with freshly made sushi and delicious canapés created by top chefs, those red packets of digestive biscuits would always be given a star place on the table.

The digestive biscuits stayed with us but some things went. The sheepskin coats, the Crombies and the eye-wateringly expensive wig that topped off my sartorial look back in those days.

Yes, I confess, I wore a wig, which does make me chuckle now when I see old photos. It wasn't actually called a wig. It wasn't even called a hair piece. When the man turned up at our door one day, and I was nineteen, what he held in his hand was described as 'a real hair system'. I was captivated. I was permanently hung up about my thinning, frizzy, ginger hair, which had started falling out when I was fourteen. 'By the looks of you, this colour would really work with your hair,' said the chap. As poker faced as I am in business, this chap probably instantly saw a sale.

'Let's try it on you.' He stepped over the threshold. I was putty in his hands, as he placed the pale brownish mop on top of my head, and set about loosely styling it. 'This is how you do it, natural like,' he muttered as he began to comb it out. I stared at myself in the mirror. Real hair was hanging casually over my ears and eyebrows. I couldn't tell where my scrappy locks ended and the luxuriant 'hair system' began. 'Looks great on you,' he said. He stepped back.

'How much?'

He gave me a pained smile. 'It's expensive. But it's really worth it. It's three hundred pounds. But we can sort something out so you can pay a few pounds every month.'

I grimaced. That was exorbitant. But I took another look at my reflection in the mirror. My hair was now thick and luxuriant. God, how I had always wanted hair like this. I had to have it. 'I'll take it.'

The 'real hair system' came four weeks later with a polystyrene mannequin head, and a complimentary bottle of shampoo. The salesman gave me detailed instructions on how to wash it and take care of it. When Kate first saw it, bless her, she didn't laugh. She simply accepted that from now on her boyfriend would be wearing what she later called 'the hamster' on his head.

'I think you are great just as you are,' she told me.

I would never believe her, no matter how many times she told me. But with my new wig I really could feel more confident. I looked after it like a precious piece of art. I wore it to work – in the filthy conditions of the Black – and I'd come home with it covered in grease and stinking. Then I'd spend half an hour washing it back to a state of perfection, and carefully arranging it on that white polystyrene head every night. As I mentioned earlier, I wore it on our wedding day. I wore it on motorbike rallies. I wore it to car auctions and I wore it on that car lot. But there are times a wig just has to go.

It was a year after we opened The Wholesale Car Centre. I was in the garage workshop, dealing with a problem. 'Why has this car not been fixed? I've got the customers waiting?'

'The exhaust needed welding and I couldn't do it.' That was an infuriating answer from one of many scruffy boiler-suited greaser mechanics.

I was apoplectic. I have high standards. I don't keep customers waiting and I can't be having mechanics standing around giving me excuses. Ignoring the fact that I was wearing a pinstriped suit, I grabbed the welding torch and goggles, pulled on the goggles, lay on a crawler board on the filthy garage floor, shimmed myself under the car and five minutes later I had welded the faulty parts back together.

I emerged from underneath the car hot, sweaty, jubilant but still furious. I'd proved my point. 'Now what is so difficult about that?' I said. 'Just do your job and don't give me any more excuses.' In the midst of chastising them to make my point all the more dramatic I ripped the goggle off my forehead and threw them across the room, but then – DISASTER!

The elastic strap of the goggles had hooked behind my hair piece, ripping off the pins that held it to my head and now it was spinning through the air like a Frisbee heading towards a huge vat of dirty old engine oil. We all watched mesmerised, the mechanics standing open-mouthed as my £300 'hair system' arced through the air towards its absolute destruction.

Incredibly, somehow it managed to land about six inches short of the gooey oil bath. I marched over, took the hair piece, plonked it on my head and as I stormed out of the workshop I shouted pompously, 'Never fail me again.'

They must have been in stitches after I left. I now had total humiliation to add to my anger and indignation – although even then I could see the funny side as soon I was out of the door and out of sight from the men. I laughed all the way back to the sales office.

It took me a few more weeks to return that wig to its box, but I knew it had to go. Times were changing. Our world was getting bigger. Kate was pregnant. I was going to be a father. I felt loved and supported by Kate and my family and things were starting to work out. I was good with cars, good with customers. I was on track to achieve my childhood dream of building an empire. That lustrous, luxuriant hair that was the male hallmark of the '70s and which I'd craved for as long as I could remember was no longer even in fashion.

I looked at my wig, ritualistically placed on its polystyrene stand and knew I didn't need it any more to give me confidence. Kate – now my wife – was right, I was good enough exactly as I was.

Chapter 10

BUMP

SOMETHING WASN'T RIGHT at home. I knew it but I couldn't quite put my finger on what it was. In many ways, everything was going so well. Even though it was early December and a few weeks into the pre-Christmas slump, The Wholesale Car Centre was really becoming established, and Kate and I had so much good news to celebrate.

We had had our first child. We named her Rebekah, an old biblical name Kate had always loved. She was perfect. Our little angel. She'd been born a few weeks earlier and it was an unexpectedly difficult birth. By the time I got to the hospital it was complete panic stations. Kate had been in labour for hours and there were monitors attached to her swollen stomach, checking the baby's heart rate. I could see Kate was scared. So was I.

'Nurse, all the machines are bleeping,' I shouted into the corridor, after each monitor sounded its alarm, one-by-one, The midwife dashed in to the room and assessed the situation. 'We're going to have to do forceps,' she said, firmly, calmly, authoritatively, and then, 'Mr Caudwell, can you please move over there, to the back of the room?'

I had a fairly good idea about childbirth but this scene playing out before me was turning more horrendous by the second. 'It's going to be all right, Kate,' I said, above the heads of doctors and nurses. A whole team of medics had suddenly appeared, and – in an instant it seemed – sheets, scissors, metal instruments and a large pair of forceps were being passed between them with an urgent sense of speed. I was immediately aware of the fragility of our baby's life, and then overwhelmed by a sharpened sense of panic as the room then went completely silent, the absolute quiet broken only when one doctor would intermittently shout a few short, tense bursts of instructions.

I could do nothing. I felt like a useless bystander. I could hardly see anything through the crowd of medics and the sheets and I didn't want to move in case I distracted anyone from what they were doing.

After an anxious 15 minutes I heard the words, 'It's a girl' followed by a scream from my wife, a sound of pure joy in a slipstream of trauma. Then finally, there was a thin, high-pitched wail and I realised that I, too, was crying as I saw our baby, alive, red-faced, her head slightly misshapen from the clutch of the forceps. 'Don't worry, babies heads are soft. It'll be fine in no time,' the nurse assured me, and she handed her to me. I didn't care what she looked like. She was here, she was ours. She was safe. And I was going to make sure that was how she would stay for the rest of her life.

*****

I WENT STRAIGHT back to work because as far as I could see it, there was now even more reason for me to make money. That little girl in the see-through plastic hospital crib was never going to have a childhood like mine. Things were going to be different for Kate and my family, and that would be down to me. I needed to work even harder.

A fortnight later Kate was discharged from hospital and returned home. She was still in a lot of pain. She had trouble walking, and even sitting was uncomfortable. When you have your first baby, it's easy to lose sight of day to day problems in the face of your newborn.

Rebekah was beautiful and nothing gave me greater joy than to hold her in my arms and just stare at her when I came home at night. But I confess, I left most of her care to Kate. I was focused on work, which to me represented security for my family. In the evenings, when I came home, I knew that Kate wasn't quite herself. She looked strained, but I knew she was exhausted and had not fully recovered from that traumatic birth. It was just a matter of time and the weeks were passing. My brain was working overtime on issues at work and home seemed like my sanctuary where for once, I didn't need to worry. Everything would be all right, I was sure.

'Mr Caudwell, can I have a word?' Kate's health visitor was calling me from the top of the stairs. I was in a hurry. I'd just shouted up to Kate to see if she knew where I'd find an ironed shirt, but now I was being summoned in a rather brusque voice. I dashed up the stairs to find out what she wanted.

'Your wife has a very serious infection,' she said as I walked into our bedroom. 'She needs a lot of help.' I looked at poor Kate who really was looking unwell and I felt a twinge of remorse for not fully noticing before. I was normally pretty hot on any form of illness but I realised Kate hadn't made a fuss or even said anything to me, outside the house I was focused on work and inside the house the two of us were focused on Rebekah. And with the feeds and broken sleep we were both shattered.

The health visitor ushered me downstairs and then said very seriously, 'Her infection will heal but that's not the real problem. I believe Kate is suffering from postnatal depression. She's not herself. Many women go through it, particularly after a difficult birth. She needs a lot of support physically and emotionally.'

I was stunned. I watched her pack her bag to leave, my mind was racing. 'Do you have family who can help?' she asked as she stood at the door to leave. I shook my head. My mum worked and Kate's mum was going through health issues of her own. I had no idea about postnatal depression. I'd vaguely heard of 'baby blues' being talked about, but back then no-one really discussed things like that. I'd grown up with the wartime generation who suffered in silence. In the case of Dad's post-traumatic stress syndrome, we'd all suffered as a result of that silence. That wasn't going to happen to me, Kate and Rebekah. I needed to do something.

*****

'MY WIFE'S NOT well. She's having problems after the baby', I said bluntly, standing in the office at Michelin. 'I have to take some time off.'

My boss looked at me. He was a traditional, working-class Stoke man who'd risen through the ranks at the car factory to become a manager. He was tough, he was smart and he was the sort of man I may have become had I not been burning on the inside with an ambition to be something far bigger.

'Sit down, Caudwell,' he said. I sat and he asked me some questions about Kate. Now, I know he knew – as did most of the staff – I had another business on the side but he never mentioned that. I think he could also tell from my manner that I was in a state of shock, not knowing quite what to do. He listened carefully as I recounted what the health visitor had said to me. Then he nodded wisely and said, 'Right, I'm signing you off on compassionate leave. Go home, and look after your family.'

This was the tail end of 1979 and the dawn of 1980, and the issue of mental health did not loom large on the social or political agenda, but my manager was an example of a dyed-in-the-wool Michelin man. Many unfortunate things have happened in my life but the older I get, the more I look at the business world from the ground up, and realise how lucky I was to have received the thorough and progressive training I had there, at Michelin.

Founded in 1889 by two brothers, Édouard and André Michelin, the company started out as a rubber factory until one day a cyclist turned up at the factory asking for his tyre to be fixed. Back then tyres were all solid and glued to the wheel rims. They took three hours to remove and repair. The brothers were inspired to invent a pneumatic tyre and in 1891 their first removable pneumatic tyres were used by the legendary Charles Terront (sponsored by the Michelin brothers) to win the world's first long distance cycle race, Paris-Brest-Paris.

Édouard and André were true business visionaries, diversifying into car tyres, air transport, agricultural and industrial tyres along with road maps and the Michelin restaurant guide which laid the foundations for today's highly-prized Michelin star rating system of restaurants. It is a name synonymous with the highest standards, and I know that its training has had a profound influence on me in business and my outlook on life and in so many other ways.

I have no idea who specifically devised the four-year training programme we all went through at Michelin. It was not only progressive but – created by a French company – it was also educational and philosophical, with a focus on physical and mental well-being. All trainees – and my manager who had come through the programme – had to complete 32 hours a week at the tyre company and 15 hours a week at college, where trainees could also study a language as well as sitting technical exams. Twice-weekly physical education was compulsory and, as part of the training to be a Michelin engineer, trainees were sent to help out in local psychiatric hospitals. Those of us in Stoke went to Stallington Hall, where we'd help staff in any way we could, from fetching and carrying equipment to assisting with certain patients.

I remember walking into the forbidding grounds of this rather crumbling, moss-covered gothic Victorian building. Some of my peers gulped. 'Why do we have to come here? What's this got to do with being an engineer?' they said. In response, I shrugged my shoulders. I had no idea what this had to do with engineering training. But I must say that I found the experience deeply fascinating and very profound – despite some of the more unnerving patients. They included one guy with almost super-human strength who jumped from the first floor onto the grass below.

In the weeks that I spent there I learned that the mind can be as frail and susceptible as the body and that mental health should carry no stigma. I learned that those who are mentally ill should be treated with the same compassion as those who are physically unwell. I also realised that it takes time to find the right cure.

That moment in the office with my manager was an example of this holistic attitude towards your workforce. 'Come back in a couple of weeks, and good luck,' he told me as I left his office. Just having been able to sit and talk to someone who was clearly sympathetic had really helped me. But I knew I was going to need more than luck to deal with this.

*****

OBVIOUSLY, THERE WAS a world of difference between what Kate was going through and everything I had witnessed at Stallington. I'd had a feeling that something wasn't right at home but I hadn't been able to put my finger on it. It had been staring me in the face all along but still it hadn't hit me until the health visitor had crystallised exactly what was wrong.

I knew that Kate felt very down, that her natural ebullience and confidence had temporarily deserted her, but this was something we had to get through. I was very worried though. I knew that Michelin would easily be able to do without me for a couple of weeks but the Wholesale Car Centre couldn't. If I let that slide, it would spell disaster for all our futures.

'Kate,' I said gently, that afternoon. 'Even though I've got this time off from Michelin, you do understand I still have to help Brian with the car lot.' She nodded. She needed me but Brian also needed me, and the business needed me or else we might go under.

'And then where will we be, Rebekah?' I said to my sleeping baby as I sat with her downstairs and tried to work out a solution. I was between a rock and a hard place. I couldn't leave Kate and the baby to go to work but I couldn't not go to work and leave Brian to deal with everything.

As crazy as it sounds, there was only one way I could think of handling the situation. I called Brian and told him what was going on. 'But don't worry,' I said. 'I have to spend more time with Kate and keep an eye on her. But I'm still going to be able to work. Michelin have given me a few weeks off so it's not going to affect our business.'

Then I spoke to Kate and told her my solution. 'So what I was thinking is that I could still go to the auctions, but you and Rebekah could come with me. It would get you out of the house and you might start feeling better.' Bless her, Kate just went along with the world's most unconventional way of trying to deal with postnatal depression – driving up and down motorways to auctions with a baby in tow.

Incredibly, we got through it. I wish I could say that I stopped working, waited on Kate hand and foot, changed every one of Rebekah's nappies and catered to her every whim, but I didn't. I couldn't. Life just wasn't like that for us. I focused on the future, on getting to the next stage and pushing forward for both Kate and the business.

Kate knew me well enough to know that this was the way it was going to be. But she also knew that we had to be a team. Actually, I really liked having them with me at the auctions. Lots of those hard-nosed dealers and auctioneers turned rather soppy at the sight of Rebekah wrapped up in her hat, mittens and blankets. And however down she felt on the inside, Kate was also a big hit. 'Alright, Mrs C. How's the baby?' She'd smile and wave. Rather typically, after a few weeks – when Kate had colour in her cheeks and seemed to me to be improving – I roped her in, helping out with the cars.

Her abiding memory of that time is me getting her to drive back from Brighouse in Yorkshire, where another of the big car auctions was regularly held. 'I'll take this car and you and Rebekah drive home in this,' I said, chirpily, pointing at a car I'd just bought but hadn't test-driven. 'I'll pop in on Brian at the site and then see you at home.'

I spent an hour or so catching up with Brian then I arrived home to find the house in darkness. No Kate, no Rebekah. It was January 1980, and a snow storm had blown up as Kate was driving home on the motorway with no hard shoulder. Inevitably, the car – which was in need of more than a few adjustments – broke down. So she had to sit, waiting for the police to rescue her, while baby Rebekah screamed for milk.

'The policemen were really lovely to us, but I was too embarrassed to breast-feed in front of them,' she told me a few hours later, when they'd been towed home. They were both cold, tired and hungry. I held our indignant daughter who screamed loudly and kicked at me as Kate hastily tore off her coat and got ready to placate Rebekah with milk.

That was the last of Kate going to the auctions. It had never been a perfect solution but it was the only one I had and miraculously Kate had improved. But, clearly, it wasn't the best way for a mother and baby to spend their days. In those minutes my little girl spent kicking and howling at me I realised then that, in any aspect of life, some solutions can only ever be very temporary and to never expect a smooth ride.

Chapter 11

COMMUNICATION BREAKDOWN

IT IS 1986, and Brian and I are fast becoming a force amongst Stoke's used-car dealerships. We are good at it, we are trusted, we have grown by pushing and scratching on every deal, trying to find value cars for our customers and doing our best to please when they want a vehicle we haven't got. We take their names and numbers, and promise to call when we've hunted one down for them.

And that is why I have spent 15 minutes queuing to use the payphone on the auction lot, and have jammed a succession of ten-pence pieces into the metal slot in order to speak to Brian. 'There's two CD Cavaliers here. Those buyers still interested?'

'Let me check. Hang on…'

Silence. Then I can hear Brian on the other line, trying to get hold of the customers who'd lost out on a CD Cavalier a few weeks earlier. I clutch the phone and check my watch. Five minutes before the auction begins. I don't look around because I know there are four guys behind me, each needing to use the phone to call his office.

'Hurry up, Caudwell.'

'Come on man! There's others waiting!'

I pull the phone closer to my ear. 'Brian,' I shout down the line. 'His wife doesn't know, and he's not going to be back till six,' Brian says after I've spent a few minutes straining to hear his muffled conversation. 'And the other guy's number is ringing out. But can you look for a F….'

111

The pips go. I don't bother inserting any more coins from my rolls of fifty and ten-pence pieces. The auction is up and running, bidding has already started on the white Cavalier and I decide not to raise my hand. I'm not sure whether the two customers have changed their minds. Or maybe they've found something else. And I'm trying to guess what Brian was after – was he about to say Ford or Fiesta, or did I mishear a 'v' for Volkswagen?

It's not the stress that gets to me – I can handle that by the bucketload – it's the lack of communication, and the damage that does to your business opportunities. Then, car auctions had one phone and generally about ten guys wanting to use it at the same time. You can make a call and miss a car that's going under the hammer, or miss the opportunity to bid for precisely what a customer had wanted.

Brian was just as frustrated as me. He tried every which way to solve the problem, the most popular seemingly ground-breaking method of instant communication back then were BT pagers which were clipped to the trouser belt enabling text-like messages to be delivered to you wherever you were. But you still needed a phone to be able to call back whoever wanted to speak to you. Then we experimented with Citizens Band radio, known as CB radio, which were hugely popular with lorry drivers on motorways. CB became pretty cool in the mid-70s after the success of the US country song and movie, Convoy. But that's about the highways of Tennessee, and the fact is, CB radio didn't seem to like some of the motorways around Stoke. By the time you'd got to the auction – where they couldn't be used – you might be no clearer than when you started.

'We might as well use a long piece of string with a plastic cup on each end,' I told Brian, after we'd spent hours trying to decipher each other's faint and crackling voices. Really, they were pretty hopeless.

But every business has its issues, its difficulties. And to succeed you just have to find a way around them. I always tried to make sure

COMMUNICATION BREAKDOWN

I was near the top of the queue for the phone, and I'd have pieces of paper in my pocket covered in phone numbers so that I could call customers direct from the auctions in case I saw a car I thought they'd like. I could run at Daley Thompson-speed (well, almost), from the phone box back to the auction floor. Plus, I trusted in my ever-growing knowledge of customers' requirements, and I had confidence in what to buy to make sure that we remained at the top of our game.

I was a well-known figure on the circuit and there was a certain camaraderie I enjoyed. I also liked a lot of the characters I'd meet. There was a certain auctioneer who could be incredibly sarcastic with the dealers, spicing up his patter about cars with rude little quips. He had nicknames for those of us he felt were clearly worth bothering with – although I'm not entirely sure if any of the names were meant as a compliment. Auctions went at breakneck speed, but if I got the winning bid he'd shout, 'Car sold to Walks On Water'.

That was my name because my initials were JC (as in Jesus Christ). Another regular was known as 'Where They Keep The Horses' because his business was located in an old coaching house. He would make me smile every now and again but going back up and down those motorways, constantly looking for the best value cars was exhausting.

And then one day I saw it.

And everything changed.

Chapter 12

DOES ANYBODY WANT A MOBILE PHONE?

THERE WAS NOTHING special about the day at all.

It was December, it was freezing cold and I was at an auction hurrying to the payphone when I saw one of the regular buyers, a dapper, little guy called Richard, waving at me. He was carrying a large, heavy-looking suitcase in one hand. 'You giving up the auctions?' I said, and I laughed and nodded towards his case. 'Looks like you're off on holiday.'

'No,' he said. He smiled, looking rather pleased with himself, as he added, 'This is a mobile phone. No more queuing up for the pay phone for me.'

I was stunned. 'Let's have a look,' I said.

He opened the case and inside was something that pretty much resembled the BT phone, but it was smaller, it was portable and it belonged to him alone. Despite the fact I was standing in Brighouse car lot in the drizzling rain, it felt like that moment in the James Bond movies when Q shows the secret agent some dazzling new piece of technology and says, 'Now pay attention, double-O seven,' before running through the intricacies of a gloriously-ingenious invention.

I was entranced. I knew at that very moment that I was looking at the future. For once I forgot about dashing to my place in the payphone queue. I did not think about racing back to the auction. Instead, I wanted to know everything about the mobile phone –

how it worked, how reliable it was, where it came from, whether you could use it anywhere and, of course: 'How much did it cost?'

'Well, that's the tough bit,' my friend said, suddenly seeming rather woebegone. 'Firstly, you need to buy the phone. Which is six hundred quid. Then you have to pay for the line rental and that is £25 a month. Then it's 25 pence per minute for each call.'

Bear in mind this was 1986. In today's money, that would be more like £71 a month rental and 71p per minute to make a call. But there was more.

'They also have something called 'full-minute billing', my friend went on.

'What does that mean?' I was genuinely puzzled.

'They charge you for the full minute, regardless of whether you're actually speaking to anyone.'

'So, if I called up and got the wrong number, I'd still be charged 25 pence even if I was only on the call for five seconds?'

'Yup,' my friend shrugged. 'And it's 33 pence per minute if you are calling from London. Mobile phones don't come cheap!'

I looked down at the bulky case he was hefting from one hand to the other. 'Do they all come in those great, big cases?' I asked.

'No, Motorola do a smaller one. It's the size of a brick with an antenna and it has a much smaller charger. It's called a Motorola 8000S. But that one is really expensive. It costs about eighteen hundred pounds.'

I couldn't get that suitcase phone out of my head. The price was ridiculously high and I tried to justify taking such a large chunk out of our business. After all, Brian and I prided ourselves on keeping a very lean ship as it was so essential to our survival. I imagined myself running around with that great big bag, remembering how my friend had quietly groaned as he picked it up when he said goodbye. I couldn't imagine being able to run fast with that thing in my hands.

And what if I left it in the car and then someone pinched it?

As much as I tried to talk myself out of it, over the next few days when I stood in one payphone queue after the next, I knew that regardless of the cost, regardless of anything, I had to have a mobile phone. The more I thought about it, the more an idea started to build in my head. I'd seen a vision of a future I wanted to be part of. I didn't simply want to have a mobile phone, I wanted to sell them. I wanted in on the act.

*****

'CAN YOU FIND out where I can get the best possible deal on a Motorola DynaTAC 8000S?' I was standing in front of Nicky, our new reception lady at The Wholesale Car Centre. She blinked and then tried to repeat what I'd said, as if I'd been speaking a different language. 'I'm sorry John, I didn't quite get that.' I spelt it out for her, checking on a piece of paper because I'd hastily scribbled the name at the auction.

Seven hours later, she approached me. She looked worried. 'Excuse me, John, no-one's heard of this Motorola thing,' she said, frowning. 'There aren't any dealers listed in The Yellow Pages. I was told to get in touch with a business called Cellnet, which is the mobile phone division of BT. But when I phoned British Telecom, they said they had never heard of Cellnet. And Cellnet isn't listed, either. It's impossible...'

I told her I was impressed she'd been so thorough, which made her smile. Then I told her I was confident she'd be able to track them down. Several days later, after many leads and many dead ends, she dashed up to me, her face beaming. 'I've found a dealer. And he's in Stoke-on-Trent, would you believe?' She was delighted to have finally got me what I wanted and she chirpily thrust a piece of paper at me. 'I've written his name and number down here.'

The difficulty in tracking the mobile phone down had really

piqued my interest in getting involved with the business. I called the number. 'Hello, how much,' I asked. 'Will a Motorola 8000S cost me?'

'Fifteen hundred pounds,' came the reply. That was £300 less than my friend had been told.

'And how much if I buy two?'

'Then it's £1,350 each,' said the dealer, with no flicker of hesitation. I hadn't even had to negotiate. This told me that profit margins on these phones must be huge. Casually, I asked him a few questions, did a bit of subtle digging. By now I knew they were an American company but they also had a UK headquarters close to London, just off the M4 corridor. That was my next port of call.

America was way ahead of us in terms of mobile phone development and technology. Motorola – founded by two brothers, Paul and Joseph Galvin – flourished in 1930, after producing the first car radio. Almost four decades later, when the first man landed on the moon, it was a Motorola transceiver that astronaut Neil Armstrong spoke into when his famous words – 'that's one small step for a man, one giant leap for mankind' – were transmitted to 650 million people watching on their television sets around the globe.

Today, I was taking my first small step towards what was to become a giant empire for two brothers from Stoke-on-Trent.

'Sales department, please,' I requested. I was put through immediately and asked how much it would cost me to buy two 8000S.

'Sorry sir, we only supply to dealers.' The reply was polite but firm. I was undeterred. 'OK. Well, how do I become a Motorola dealer?'

The London office proved to be highly efficient. I was impressed. A week later, an accounts manager called John Rudge turned up with a variety of forms which I filled in. I made an order of 26 phones to be supplied as soon as my status as a dealer was rubber-stamped. I was given a great deal on my phones because – unbelievably, given how times have changed – an order for 26 mobiles was the largest they had received. I was very impressed.

But I was also very naïve. The mobile phone industry was to become a place not too dissimilar to the old Wild West, with cold-blooded cowboys, ruthless scalping techniques and double dealers on every corner, all ready to snatch anyone's gold. But these were the early days, John Rudge was giving me the advice he thought was best at the time.

Motorola mobiles came in four different styles, the simple car phone, the car phone plus kit so you can make hands free calls, the portable DynaTAC 8000S (aka the brick phone) and the transportable which came in the heavy suitcase.

I was advised to buy a whole range of Motorola products and just one DynaTAC 8000S. 'People want car phones and they're the easiest to sell,' I was told.

'But,' I argued, 'they aren't voice activated. That means you have to dial as you are driving, which is impossible. The ones with the car kit already are a better buy.' In order to make them hands-free you had to buy the kit which was going to set you back another £150. Buying the phone with the car kit already was more expensive but about £100 less than buying each item separately.

'Seriously John, we know what sells, and it's the car phones. It doesn't matter that you have to dial as you are driving. They're a lot cheaper and they will be easier to sell.'

I wasn't expecting to be given the wrong advice by Motorola, even though my gut instinct told me the brick phone – which you could carry around – was the best option of the lot. My order consisted of largely car phones and transportables – and just one brick phone. It didn't seem right but I thought of my friend who'd opted to buy the suitcase version, so maybe they were right. I was very definitely made to feel Motorola knew exactly what they were talking about which turned out to be a big mistake.

I could not shift a single one. No-one wanted a car phone, which involved pulling over in order to make a call. It took two months to sell a phone to a taxi driver who had so many problems with its signal coverage that I was haunted by him for another two years as we tried to resolve his complaints. I tried to negotiate with John Rudge to get him to swap the phones or supply me with the extra equipment I needed to make the car phones hands free, but he refused point blank, telling me it wasn't 'Motorola policy.'

It felt like Belstaff all over again. I was not impressed. But I was stuck with a cupboard full of useless phones. I'd made a massive mistake but there was no turning back. I was going to grit my teeth, dig into my reserves, buy the right phones and try and turn my bad deal around by working like crazy to make sales. But now, with Motorola, I was on my guard.

*****

TO UNDERSTAND THE mobile phone industry of the '80s you had to be knowledgable. Pricing structures were complex, and there were few retail outlets selling direct to customers. If you sold a phone, the profit you made came from arranging a connection to a network provider who paid a commission. This would cover some of the cost of the phone.

So, let's say a customer bought a phone from me for £1,300. Now, it would most likely have cost me £1,500 to buy it from Motorola. But my commission from the phone network would cover my costs, and with a reasonable profit on top.

It wasn't big money but I just believed this was a market that would grow. I thought back to being a little boy, when few people had phones in their homes – even as a teenager Kate had to use a phone box to call me – but now everyone I knew had BT lines in their houses. So surely, the same would follow in this business.

Not everyone shared my vision. In the first few weeks I'd approach other car traders at auctions, admittedly with my rather poor selection of non-hand-free phones. 'If you have one of these there's no need to wait in the pay phone queue. You can get business done immediately... And make more profit,' I'd explain to a group of guys who looked at these bulky, cellular objects with their rubber push-buttons and black plastic casing.

'How much?' was always the first question. I'd run through the pricing options but quickly would notice most of the guys shifting on their feet, put off by the high toll.

'Not sure I can justify that price, John?' I was told on several occasions. I went to a local car agent called Ken, who was a friend and suggested he joined forces with me in the business. He shook his head. 'I don't think it's going to work,' he said.

Lots of people told me they would never catch on. I wasn't disheartened. I knew I had a challenge on my hands. But I also knew the guys at the auction were exactly the right customer for these phones. It was a question of getting the right product at the right price.

These days it's unusual to find someone who doesn't own a mobile phone. In 2017, a survey showed there were 79.17 million mobile subscriptions in the United Kingdom, across the entire population of 66.04 million inhabitants. However, in 1986, when I first saw a mobile phone – albeit a very unwieldy one – the airtime providers Cellnet and Vodafone had only 56,000 mobile phone accounts between them. In other words, about one in every thousand Brits had a mobile phone.

Like everything innovative and different, mobile phones seemed rather alien and unnecessary to the average person. The comedian

DOES ANYBODY WANT A MOBILE PHONE?

Ernie Wise made Britain's first official call on a mobile. It was a televised event on New Year's Day in 1985, and he phoned Vodafone chairman, Sir Ernest Harrison (although it later transpired Sir Ernest's son, Michael, had cheekily made a call a few hours earlier). Ernie confessed he handed the mobile back to Vodafone straight after the event, believing that he'd never have a use for it again. 'I wouldn't even know where to put it,' he said.

But two years later, the biggest movie of the year was Wall Street starring the legendary actor Michael Douglas as the ruthless stockbroker, Gordon Gekko. There's an iconic scene when he's standing on a beach making a call using a Motorola DynaTAC 8000S.

The film won Douglas an Oscar for Best Actor, but it won Motorola a following among highly-paid top business executives and City traders. We didn't have many – or any – of those in Stoke. Most of them were down in London and rich enough not even to care that it meant they were paying the premium 33 pence a minute per call. I didn't know any City traders, just car traders, but I believed I could get a fair few of them to eventually become my customers.

As enthused as I was by mobiles, I couldn't afford to focus on them full time. I still had to buy and sell cars because in the early stages it was the car sales that were propping up our fledgling mobile phone business. Even Brian admits now that he couldn't quite see the future I saw, and he was keen to keep expanding The Wholesale Car Centre, playing to our strengths.

I moved one of our sales team, Paul Ridge, to run the phone business and – as usual – I tried to split my time, working 18 hours a day, seven days a week, trying to keep everything going. There were problems with Motorola, problems with cars, problems with staff, but that all comes with the territory.

I remember feeling constantly exhausted but never stopping to rest because my eyes were firmly fixed on the future.

LOVE, PAIN & MONEY

Every instinct told me that something huge was on the horizon but I would have to climb a mountain to get there. I was going to keep on climbing because I had to make this happen.

My mum loved my curly hair. It is safe to say I did not

Me at around 12 months old

Walter Caudwell, aged four. Dad was a tough man to love and a man who had experienced a lot during the Second World War. I never felt like I got to really know him and winning his approval was as good as impossible

Dad in the African desert during the Second World War. He was, like many men of his generation, scarred by the conflict and reluctant to discuss what he had seen and what he had gone through

Aged about six. It looks like butter wouldn't melt in my mouth. Trust me, it would!

At the seaside with Mum, Dad and Grandma Caudwell. We took her everywhere with us

Mum, Brian and me, on Newquay beach before Dad's stroke. The stroke changed everything, and made Mum's already difficult life a whole lot tougher. I have my arm around Brian here and that typifies just how close we were then and remain to this day. Having my brother right next to me during my career helped in so many ways

Kate outside our caravan home on Mum's lawn. When we first met I could not quite believe she was interested in me, or that she wanted a future together. She was, and is, a fantastically intelligent, fascinating and brilliant woman, mother and friend

Two becomes three as Kate feeds our newborn daughter, Rebekah. Becoming a father was an indescribable feeling – doing it six times even more so!

Kate and I on holiday in Tenerife

A 70th birthday party for Dennis with Jean, Kate, and Libby. Note the neck brace – this was the first of my three broken necks. Injuries have always been part and parcel of my life and have never stopped me from cycling, skiing and generally being as active as possible

The offices in Stoke where I first founded my mobile phone business. I realised very early on that mobile phones were going to change the way we live our lives

The famous Motorola 4500X. The phone that helped put me on my path to success

In my office and showroom for a publicity shot. When mobile phones started to become increasingly popular, we knew we could transform our business into a massive success

An early photo with the revolutionary Motorola 8000X. It is hard now to comprehend what a game-changing phone this was

A bad hair day with Kate, Rebekah, Rufus, Mum, and our friend Kim

I sponsored a stand at Port Vale Football Club. Here I am shaking hands with the late Bill Bell, the club's chairman at the time

I stand outside Broughton Hall with my helicopter – I flew it myself – and Bentley in a shot for *The Sunday Times* Rich List

In Moscow with Hugh Grant, Claire and our Russian guide prior to having dinner with President Gorbachev. Hugh is a very charming, intelligent and interesting man, he is great company and we always had fun when we got together

Jacobi in Elton John's suite, where he'd been playing football with his boys. Nothing is ever too much trouble for Elton, he has played gigs for me for free in order to raise funds and he is one of the greatest entertainers Britain has ever produced

With President Bill Clinton and my former partner Claire, talking about charitable works

Claire and myself joke around with the simply amazing Muhammad Ali. He still had a sense of humour even when suffering so badly from Parkinson's disease

Rod Stewart is another absolute pro and absolute gentleman. He always delivers when I ask him for charity help and I really admire him and the career he has had

I met Maggie Thatcher several times, this occasion was at the RHS Chelsea Flower Show, and hosting her at Broughton Hall was a massive honour for me and my family

My 'Queen' with princess Tilly Griffiths, who writes with such passion and clarity in this book. Helping her, and thousands of other children, has become the true driving force in my life

Cycling with Jacobi in the Ardèche. Cycling has always been one of my massive passions and it helps to keep me physically and mentally fit – something I really take pride in

Chapter 13

GIANT

A YEAR ON and Brian and I are still standing. Well, that's not actually true because we were never standing and we were never still. All we did was race from one thing to the next, building sales, buying cars, selling cars, checking on phone sales, dealing with problems, hiring staff, firing staff, and coming up with ideas to make our business bigger, better and more efficient.

I would look at Brian and know I could not have done this without him. When we started The Wholesale Car Centre he was a teenager – albeit, a mature one – and now, in 1988, we are both grown men. When we started Brian was young enough to be going out to clubs with his hair half shaved on one side, long on the other and his favourite outfit a yellow, green and purple flying suit – very Wham! Now the flying suit is long gone. He is married to the wonderful Paula and they have started a family, and I have another beautiful, baby girl, Libby. The Caudwells are growing, prospering and building an empire. I don't know if she ever saw this in her crystal ball but I do know Grandma would be especially proud.

It wasn't easy – nothing in my life has ever been easy – but I felt we were winning. We had built up a strong team, with a car sales manager and a car trade manager who I'd trained to supplement more auction buying. Then there was Paul, who was running the mobile outfit with a dedicated sales team. By then we were selling around 150 phones a month, but we were continuing to make a monthly loss of roughly £2,000. It was hitting us hard, but that's often the way with a new venture – in business textbooks they call it the 'J Curve', an initial loss followed by an exponential growth. It can, in many cases, be a precursor to bankruptcy but I knew that growth would come.

The car business worked because both Brian and I understood cars, we got to understand the customers and kept improving. We had expanded, adding a service station with our own mechanics, and I decided that I'd do the same on the phone front. I created a space within our existing building, just up the road from the car lot, to create a service centre for phone repairs, and I hired a technician along with the high-tech equipment that was needed for the phones we had slowly but steadily started to sell. This gave the business credibility, provided customers with another service and also meant that we weren't merely salesmen – we also had the technical knowledge and ability.

It also gave us – on one occasion – a very different problem to deal with. One day our very quiet, geeky technician, who shall be nameless, didn't turn up for work. We had a queue of customers waiting and there was absolutely no sign of him which was incredibly frustrating. We tried calling him at home but there was no answer. He came back to work the following day, full of assurances it would never happen again.

A few days later, I discovered from another member of staff that he'd been in A&E having inserted one of the electrical wires he used at work into his private parts and was unable to get it out. Clearly he was more adept with mobile phone equipment than his own equipment. God knows what he was doing and I can only imagine it was eye-watering. But often it's the quiet unassuming types that can surprise you the most.

*****

MY MIND WAS forever racing and I was constantly trying to absorb as much information as possible about the world of mobile phones. The previous year, I'd been invited by Motorola to spend a day at a luxury spa; a bonus trip in return for exceeding sales targets.

Normally, I'd never take a day out of the office and I had little interest in spas. However, I knew this would be the ideal fishing expedition in which to gather valuable information. After all, I was now in the business of communication and talk might be cheap, but to me it also had great value.

In the mid-to-late '80s, Motorola was the biggest mobile company in the world but most of its business was in something called Professional Mobile Radio (PMR). This was a device used by dispatchers, van drivers and taxi drivers that relied on a mast, a service operator and a base station to communicate with groups of drivers. At the spa and relaxing in the hot tubs were a bunch of PMR guys who had added mobile phone sales to their portfolio. These guys were the oldest hands in the mobile world and I thought they might provide me with a perfect research opportunity.

'I'm John Caudwell,' I said, introducing myself to each and every one of them.

I explained to them I'd only been invited because I'd managed to sell one mobile phone but in selling that one phone, immediately I had their attention.

'You guys have probably sold hundreds,' I laughed. 'But Motorola didn't expect me to sell any. My target was zero phones. So because I managed to sell one phone, I'm actually over my target!'

They all burst out laughing. They loved that I was being so self-deprecating and presenting myself as the underdog straight away so I was immediately taken into the circle.

We spent the rest of the afternoon chatting away, getting on like a house on fire, and every now and again I'd throw in a few subtle questions. But they were, in fact, a good bunch who surprisingly had no issue with me carefully filleting them for insight and information.

'Telesales,' said one guy. 'That's the way to sell those phones. You need direct and targeted contact with your customer.'

'You've got to think,' said another, 'of all those small businesses – plumbers, electricians, TV repairmen – all the sole traders who would make more profit if they could be contacted when they are out on jobs.'

I nodded and told them they were right. I realised that I'd been on the right track, selling phones to other car salesmen at auctions, but these guys were genuinely opening my eyes to other new strategies. A lot of it may seem like common sense, but it beat learning through making mistakes and I was taking it all in.

'Yellow Pages,' said another of these sages, as he sipped a glass of complimentary sparkling wine. 'Work your way through it and target the sole traders. That's the way to build it.'

I learnt a lot that afternoon and left with real confidence because these were the big boys of the mobile phone world yet none of them had seen me as someone with an agenda or as any sort of a rival with my paltry sale record of one phone. Getting information from them had been pretty easy. And if they were my competition, then I didn't have much to worry about because these guys had been easy to play. I also knew that I was on the right track thanks to a newer product, a Motorola DynaTAC 8000S which was going down well with the car traders. I was now killing two birds with one stone at the auctions, I'd turn up to buy cars with a boot full of mobiles and I'd be selling phones between lots. I'd also acquired a nickname. I was no longer John Caudwell. I was simply 'Motorola Man'.

*****

'WHAT'S WRONG BRIAN?' I'd walked into the office and my brother was looking glum.

'We've lost our car sales manager and trade manager – they've been poached by the competition.'

I sighed as I sat down. This was bad news. Seriously bad news. I couldn't quite believe it. The phone rang. It was Paul who ran the mobile phone operation.

'John, hi. Look, I'm sorry,' he began. 'But I've been offered a job by Motorola. It's good money and I've said yes. Sorry. I need to start in a couple of weeks.'

I put down the phone. Brian had heard every word. We stared at each other, speechless. This was a massive body blow to our fledgling operation. Seventy-five percent of our total workforce had gone in a space of minutes – and all of them senior members of our small team. My mind was a mish-mash of thoughts as well as the image of the strimmer flinging that stinking dog mess in my face just as I thought I was getting everything in good order.

But that's business. You are forever building a house of cards and it takes the slightest knock to shake it, or raze it to the ground. So you have to keep running, hold it up, use every ounce of Herculean strength just as I did when I single-handedly hoisted that RSJ into place in the very building I was in right now. You have to think and then you have to move – and be quick with it, or everything will collapse.

'So, we'll split it up,' I said decisively. 'You run this place and I'll run the mobile phones. I'll still do the auctions and we'll train up new people. We'll make it work.'

Brian looked at me, nodded and we both got straight to work. Two brothers. Total trust. A perfect working relationship.

*****

I STEPPED INTO our mobile phone offices, Midland Mobile Phones, which was just around the corner from the car lot, and I thought, 'How am I going to turn this latest sucker punch into a victory blow?'

I genuinely believe something chemical happens within my body in moments of stress. Adrenaline was pumping through me, obviously, but my brain was in a different gear. I was calm. I was focused. I was thinking extremely clearly, and now I knew exactly what I had to do.

Problems to me can be like the jumbled coloured squares on a Rubik's Cube. They will all line up in perfect order if you think, make the right moves and keep making incremental little shifts and turns until you get it right. I had absolute confidence that I was going to do exactly that. First, however, I needed to look at all the problems I had to solve and to work out how I could reverse the company's fortunes by ending the monthly losses of £2,000. You can't keep on losing money in business, if you do you have to work out why and see how you can start moving towards breaking even and then profit. But profit is always your goal.

Day one I realised one major issue. At precisely 5pm, every member of my sales team stood up, stepped away from their desks and started putting on their coats. 'Where are you all going?' I said, puzzled.

'Er... home. It's five o'clock,' said one of them.

I was beginning to see why the guys in my sales team were not performing as well as I believed they could. When the team came into work the next day, I sat them down in front of a bar chart. On the chart, each team member's name was written beside a column which would be filled.

This crucial column would show the number of phones they had sold each month. I realised my staff of nine-to-fivers were in need of a stick and carrot approach. In other words a swift kick up the backside with the promise of a treat to make them hungry.

'So, I'm introducing a bonus system,' I announced. 'The person who sells the most phones in a month gets a cash reward...' I had their attention, they looked interested.

My name was also on the chart because even though I was managing them all, I was also, like them, selling. It was all hands on deck and as far as I was concerned, I needed to understand the issues of selling in order to understand and motivate my team. I managed and I sold. In month one and month two I was the top seller on the board. Theoretically, I was entitled to the cash reward. This wasn't quite right, there was no incentive, so I amended the rules. The bonus was awarded instead to the next best salesman, the person who sold the maximum number after me. It all took a lot of cajoling to keep everyone on track. The office wasn't transformed overnight. At 5pm someone would still put their coat on.

'Oh,' I'd say from my desk where I was working flat out. 'Have you hit your weekly target then?'

Sometimes the coat would stay on, other times they might laugh and take it off again. It took time for things to change but I always made sure I was there in the office, working and managing, and slowly things began to change and the 5pm home time became a thing of the past.

I continued to go to car auctions. I made flyers for the phones and took someone with me to put them on every car in the parking lot. Eventually, thanks to me pushing hard for airtime commission going up and negotiating even harder for my cost price on mobiles to be reduced, we managed to hit the magic price point of £999 for a phone.

To me, this was psychologically the perfect number: just one single pound less a thousand pounds made the price so much more appealing. More importantly it was £200 less than any competitor. It was a huge step and made an immediate impact on sales.

Back in the office, I got to know each member of my team individually. I was a very tough coach. I'd push them constantly, driving them to get a higher volume of sales. But I also led by example. I stayed longer hours selling phones and devising strategies. I made it exciting with bar charts, bonuses and banter – which was generally on the sarcastic side. I was extremely demanding and I admit that some people couldn't take it. But others thrived and grew. Several people left, they couldn't fit the mould I was creating for my team, but I only wanted winners so I recruited carefully and took on more staff. I'm proud to say that after I sold my business in 2006 nearly all my senior people went on to become directors or even managing directors in their own right.

I had my own idea of the perfect salesman and it was the exact opposite of the loud, flashy image most people have in their minds when they think of those guys selling phones in the 1980s. I wanted smart, clean cut, responsible young men and women. I had my rules about tattoos – I would never employ someone covered in tattoos and believe they should not be on display to the customer because you never know if someone may take offence to any of those tattoos. I preferred the quieter, thoughtful types but in terms of sex, creed and colour no-one was ever discriminated against.

'When you talk to a customer,' I told them at one of the first sales meetings. 'Be absolutely straight with them. Tell them about any network coverage issues. Explain every single negative first, and then tell them the positives.

'I will always tell a customer that these phones are rubbish. But they serve a purpose, they can start to change your business and they will get better and they will become your lifeline but they will also annoy you so much you will want to fling them on the floor and stamp on them.'

A couple of them looked at me as if I'd lost my mind. But Brian and

I had always followed the honesty-is-the-best-policy route. 'It makes you more trustworthy,' I explained. 'And they will always come back to you. I want new customers but I also want returning customers, loyal customers. You only achieve this by really caring about your customers and being completely honest.'

I carved out hours here and there for my research. I dug myself into the numbers of the business. I am fascinated by numbers, percentages, margins, profit – how to squeeze that bit here and there, and how to find routes no-one else has considered. I immersed myself in figures. I'd been working on a price graph ever since I'd started dealing with Motorola.

I knew I was paying more for handsets – around £50 or £60 per phone – than the service providers. I carried on trying to find any snippets of information I could and stored everything away, making notes. I gradually found out how much Motorola were charging others for phones and began putting everything onto a price and volume graph of all Motorola products. I did the same with a graph of phone commissions. Whenever I could I'd find out how much commission someone else was being paid and that information was then plotted on another graph.

The important take-away from all this was that there was more commission to be had. It was a big leap between £50 to £100, but if they were giving £100 I was sure there was more to be had. If someone was smart, they may even be able to get a lot more.

*****

WHEN MOTOROLA POACHED my sales manager it was, to my mind, a deeply underhand move.

It could have seriously affected my fledgling business. But in actual fact they did me a favour. Whereas previously I'd always been in fight mode, now I was in war mode and there was no stopping me.

A lot of people like to be loved. To be constantly getting on well with your suppliers and being told that your company is marvellous. But that's not the reality of business. The most liberating thing of all is to know exactly where you stand and – even though they were often delighted with my sales – I knew exactly where I stood with Motorola.

My animosity towards them was steadily increasing. Firstly, they had advised me very badly on the product in the early days and refused to give me compensation. Then as a result of my carefully kept graph on price and volume, I knew I was being charged more for the product than other Motorola customers. And now they had taken away the man who ran my mobile phone business.

I knew I needed to tip the whole playing field so that the ball rolled in my favour. And I had a plan.

So at the time, as I have explained, a business like mine would buy a phone for say £1,000 and it would then be up to me to negotiate a deal with an airtime provider, who would give me commission once I sold the phone to a retail customer and signed them up with the airtime provider.

Things were quickly changing, however. In 1988 there was a Stock Market flotation of a 20 percent stake in Vodafone's parent company, Racal Telecom. In various disclosures that were then made available, documents estimated that each mobile phone customer was worth a thousand pounds to the networks. So if a network provider paid a commission of £200 or £300 for a new customer then it was still a great deal because every customer was an asset worth £1,000. At a similar time, one of the service providers sold up at a price of £1,000 a customer. Now I knew exactly what each customer was worth.

The networks steadily became desperate for new connections, so the service providers began to up their commissions and they pushed businesses like mine to work with them. I was fully aware of the value that had been ascribed to new network customers. And I pushed back harder for higher commissions. The prices of handsets were continuing to drop, and the old Motorola Transportable was gathering in popularity as the price continued to go down. But they were in short supply.

The service providers were desperate for them. Motorola would sell the phones to them at a lower price, but they wouldn't sell them in large quantities because they could get more money out of me for each Transportable.

By now I had very good relationships with some service providers and – using my ability to see how the coloured squares in the Rubik's Cube could line up – I spotted a way of cutting myself a very good deal.

First off, I wanted to know how much they were paying for the phones, and those figures went straight on my graph. Then I made a suggestion: 'What if I provide you with Transportables without you letting Motorola know that you are getting them directly from me. You can sign up customers but I have to pay more for the phones from Motorola so you will have to pay my cost price.'

'Sounds good,' came the reply.

'My only fee will be the retrospective commission,' I said. I knew I would be making a retrospective volume rebate of four percent. I put in an order for 100 phones – an £80,000 shipment. From that one order, I made an immediate £3,000.

I am fully aware that this may be mind-bogglingly complicated to many people. But I'd found a golden opportunity which in business terms is known as an 'arbitrage' – the purchase and sale of an asset in order to make a profit from a difference in that asset's price between those two markets. In simple terms, by them buying from me at a higher price, I was getting more of a margin and they were able to sign up more of those £1,000 customers. We were both winning. The service providers didn't need persuading because now they had a guaranteed stream of highly desirable Transportables enabling them to keep their dealers trading and selling the lucrative airtime contracts.

Thanks to this move, as well as my newly-enthused sales team, we progressed swiftly, from that £2,000-a-month loss to a profit of £20,000 in the first month. In the second month, our profit was £25,000. And in the third month we hit profits of £30,000. On it went, out of the curve and up into the beautiful, straight, skywards – the exponential growth as illustrated in the J Curve.

The people at Motorola were delighted to be charging me the maximum price for Transportable sets, so they were shipping vast orders to me and, meanwhile, other service providers had no choice but to knock on my door. Like our used-car business, our mobile phone company had suddenly gone wholesale and rapidly I was becoming the biggest mobile phone retailer and wholesaler in Britain.

*****

YEARS AGO, WHEN I was a mischievous kid, I sneaked into the Odeon cinema and I saw James Dean in the classic movie, Giant.

There's that moment when, as the humble ranch hand Jett Rink, he strikes oil on his little piece of land. All this black goo shoots up into the air. Jett stumbles back and then he opens his arms. He lets this dirty liquid spray all over himself because he knows he's hit gold, and that means it's the end of his kowtowing to the arrogant ranch owners. And that oil, it keeps on gushing up out of the ground, unstoppable as the music suddenly rises. It's a glorious scene.

For a brief moment, it felt like that with the Transportables but unlike Jett Rink's oil, the money didn't keep pouring in forever and I had to keep on pushing and pushing to discover new money revenues.

There were too many of these moments to recount. Quite early on I began exporting the MicroTac phones to China. It took months of laborious work to set up meetings and do the deals but I had many more months of very healthy trade with China. Motorola knew exactly what I was doing and were delighted, until the American office discovered I was distributing their product. They expressed their great dissatisfaction to the UK office, who promptly claimed they knew nothing about it and did everything they could to shut down my Chinese trade.

Another situation involved a process called 'netting' whereby phones were sold at a very cheap rate to other dealers. It was a higher risk strategy because you had to wait for your commission from the service providers and try to ensure phones were being sold to genuine customers with credit to pay for their connection. I did this slowly, trying to make as many checks as possible.

One of my competitors did the opposite and ended up supplying a group with hundreds of thousands of pounds worth of phones. They turned out to be a criminal Birmingham gang who had just sold the handsets. There was no commission ever coming and when he tried to get his money back he was warned in no uncertain terms that he and his family would be dead if he tried. I felt incredibly sorry for him but I also knew he'd fallen foul of being too greedy. That was the world of mobile phones back then.

I worked hard to keep coming up with new strategies. I was expanding fast and I knew there was a lot of money to be had. I was buying more and more buildings around the car lot in Shelton Old Road as we grew and grew.

As for the car business, we had plans to open a second site but compared to mobile phones, the cars – which had served us so well – suddenly seemed like those mushrooms I'd grown years earlier. Cars were like a part of our heritage, but they were never going to provide the future that I could now see for us. I was hunting down more opportunities for revenue and profit growth in the mobile phone world, I knew there were even more and I needed Brian by my side to help me.

I went to his office to see him. 'I don't think we should get a second site,' I said. 'In fact, I think we should sell this place. The car business just isn't scalable or saleable in the way the phone business is. But I need you with me to make it bigger and better.'

Brian took a few minutes. Then he nodded. Being a used-car salesman is a tough gig and he'd been at the sharp end for just over a decade, constantly striving, always at the mercy of the weather and the economy. He'd seen what I'd done already with the phones and was savvy enough to see how much more could be achieved. 'OK,' he said. 'I think you're right. Let's make it work.'

We did.

By 1990, Midland Mobile Phones (which, after a run-in with the Midland Bank became Caudwell Communications) had a turnover of £13 million.

I was 38 years old.

Chapter 14

LAMB CHOPS, LLORET DE MAR AND PINK CARPETS

I AM A very privileged man.

In the press I became known largely for the money I have made. I own the most expensive house in London which is twice the size of the Royal Albert Hall and the largest private dining room next to Buckingham Palace. It even has an indoor river. You might see a publicity photograph of me in a magazine with my helicopter, or on the deck of my 73-metre superyacht, and you'd nod and think, 'Oh yes, he looks like a billionaire.'

But that image is not a representation of who I really am. Those possessions reflect years of monstrously difficult graft and grind. They show the world who I am now but they do not hint at where I have come from. People need to look a little closer, not judge by the fancy exterior. If you happened to see me in the grounds of my stunning home in Monaco, that looks over the glittering Mediterranean, then you would probably mistake me for a workman. I am more likely to be in shorts and a vest, suspended half way up a tree, manhandling a large electrical trimmer. That is who I am.

I refuse to pay local gardeners 40 euros-an-hour to come late, take long lunch breaks, leave early and achieve very little, so I'd rather do it myself. If you are not going to take pride in your work, if you are not going to work hard and do your utmost, I don't want you in my garden at all. I have too much respect for a true work ethic.

On a recent trip to Monaco I needed some landscaping work done. My friend, the gentlemanly Andrew, who owns his own building company, knew I had had issues finding workers who fitted my standards. 'John,' he said. 'Let me help you. I will work with you.'

Now Andrew is a very successful man, wealthy in his own right and I know he has a lot of his own business to deal with. I was unsure whether he knew what he was getting himself into.

'I start at 8am,' I warned him, thinking that might put him off.

'That's OK with me,' he said, and he smiled.

After several hours toiling in the red-hot sun, we stopped for a short tea break. I was pleasantly surprised that Andrew knew exactly what he was doing and he was resourceful, hard-working and keen to get the job done. However, he already looked exhausted. We started again, clearing the masses of tough foliage and branches that were blocking the view of the ocean. By four o'clock I saw him, red-faced and checking his watch. I smiled to myself and got back to wrestling with the trimmer, clambering up and down trees, spotting patches of tangled undergrowth that needed to be dealt with. Sweat was pouring down my back in a steady stream. Time passed, then I heard Andrew clearing his throat a few feet from where I was working. 'So, John, it is five o'clock. Have we finished do you think?' he said hopefully, as he came round to my side. He looked exhausted.

'No,' I answered. 'I work till the sun goes down.' His face fell then I remembered something that I thought would cheer him up. 'Oh, actually, Andrew, I have to meet someone for dinner at eight,' I said. 'So we can call it a day at 7.30 if you like.'

He must have bitterly regretted ever offering to help, and I will respect him forever for battling through by my side when he must have felt fit to drop. Andrew would have probably preferred to spend part of the day back in his smart business clothes, running his own concerns. And on that day Andrew probably got to know me better than he had done in all the years we had known each other.

If there's something to be done, I will do it myself and I won't stop. I am rarely lounging about like the wealthy man of those publicity shots. Like my dad, I'm more comfortable working and if I'm not working I will busy myself doing chores or riding my bike. The most incredible food I've ever eaten is my special recipe of Knorr powdered soup, Yeoman tinned potatoes and Fray Bentos corned beef after a 90 mile bike ride, sitting on the side of the road out of a simple plastic bowl. No elaborate, gourmet meal in a Michelin starred restaurant can ever compare with that.

In 2012, my daughter Libby joined me and Brian on a charity bike ride from Land's End to John O'Groats to raise money for Caudwell Children. She learnt a lot on that trip about everything from chafing thighs to overcoming physical and mental abject misery (it was freezing cold and very wet for many hundreds of miles) and the power of dogged determination. I was extremely proud of her. She also learnt that hunger really is the best sauce and nothing in the world can beat those roadside snacks. She wrote a diary of the trip and it made me laugh out loud when I read these words written by my very health conscious daughter: *Hotdogs and soup and jaffa cakes and salt n vinegar crisps. That combination will forever more hold for me a peculiar kind of beauty.*

There are the real moments in life, the times when you know who you are and what you are all about. Regardless of how wealthy I have become, I have never lost sight of who I am, where I come from and the things that mean the most to me.

*****

SO IN 1990, our business has a turnover of £13 million, and some people might think that suddenly I started to behave as one would expect of a wealthy young businessman, starting to relax and spend money. Wrong.

The value of a business takes into account the turnover, the running costs, the margin and the cash flow. But even if all of these numbers are good you can still be left with the constant feeling that the house of cards could tumble at any moment. I was still working those 18-hour days. True, I drove a better car but I wore suits from Marks & Spencer and I bought milk from the Happy Shopper.

I would have been able to tell you on any given day of the week, the exact state of my finances. The red and the black. Red would have figured prominently but I knew the black would always be coming through.

Kate had her own way of gauging our steadily-rising fortunes. She was never, by any stretch of the imagination, a materialistic woman. She did not ask if she could have a designer dress or a pair of expensive shoes. But once my business was doing well, there were events we were invited to which often required her to wear an evening dress. Kate had never owned an evening dress but dutifully went shopping in Chester and after a couple of hours of going in and out of the more upmarket boutiques, she finally found the perfect outfit for the occasion. She walked in to take a closer look at the gown.

Then she returned home without it.

'It was £350, John!' She told me later that night. She was horrified by the price tag. At one point in our lives that would have been as much as we spent on food in a year.

I laughed. 'Kate, just get it. I bet you will look fabulous in it.' She shook her head. 'It's too much,' and I spent the next hour persuading her to forget about the money and buy it. The following day she went back to Chester and returned with it wrapped up in fine white paper inside a very fancy bag. Kate looked wonderful in that dress but she never forgot how special it was. It was inspected for damage afterwards in case a drop of wine had split on it or a scuff mark had somehow appeared then cleaned and hung in a covering on a special hanger in her wardrobe. She treated that dress like a piece of fine art, never once taking for granted the money spent on her outfit.

There was, I remember, only one time Kate asked me to spend money on something that she really wanted. Libby was two and a half years old, and we had outgrown our little bungalow.

A former pig farm in the countryside came on the market and we went to have a look at it. It was called Woodlands. We viewed it on a sunny day in late July, and it was in a dip in the middle of fields which were covered with red poppies, their pretty heads gently swaying in the breeze. There were plenty of muddy patches, broken down outhouses and signs of wear and tear. But regardless of this, all around you could hear the sound of birdsong and the leaves rustling in the trees.

Kate instantly fell in love. The house was going under auction in a matter of weeks. She had barely stepped foot inside when she turned around to me and said, 'John, we have to have this house. Do not come back from the auction without it.'

It wasn't a palace. We moved in on Christmas Eve and somehow ended up with two removal men, one who had a wooden leg which made things complicated as it was so muddy by the entrance to the house that I'd had to lay a ramp of planks to keep the mess out.

Kate, who had again suffered the most crippling postnatal depression after Libby's birth, could not have been happier. Her eyes were gleaming as she looked around her, clearly seeing right through the mess and chaos to the family home she knew she could create.

Rather foolishly given the circumstances, we had invited both families to Christmas lunch the following day. So in addition to unpacking, she had to work out how to cook the turkey we'd brought with us in an old Aga which she had no idea how to use.

'I've been up all night but I think I've got it working,' she told me the following morning brightly. This run down old house had certainly had a magical effect on her. She hadn't stopped. All our presents had been wrapped in bin bags but the table had been laid, holly and mistletoe spread everywhere and enticing smells coming from the kitchen of the feast to come. The turkey was succulent and piping hot and it was a wonderful Christmas celebration.

Kate loved that house. In the bungalow, the whole place had been finished throughout with bright pink carpeting that I'd got cheap because no-one else would buy it and it was taking up room in the warehouse. In the days after we moved in Kate hesitantly asked me, 'Have you got any thoughts about carpets, or anything?' I knew that this time she had her own vision for this place. I also knew how creative she was and how much she would love to decorate Woodlands to her own style.

'No,' I said, and laughed. 'You do exactly what you want. But don't spend too much.'

'As if,' she said.

She did a fantastic job creating an incredible cosy, rustic family home. Everyone who ever came to Woodlands always wanted to know who had designed the interiors and she was always being asked, 'Where did you buy this?' or 'Was this expensive?' Kate would look at me and laugh because we both knew she'd created miracles on a very small budget.

*****

KATE WOULD SAY if she really thought about it, she would best track our financial ascension through our holidays. Our honeymoon in a one-star hotel in Majorca cost us – in total – £29 each. We got what we paid for. Our room looked out onto a flat roof that was covered in bottles filled with urine and used condoms. What a view. The wardrobe was so bashed about that it barely stood upright. The door knob had been knocked off it and in its place a piece of string hung through the hole where the handle had once been. But it was hot. It was 'abroad' and we didn't really care.

That wardrobe used to make us laugh hysterically every time we opened it. We were so happy to be there. On the way down to the airport, Kate – who had never been on a plane before – had been convinced we weren't going to make it. The head gasket went on our Hillman Imp which caused it to overheat and meant we'd have to stop every 20 miles or so to top up the water. We drove down to Luton with a five-gallon drum of water in the car but as we got closer to the airport we were stopping every ten minutes, then every five minutes, then I had to pull into a petrol station to get more water as Kate clutched our passports and prayed that our clapped-out car would get us there in time. It did – just about. We spent most of the short flight giggling as we talked about how we'd probably have to push the car home (miraculously it made it with water stops every ten minutes). Adversity brought out the best in us.

We still crack jokes about our terrible holidays which were never that terrible after all – Lloret de Mar was as exotic as it got for us in those days. They are some of my fondest, funniest memories and even now my mum loves me to retell them because they make her smile. Another time, we went up to Scotland camping with around twenty pounds in our pockets. We had a great time but there was only a matter of a few pounds left when it came to getting back home.

'Don't worry, I'm going to work out the shortest route and if there's no traffic jams, we'll be OK,' I said. 'But we need all the money for petrol so we can't have any breakfast or lunch.'

The plan was going well. I came off the motorway to avoid queues and to drive slowly at 30-40 miles per hour to save petrol – and then we hit Matlock – 30 miles from home – where the car just stopped. The petrol light was on red. I kept an emergency bag of change in the car, any coppers I had went into that bag. Kate got down on her hands and knees rifling under seats, checking every spare inch of the car for any coins that may have rolled out of the bag or our pockets. I went through our bags checking every single pocket for coins. We managed to scrape together a few more forgotten pennies. We were bang opposite a pub and a petrol station. I sat and counted up our money.

'Hey, this is great,' I said triumphantly. 'We've got enough for petrol to get us past the last leg AND enough for a pint of shandy and a sandwich between us in the pub.'

With that handful of coppers, it felt like we'd won the lottery. Kate was over the moon. She threw her arms around me and we walked to the pub hand in hand, laughing at our miraculous little scavenger hunt.

Kate and I always seemed to have hilarious adventures together but everything was so simple back then. Once, I took Kate on a romantic trip to Blackpool despite the fact we were completely broke. We paraded around all the bed-and-breakfasts that always did good full English breakfast and also provided dinner. Unbelievably these places would charge less than five pounds for the lot. I was always a real foodie, so we both spent time looking in the windows of each one where they'd have a menu pinned up and the longer you walked round looking at the meals on offer, the hungrier you got. Then we arrived at one which had no menu in the window.

'Knock on the door and ask what's for dinner,' giggled Kate.

I did. A man answered. 'What's the food like here?' I said.

He loomed towards me, put his face close to mine and in a broad Yorkshire accent said, 'Put it this way lad, do you like lamb chops?'

Kate was practically stuffing her hand down her mouth to stop herself laughing. But, as it happened, I loved lamb chops. So I marched in, my mouth watering, leaving Kate to follow behind. She was trying desperately not to break into hysterics in the tiny hallway, where we were now being given the run-down of the rules.

From our one-star honeymoon hotel we jumped to a three-star in Majorca, and then a four-star in Tenerife. After that we would book a cottage for two weeks in Saint Raphael on the Côte d'Azur. I would spend the first week laid flat out, sleeping in the sun surrounded by Stephen King novels I was too exhausted to read. In the second week, I'd emerge from the sofa in the lounge where I'd been sleeping all week and play with the girls in the pool, having recharged my batteries with enough sleep to enable me to do months more of those 18-hour days when I got back to England.

These days I have my pick of holiday destinations or I can travel by boat to as many countries as I chose. I love to go away. I love to be with my family and friends eating great food in the sunshine and I am a very well-travelled man. But I've never forgotten those early experiences of cheap and cheerful holidays, how much sheer fun I got out of them and how much they are still part of me.

And I still like lamb chops.

Chapter 15

THE DANGEROUS BROTHERS

BRIAN AND I were getting a reputation. The two penniless boys from Stoke – the ones who grew up jumping free rides on Hanley Park boats and sneaking into cinemas for free – were making waves and making money.

People were starting to talk about this pair of used-car salesmen who were now selling mobile phones. It's true, our business was rocketing. Due to the enormous levels of sales we were providing, we were regularly invited on Motorola jollies, as well as other corporate weekends hosted by other companies – and there were many – that were part of this ever-growing industry.

These weekends were a great chance to network and, given my success at gathering information at my very first spa visit on Motorola's penny, I regarded them as an opportunity of finding new ways to expand our business. Usually, they involved some form of activity which was appealing, as both of us have always been very fit and any form of physical exercise was right up our street, whether we knew how to do it or not.

'Have you ever skied before?' was the question from the ski leader as Brian and I were strapping on skis.

'Yes,' I said. 'I've broken a few ribs and my collar bone but I'm pretty proficient now.'

'So, I would advise you to go to the green slopes for the day,' he

146

said, clearly concerned he'd have an accident on his hands. On these sort of trips, instructors like to be very cautious.

'No,' I answered, smiling. 'We're going straight to the black slopes.'

Within hours, Brian and I were hurling ourselves down the black slope. We were so competitive – we still are – that if we were going to do something, we had to push ourselves to the limits to prove that we could handle it. Skiing is something I still love. I have a wonderful ski lodge in Vail, the resort in Colorado, which is a place of great joy for my children, friends and family. Even with my broken ribs on my very first trip, I couldn't wait to get back on the slopes and skiing remains one of the greatest passions of my life.

On another spa trip, somewhere down in the south of England, I was invited to go horse riding. I am, in fact, rather wary of horses as there's a large element of the control being out of your hands. But I will always give anything a go and the fact it was pushing me out of my comfort zone appealed to me. Off I went, along with a lady who seemed pretty competent, as we set off, she was just a few yards ahead of me. Fifteen minutes in and our horses – which seemed to have some sort of telepathic communication going on – began to gallop at a fair clip. This was faster than I was used to and pretty quickly the horses started to really pick up speed.

I was hanging on for grim death, telling myself I just needed to focus on clinging on when suddenly I saw the lady in front of me fall from her horse. It happened incredibly quickly. But horrifically her foot stayed stuck in a stirrup and the horse carried on galloping, dragging her along the ground. I started screaming at my horse, 'Stop!' Then miraculously the horse in front halted. My horse then stopped suddenly, and I jumped off and ran towards the woman who was now semi-conscious with blood gushing from her neck.

I dashed towards her. As I assessed the damage, I realised the horse's hoof had clipped her neck, cutting an artery. That accounted for the massive amount of blood. My own hands were covered in cuts, but I used my thumb to quickly cover the wound, trying to stem the bleeding as best I could. The others on the ride and the instructor – who were in front of us – had heard my screams and realised we were in trouble. Now they were coming towards us. 'Call an ambulance,' I yelled. 'Tell them her artery is punctured. I'm holding it steady.'

This was the early '90s. Everyone was aware of the dangers of Aids, which could be contracted by open cuts in the body. It's rather like how it has been over the past few years with the anxiety about contracting Covid-19. The ambulance men swiftly dealt with my companion and then took one look at the cuts on my hands and gave me an anti-HIV foam to rub all over them. I hadn't even thought I could have been in any danger from Aids because I'd been so concerned about her. It was actually quite a shock when the ambulance man handed me that foam. But I was as logical about Aids as I have been about Covid-19 and I have never fallen prey to paranoia. I reasoned I had about a one-in-a-thousand chance of contracting it and I also knew that regardless, I would have done exactly the same thing all over again.

I saw my riding companion again at dinner the following evening. She seemed to have recovered, and was clearly well enough to go out for dinner despite the large dressing around her neck covering her stitches. She was full of gratitude for my quick thinking. She also told me she'd been tested for HIV, and was negative, which I admit was an added relief. But I have remained to this day somewhat wary of horses.

I have had my own fair share of sporting accidents. I've broken my neck three times, once when racing a motorboat, once when kart racing and once when trampolining. I've broken pretty much every bone in my body, cycling, motor biking, car racing and skiing.

I was – I am – always pushing myself to win if I think there's even a fraction of a chance of me succeeding, rather like when I was a kid at school and I'd take a jump from a high building. The jump seemed impossible but I wanted to prove that no-one could beat me, even if I did happen to break an ankle in the process. The only person I know who was as competitive as me – if not more in the case of motor-racing, something he excels at – was Brian. Like me, he cannot resist a challenge.

I can't help it. Challenge me to water-ski backwards blindfolded on one leg and I'll do it. Even at 69. My teenage son, Jacobi, mastered the art of a Unicycle a few years back, riding it backwards and forwards on my yacht. I had to be able to do it too, so I bought one and have spent many hours travelling a few inches and falling on my backside. It's not really a sport you'd advise a man in his sixties to take up, I've dislocated several fingers but I'm persevering.

I know my partner Modesta worries about this aspect of my personality. She doesn't want to lose me but believe me, as extreme as I like to take things, I never want to put my life at risk. A few years ago, I almost died after a cycling accident near Florence in Italy.

It was a perfect day, I'm an experienced cyclist and was enjoying a rigorous ride through the countryside. Then as I was going around 25mph downhill there was a tremendous bang and I was thrown at high speed off my bike. I was concussed, fighting to breathe with horrendous pain all over my body and for the first time in my life I knew I was in real trouble.

I managed to get my phone and call Modesta. 'I've had an accident,' were pretty much the only words I could get out. Luckily a passing motorist called an ambulance but I honestly believed I was going to die on the way to hospital. It's the first time in my life I've felt that. I thought of my family and my children but I was in so much agony I couldn't really think straight.

At the hospital the nightmare just escalated. A blood test showed I had Covid-19. I'd broken 11 bones in my body, shattered my shoulder and punctured my lung but all I could see around me were people masked up with big gloves and aprons, no-one spoke English. I was pushed and prodded and then left for hours, then once stripped naked and just stared at by two nurses. I desperately needed water but I had no way of reaching the jug by the side of my bed.

Meanwhile Modesta was frantically going from hospital to hospital trying to find me. She had no idea where I was. And as I was in a Covid-19 ward no-one could come near me. I spent five days in a delirium of pain and anxiety before Modesta – who had tracked me down – insisted I was helicoptered out of there to a different hospital.

I was haunted by the experience for months. It took me to a dark place. It wasn't just the accident, it wasn't just the pain, it was the utter helplessness I felt, the inhumanity and the lack of care and compassion from the staff.

It did not put me off cycling, it simply delayed my return to my bike. It was an accident, my worst accident, but I got through it. The helmet I was wearing saved my life (I have kept the smashed up helmet and will never get rid of it). It did make me aware of my mortality – my life hung by a thread. But if anything it made me extremely grateful for the friends and family I have and more determined than ever to show compassion for others through my charity work.

*****

I AM FULLY aware I take a challenge to the extreme, in business and in life. My great friend David Lewis, who runs Sunseeker, once mentioned to me in passing one night that he made the best chips. 'I'm sorry, David,' I said. 'But I make the best chips.'

'Well, John,' he laughed. 'I don't think you could beat mine.' He probably thought that was the end of it. He thought wrong.

'Let's do a chip-off,' I said. 'My house, thirteen guests, thirteen chips, identical sizes, identical potatoes and then we will see who makes the best ones.'

So the scene was set at my house, Broughton Hall, with guests gathered, candles glowing, fine cutlery and all the condiments – ketchup, mayonnaise, brown sauce, malt vinegar and salt– on the table. David and I were in the kitchen slaving over our chips. Guests were given a score card to give marks out of ten for a variety of factors, including taste, appearance, fluffiness, crispiness and so on, and a final preference.

Finally, with great ceremony, Chips A and B were handed around. The guests chewed, cogitated and scribbled down scores – no-one knew who made Chip A or Chip B. The scores were then given to my housekeeper, Kathy.

Kathy went away, counted and then returned. We were all on tenterhooks. 'It's very close. There's only one point in it out of thirteen of you,' she said as she walked into the room. I leapt up before she could say a name.

'No – Kathy,' I interrupted. 'That's impossible. There's not just 13 votes, there's 650 points in total,' I said. 'We need the full points calculated.'

'Oh, sorry I didn't do it that way... I just did the final score,' she answered, looking rather crestfallen.

'Well go back,' I said, completely pumped because this had to be absolutely accurate and without any room for argument. 'You have to add them all up. We need a proper result.'

She disappeared again, and the tension increased. There's nothing like a false start to build the pressure. David looked nervous and, I confess, I was feeling more than a little on edge. After a good ten minutes Kathy came back into the dining room. She was looking rather stunned.

'You both have identical scores,' she said. 'Chip A has 579 out of a possible 650 and Chip B has 579 out of 650.' Everyone roared. David had his head in his hands. This wasn't the way it was supposed to end.

'Go back to your original count, then,' I tell her. 'Who was the winner then. We can't have a draw.'

'Well, it's chip A, and chip A is…'

David's face was glistening in the candle-light. One guest had a napkin almost stuffed into his mouth with the anticipation.

'…John!'

I was already leaping to my feet, absolutely jubilant. David was trying to look like he wasn't bothered, telling everyone the score cards were even. But in the final reckoning it was mine that got the vote. I won. I was the champion. The King of Chips.

Anyhow, I'm afraid that is how far I will go over a chip.

I don't always come out on top. In 2019, my son-in-law Nick generously invited us to Necker Island, Richard Branson's idyll in the British Virgin Islands, as a 40th birthday celebration for Rebekah. It was great to be in such a beautiful place where we could all be together. Branson was also on the island.

Now, Branson is a man whose business skills I admire – the way he's managed to use publicity to push his brand is absolute genius to me, and I love his fearless adventures, like crossing the Atlantic in a hot air balloon.

I'd played tennis with him and lost, but that was OK as I don't play regularly (needless to say I've since taken it up) and he has two-hour sessions from a top coach every single day. But, as a keen and well-practised cyclist, I thought maybe it would be good to suggest a bike ride. He's two years older than I am but like me, he's into active sport.

We had to get a boat to a different island to ride our bikes. As we jumped out, I thought he looked a bit wobbly. He wasn't wearing performance cycling shoes, just old tennis pumps. Then he put his feet into some old fashioned bicycle pedal clips and – rather unsteadily – got on his bike.

'Are you alright there, Richard,' I called, because at this point I was actually feeling concerned for him.

'Fine,' he said quite casually and we set off, with me initially watching him to check he was OK. And then we came to the hills. Richard cycled past me. The hills were monsters but up he went, cycling steadily, his figure disappearing into a tiny speck. As I crested one hill, already sweating from the exertion and the heat from the morning sun, I saw him already at the top of another steep mound looking for all the world as if it was barely costing him the slightest effort. It was a lesson in never underestimating Richard Branson.

That moment remains a vivid memory and obviously, when it comes to cycling, I have vowed to up my game.

*****

LOOKING BACK, I was very much a different sort of businessman. The mobile phone industry was a new world, so there were no rules. And I was determined to do it my way, and my way often caused a stir. Aside from those daredevil feats on corporate away-days, I did other things that got me noticed, some of which I'm not so proud of now.

There was a period of time in the '90s when our accountants – who have long since gone – suggested to us, in their fee-grabbing way, that we should be paid in fine wines or gold bullion. This meant that although we were paying tax, we weren't paying National Insurance.

It wasn't tax evasion but it was definitely tax avoidance, which

I strongly feel is morally unacceptable. I am very passionate about paying my taxes. I am one of the biggest tax payers in this country, paying around £300 million in a ten-year period. It's my duty and it's for the good of the country. My only excuse for my tax avoidance back then is that we were grubbing to keep hold of every penny because we needed cash to grow and taxes were damaging our growth. I've long since believed the government should have a scheme to enable certain young businesses with a proven record for growth to defer paying taxes in order to enable them to flourish. Ultimately this would be an investment for the country as a whole.

I was also very tough on my staff. I wanted results, I wanted winners and, as I drove myself hard, I believed everyone should try to keep up with me. I'd schedule meetings for 6.30am and if I travelled and had a new personal assistant, she would inevitably try to book me a first-class flight. 'I want the cheapest deal you can get,' I'd tell her. 'Look on EasyJet.' I went through several personal assistants, although I found my perfect one in Michele Owen. She has been with me for almost two decades and understands all my ways and foibles better than anyone. She's also a down-to-earth, hard working woman from Staffordshire so we are perfectly well matched.

A mythology grew up about how 'ruthless' I was. In my boardroom there were two doors: one led to my office; the other back out onto the floor. The second door became known as the 'Firing Door'. If an executive came into the boardroom and left within minutes through the second door, everyone knew they were about to clear their desk.

It is true, I was hard. Business makes you hard. Your empathy becomes buried beneath years of having to fight to survive, of being cheated or losing good staff and discovering someone who made you believe they were brilliant was, in fact, a complete dud. If you want your business to survive and flourish, you need to chop away the dead wood. Gardeners remove weeds because they stifle the flourishing plants – it's similar in an office where, as the boss, you have to make these decisions and act. But like all mythologies, not everything is accurate. I distinctly remember in the early days one of my salesmen ringing me at 8am. When I answered the phone I heard only the sound of a man sobbing, followed by, 'I can't come in, John.'

'What's the problem,' I asked him.

'I don't know. I don't feel good. I feel really stressed. I had to pull over because I can't drive my car. I think I'm depressed.'

'Tell me where you are and I'll come and get you.'

I took him home to his wife, told him to call me when he felt better. I told him his salary would remain unchanged and, when he finally did call a few weeks later, we had a long talk. We agreed it was best for me to find someone else to take on the full responsibility of his job, he could work alongside them and then when he felt better, the job would be his again. I admired his direct and honest approach: he told me the problem and was willing to take my advice and eventually returned to his job full time, when he was ready. It takes a certain person to be able to deal with high levels of stress and you have to know what you can cope with.

Brian and I were well used to coping with whatever was thrown at us. Both in and out of the office, we thrived on adrenaline, we loved new challenges and we weren't afraid of anything.

So all in all, in the mobile phone world we were causing a stir. On one trip, after witnessing our exploits on the ski slopes, Charles Dunstone – who headed up a rival company to ours, Carphone Warehouse – dubbed Brian and I 'The Dangerous Brothers'.

That made us laugh. But not as much as when we discovered what the wives on that same trip had nicknamed us. Kate had confessed that we never took anything out of the hotel mini bars because everything in there was so expensive. Word also got about that I still bought my groceries from Happy Shopper, and that I owned only two suits, both of which were inexpensive and from M&S. Brian was just as frugal, so the ladies named us 'The Careful Caudwells'. I took that as a compliment.

Even now I will never take anything from a hotel mini bar.

Chapter 16

SNAKES IN THE GRASS

I AM ABOUT to hit 40 which means, in my mind, I haven't got long left to live.

Time is running out for me so I need to think very carefully about driving everything forward because I am nowhere near the place I want to be.

This is how I thought at that time. I am being completely honest. I believed I would die in my forties because I thought that neither my father nor my grandfather made it to the age of 50. It is only recently I discovered when writing this book that, in fact, both men were in their fifties when they died. That came as a shock to me because that belief of their very premature deaths had been lodged in my brain since I was a teenager.

I also believed – quite rightly – that my fledgling empire could collapse any day because no business is ever safe. This may make me sound like a fearful man, though nothing could be further from the truth. I am not fearful. I am a realist, I am logical. Who could have predicted the devastation caused by Covid-19? It's foolish to be complacent.

January, 1991. I gather my staff for a meeting. The atmosphere amongst the staff was fizzing from the success of 1990. No-one can quite believe that in less than three years we have gone from losing £2,000 every month to building a business with a turnover of £13 million and a profit of £1 million. 'This year,' I announce to the small sea of attentive, happy faces in front of me, 'Is not going to be about growth and profit.' Smiles drop, feet shift and an uncomfortable silence falls on the room.

'This year is about consolidation,' I continue. 'We need to get ourselves in order, stabilise our foundations to facilitate future growth.' I pause. 'If we don't do this we won't survive. But in five years' time we will have a turnover of £250 million.' Jaws drop. An audible gasp escapes from one side of the room. Brian and I walk back to our office and the staff return to their desks, most of them probably thinking the boss has lost his marbles.

Thirteen million pounds is an awful lot of money. It sounds great. But that was the turnover of the business. It didn't account for money spent on wages, orders, growth, taxes and running costs. And whilst I was massively ambitious and passionate to grow sales I was also equally passionate – as any good businessman should be – to keep our expenses as lean and efficient as possible.

But money wasn't the main problem. The reality was I was driving growth so hard that we were growing too fast, like Topsy, and our infrastructure was practically non-existent and had in fact collapsed. Orders would come in with the wrong number of phones – too many or too few, or just the wrong phones. Our stockroom system was all over the place. The time spent locating the right orders, returning the wrong orders, tracking down deliveries and chasing up orders amounted to hours and hours that were wasted each day and our inefficiency was causing us to haemorrhage money. I explained this in no uncertain terms to my team.

I wanted order. I craved order. I love order. I can tell you exactly where everything is in each one of my kitchens because I designed all of the kitchens in my homes and every little thing has its place. I cannot stand mess and I cannot work without a logical system because it creates more work than necessary. When everything is clear, tidy and ordered I can think more clearly, see more clearly –

like wiping away filthy, dark pools of thick oil from the body of a machine. Wipe away, and then you can see the parts that are working efficiently and those that need attention or, perhaps, replacing. Fixing my business meant following the principles that I had learnt when mending machinery as a trainee engineer at Michelin. Strip it back, clean the pieces, fix any damage then put it back together and watch it run smoothly.

It takes time and energy, and both Brian and I gave all our time and energy. No detail is ever too small for me, and nothing escapes my eye. For days, Brian and I sat in the office working away, compiling a database of mobile phone dealers on an Amstrad PC 1512, a computer that seemed state-of-the-art back then, but now – with its green typeface and unwieldy hard discs – looks like a museum piece.

I had a vision for what I wanted our company to be and it was way beyond what we had now. I reflected on those cold, dark days in my bedroom in Wellesley Street, and the dream I had of an empire big enough to fund a charity that could change the lives of those less fortunate, children who'd never been given a chance due to ill health, parents not able to afford treatment. I thought of the poor women who'd knock on our door to see Grandma, and of the time she'd spend to give them treatments (she helped them more than any doctors). I knew I could grow this business and realise my childhood philanthropic vision but I thought – back then – that I had only a few years left to achieve these dreams.

First however, I had to get my own house in order.

*****

A YEAR ON, we were in good shape. We still weren't safe but we were in order. It's a principle that applies to anything with an inbuilt risk of danger. If you can't be safe, you can do everything you can to protect yourself. If you are cycling, check your tyres, get the right gear, the best cycling footwear, a decent helmet. Make sure you have water, a pump and a medical kit. It won't stop you having an accident but at least you will be prepared.

I was always prepared for battle with Motorola. That game had been set since day dot of our dealings, and there was no way out of it since 95 percent of my business was Motorola phones. As far as Motorola was concerned, they loved the business I was bringing in but felt I was getting too powerful. I was constantly being asked to sign new agreements. I refused to do so because the contracts were grossly unfair, draconian and disastrously restrictive. So I was constantly threatened with having my supply cut if I didn't do exactly what they wanted.

I was used to regular difficult meetings and conversations, including one with the European Director of Distribution. Thanks to the situation I'd created a few years earlier, I was retailing direct and distributing to trade, service providers and international buyers. It was a huge part of the reason we were doing so well.

But this, according to the director, was a problem. He knew how big my outfit had become. He also knew how well my operation was running. 'If anyone is doing distribution, it will be me,' he told me.

I took this to mean that Motorola would take over what I was doing, and took it as just another jab from high up. There were always conversations with Motorola going on that were aimed at significantly trying to restrict my rights.

Shortly after that meeting, Motorola terminated my contract to supply me with phones.

That was it. My business felled in one swoop on one day. Over. There was no way I could fight it. It was a done deal. The entire rug had been pulled out from under me. I was devastated.

So what do you do when your business is 95 percent Motorola

phones and you've been sacked by Motorola? It took me right back to that day in the Belstaff boardroom when, enraged by the injustice of the executives' behaviour, I fought like a wounded tiger to claw back as much compensation as I could; to survive financially and make sure my customers' outstanding orders were honoured.

But now the stakes were far higher. I had employees, offices, orders by the thousand and a business that had cost me blood, sweat and tears that no-one was going to stamp into the ground. I explained the situation to Brian and he was equally horrified. 'What do you think we should do?' he asked.

'I've got a few possible solutions,' I said. 'I just need to see if they could work.' My brain was on overdrive. My model of a Rubik's Cube had been smashed to pieces and I had to piece it together again. I couldn't sleep for days, my head spinning trying to think of ways to survive. I had to think fast because orders were coming in and speed was everything at that time.

I decided to reverse the plan that I had made last time with the service providers. Then I'd made a deal with the service providers to supply them with the hugely popular mobile Transportables and they had to give me a guarantee that they would say nothing to Motorola to ensure my supply wouldn't be cut off. Now, I was going to ask them to provide me with Motorola products and guarantee them absolute confidentiality so Motorola wouldn't cut off their supply. I picked up the phone and made a call to one of the guys who I considered a friend.

'So, I've got an idea,' I said.

'Oh yes.' He was always open to any new plans I had.

'We join forces to buy phones from Motorola which would work well for both of us,' I said confidently, not revealing anything about my disastrous situation.

'We will get a better price because of my volumes and increase your percentage discount. I will guarantee that I will keep this confidential from Motorola.'

There was silence, and then, 'Yes, great idea. Let's start.'

I made a similar call to another contact, again making sure it came over as me doing him a favour rather than desperately trying to save my business.

These discussions gave me much better buy prices but left me in grave danger of losing my supply if Motorola found out

I knew that this might only be a short term solution. I was giving Caudwell Communications the kiss of life, but I had to keep it breathing. I had to keep thinking of other strategies, looking at our operation from every possible angle just in case something went wrong with my first plan.

What happened next would change the entire complexion of the mobile phone industry in the '90s. For anyone interested in business, or anyone intrigued by the rise of the product which has become such an essential part of our everyday life – the mobile phone – this is the story of a lightning rod moment.

As Brian and I sat and pulled apart our business model, we realised that if Motorola represented 95 percent of the business then we needed to look at the remaining five percent to try to de-risk. This was made up by smaller companies, such as Nokia and Panasonic.

The Finnish company, Nokia, made a great product, but back in 1992 they only had two percent of the total market share. This intrigued me. Clearly, they lacked aggression and that was something – along with sales and distribution – that I could provide. Interestingly, I discovered there was a link with my personal history going back to Michelin and my years as a car trader. Years before they had focused on mobile phones, Nokia had been a factory in Finland which made rubber tyres.

I contacted Nokia's sales manager, Phil Rider, and asked him to come and see me. I told him that if they supplied me with the right product at the right time, I could massively grow their business. We had a great meeting. Phil was impressed by our infrastructure, our ability to distribute to wholesalers and to sell to retail.

'There's just one problem, John,' he said. 'I can't make this decision. It has to go to my boss, Chris Jones. If he doesn't like you it won't happen. But you will have to go and see him because he never visits anyone.'

Now I had a challenge.

Chris Jones was clearly an almighty ogre. But I wasn't going to him. I couldn't afford the time to travel to the Nokia headquarters in Cambridge and psychologically, it would put me at a disadvantage. He needed to see the power of our distribution. I had to lure this ogre into my den. That way I'd be able to show him exactly how we could grow his business.

My war of attrition began.

*****

A FEW WEEKS later, after a day with Brian taking a tour of our operations, this great ogre – who turned out to be a great guy who has become a lifelong friend – was settled into a cosy armchair at Woodlands, with a glass of exceptional whisky in his hand. 'I've got three thousand Cityman100 Nokias,' he told me. 'But they cost £350 a piece.' That was too high, too dear and I already knew they were an end of line model and no one would pay that price.

We carried on talking. I knew, if things went well, Chris would have been given the authority from Finland to do a deal. I just had to get the right deal.

At 4am after a tense but amicable negotiation we shook hands on an agreement for an unbelievable life-changing £50 a phone. But there was a problem. I didn't have the cash to buy them and Nokia couldn't give me credit.

We carried on talking. Chris, by now, could see that I had the ability to make Nokia a key player but he just wasn't able to go any further without speaking to Finland, and so wasn't able to finalise the deal. 'But give me time,' he said. 'And I will come up with something.'

Two weeks later – after Nokia had done exhaustive credit checks on my company – he called me and said that I could have his full stock for £50-a-phone with a creative combination of cash up front and enough short term credit for me (at a big stretch) to do the deal. I have no idea what strings he managed to pull, but it was the game changer I needed. I started off with a shipment of one thousand.

I knew the Nokia deal was a life-saver.

But I had to reflect on what had happened. Relying on Motorola for most of my business had created an Achilles heel which made my company vulnerable. I was never going to make that mistake again. I decided from now on never to depend so much on any one organisation – ideally to never to be reliant on any one company for more than 10 percent of business. It's the old adage. Never keep all your eggs in one basket.

Even though I had a great new partnership with Nokia and I was still selling Motorola phones through my deal with the service providers, I had to think how long either would last. What would happen when we sold all the Citymen phones? What if Motorola terminated their relationship with the service providers as they had done with me? What if the service providers pulled out of our deal? I was never going to rely on any one relationship ever again if I could avoid it.

But for the time being I focused on Nokia. Brian and I got our sales team together. 'Now you are going to push on Nokia phones,' we told them. 'Forget Motorola. These Nokia phones are our future.

Familiarise yourselves with the products and sell. Use every resource we have to sell these phones.'

We devised multiple methodologies of selling, going at it like Olympic athletes hell-bent on winning the race. I was completely driven. The wounded tiger in me didn't want to just get even with Motorola. I wanted to damage them where it hurt – in sales, distribution and volume.

It was at this point I discovered something that increased my desire for revenge. The man who had manoeuvred my departure from Motorola had just set up a business following my distribution model. I couldn't believe it. When he had told me months previously if anyone was going to be doing the distribution it would be Motorola, I had never, for one second, believed he meant himself. After being stabbed in the back, I was now being attacked head on – but if anything that news just put more fire in my belly.

We were now actively selling against Motorola and we were growing stronger. Then, the greatest thing happened; Nokia brought out the 101 handset – a candy bar-sized phone that came in a variety of colours – a giant step away from the brick phones. Nokia was so thrilled with my performance with the Cityman that they considered me their number one seller and gave me hugely favourable rates to sell the 101, which was another massive boost because I knew these phones were a gift to sell.

This new phone model, designed by Italian-American Frank Nuovo, and with its pretty jewel colours, large screens and lightweight, pocket size appealed to women. The phone also came with a range of batteries that could fully recharge the phone within 30 minutes, as opposed to the hours needed for some of the older brick models. They were hot property and we were the main suppliers and distributors.

We were killing it. Within a year, we drove Nokia sales from two percent to 20 percent of the market. To cap it all, we all loved working with Chris. Later, he came to work for me at Phones 4u and was one of the guests at my fabled 'chip-off' dinner party.

Unsurprisingly within a year, Motorola came back. I calmly negotiated a more favourable deal but from then on Nokia had my loyalty, even if Motorola regained my custom.

When I told my staff in 1991 that in five years' time, the company would have a turnover of £250 million, I know many of them thought that I was crazy. I was, in fact, wrong. By 1994 we had hit that target two years earlier and we were the biggest distributors in the whole of Europe.

In business, revenge is a dish best served red hot.

Chapter 17

ICARUS MELTS

THERE IS ALWAYS a price to pay for success. I knew it, even as I fought like Kratos to construct the empire I dreamed of, in order to create the future I wanted for my family.

My dreams weren't big. They were vast. Infinite. I could see how I could keep expanding and expanding to cover every aspect of my industry, from high street retail shops to making accessories, repairs, logistics, and being a service provider as well as wholesaler and distributor. I was like a boy with a box of Lego. My business had a firmer foundation, and now I was adding more and more blocks to my structure, thinking laterally about new opportunities to exploit. I was no longer one small part of a system, reliant on distributors, retailers and providers. I was building my own system, although still very vulnerable to manufacturers and networks.

But, as I say, success comes at a price, and I was caught in that trap that many ambitious men and women will appreciate. I had to work hard because I wanted to provide the very best for my family, but in order to do that it meant long hours away from them.

My family is – and always will be – the beginning and end of my world. But, that said, I was also unbelievably driven. There was no limit whatsoever to my goals. I spent years working insanely long hours but I was a father of two little girls, and I wanted to be a good dad to them. Kate was – and still is – an incredible mother, and life at Woodlands was happy, but the majority of time I spent with my girls was first thing in the morning and last thing at night. Even now, Rebekah remembers how I used to stroke her hair until she fell asleep, a memory that is special for both of us.

Kate did a great job of making our home look stylish and cosy, and I was incredibly proud of my three girls. Rebekah was proving to be an extremely smart young lady, combining my logical mind with Kate's creative abilities. Libby was just a joy, a gentle, deep-thinking empathetic soul who could also have me in stitches with her funny observations. From the moment Libby was born, Rebekah was her guide and companion. They absolutely adored each other, which was just wonderful.

Whatever was going on at work, my children provided a welcome distraction. When Rebekah was only about six years old, Kate was asked to go in to see her teacher. When I came home, she filled me in on what had happened. 'Apparently, she's been cutting hair in the playground at break times,' she told me.

'OK,' I said, waiting for the rest of the story. Had she sneaked in a pair of dangerous scissors? Had she chopped off a little girl's prized ponytail?

'But the problem is she's been charging them all money for their haircuts,' Kate continued, barely suppressing her laugh. 'I've had to tell her she mustn't ever do it again, but clearly she thought she was just setting up a good little business.'

My daughter, the playground entrepreneur!

Rebekah, like me, always knows her own mind and, like Kate, the girls were obsessed with books. Rebekah particularly loved Malory Towers, Enid Blyton's tales of boarding school life. When she was about ten, Rebekah began begging us to let her go to boarding school. One of her best friends had started boarding at Packwood Haugh, about an hour away from Stoke, and, inspired by her beloved Malory Towers, Rebekah wanted to join her and have lovely adventures at a real boarding school. I was dead set against it. It wasn't a matter of money; it was a matter of principal. I didn't agree with private education. I thought that if you were smart and you worked hard then you would achieve, no matter what. But I listened to what Rebekah had to say. Kate also believed it would give her a lot of good opportunities and eventually agreed that she could go.

Five days after Rebekah began at the school, I got a letter from her, telling me how fantastic it was. Five days later, and for the next week, I got a succession of heart breaking letters telling me how she hated it, that she'd made the biggest mistake of her life, and pleading with me to rescue her. I thought hard about what to do. Obviously, a parent's instinct is to rush over and pick up the unhappy child. But that wasn't going to teach her anything about life. I wrote back to her, saying this was a decision that she'd made, and that she had to give it at least six months. I told her she had to fight through and not fall at the first hurdle. It was a tough letter to write but this, for me, was a life lesson.

Soon afterwards, another letter arrived from Rebekah. 'Daddy, I do love it here. I was over-reacting before because I was just getting used to everything. But I definitely want to stay, and I love you, too.'

*****

IN 1994, KATE was pregnant. I was delighted but also felt some trepidation. With both Rebekah and Libby, Kate had suffered terrible postnatal depression. I worried for her, but we both really wanted more children.

On the work front, I was racing, building my Lego empire at top speed. In 1993 I had set up my own independent mobile phone network service provider called Singlepoint and I was now full pelt in the middle of an exciting new plan to open a chain of online and high street retail shops that would sell phones and mobile contracts.

Phones 4u would eventually expand to 600 shops throughout Britain and it would be those shops that would really make my name. Everyone knew Phones 4u because they were on every high street in the country, they were a one-stop shop for mobiles and extremely high profile because of our huge advertising campaigns.

But logistics aside, this involved long hours overseeing everything, from hiring the right management and sales teams, to the branding, shop design, training, legal issues, locations, and even the colour of the carpets. I am – as everyone who has ever worked with me can confirm – all about the detail. That is because the seemingly smallest details can make the greatest difference.

It was a Friday, 6th October, the day before my 42nd birthday. Kate was about three months pregnant, and she was waiting outside Libby's school at pick-up time. My phone rang. It was Kate, she could barely breathe and sounded unbelievably distressed. 'John,' she said. 'Can you get Libby?'

'What's the matter? Are you okay?... Where are you, Kate?' I was anxious.

'I'm outside the school,' she said, in a faraway voice.

What happened? I asked her, 'Have you had an accident, Kate? Is it the baby?'

'No... I just can't... I can't get out of the car.'

In the back of my mind I knew what was happening, but it was way too soon for postnatal depression – the baby was five months away. 'Kate,' I said. 'Everything is OK. Just sit calmly and ask someone to get Libby for you. I will see you back at home.'

When I got home, Libby was her usual happy self, clearly oblivious to any problems but although she was managing, Kate clearly was not. 'It was just a bit of a panic attack,' I reassured her, hoping my words would turn out to be true. 'You'll feel better tomorrow.' But she didn't. The following day, Kate told me she needed to go to the maternity hospital. I told her to call me if there were any problems, but I had to stay at home with Libby. My birthday was not going to be any sort of celebration.

I had no idea how bad it was. I thought that it was maybe a sign that Kate felt nervous – as I did – about what was to come. But this was not just a panic attack, it was part of a much bigger issue. At the hospital Kate waited for three or four hours, but there were no doctors available to see her. She wasn't bleeding and the baby wasn't in distress. The problem was what was going on in her head. In desperation, she stopped a nurse. Later she told me she had just grabbed her hand.

'I need help,' she told her. 'I'm pregnant and I'm losing my mind.'

*****

KATE WAS DIAGNOSED with prenatal depression. I had no idea of this condition but it was terrible for Kate. She was exhausted all of the time. She suffered from more of those evil panic attacks, and she worried sick about the baby growing inside her.

We were all beside ourselves. We saw doctors, we saw psychiatrists, we spoke to family, but none of it made any difference. There is no medication you can really take for prenatal depression – for obvious reasons – so we were between a rock and a hard place.

My focus was Kate and the business. But if I'm being totally honest, all the problems I was having at work were at times a welcome distraction from what was going on at home. Every day I went to the office and there were more issues. I was burying myself in work because I had to and, to be honest, because I wanted to.

My days were frantic with endless issues to deal with. One way or another we would lose dozens of people in our quest for perfection. Very few employees were up to our exacting standards. The trouble is the rest of the world knew that and were constantly trying to recruit the people we did employ. Poaching was an endless source of frustration, but we very rarely lost really good people. We would do everything in our power to keep them.

Cash flow was a continual problem due to our ever-increasing turnover. On a daily basis I was fire-fighting more issues with suppliers, battling to improve our customer service and pushing every minute of the day because those bouts I'd had with Motorola had been just a taste of what was to come with multiple companies and suppliers. Business is a war but I was becoming increasingly hardened to it as I picked up more battle scars. Although I liked to think I was building an empire, in reality I saw it as a house of cards.

When I came home, I was not, however, hardened to what was going on with Kate. I couldn't bear to see her in such a terrible place. Her pregnancy continued agonisingly, and all I could do was try to make sure every form of the best care was available to her. At the time, we had a local lady working for us as a cleaner.

I asked her if she could help out more. She could be there for both Kate and Libby, which gave me some peace of mind.

And as my business was growing, all sorts of people were reaching out to me. A month before Rufus was born, I was invited by the Trade Secretary, Sir Michael Heseltine, to join a trade mission to South Africa, another possible outlet for my phones. As much as I agonised, I couldn't turn this down because it would be a massive boost for our business profile and a huge step for me, so I was very grateful to have sorted out extra help at home.

The trip was eye-opening for me on many levels, thanks to some information given to me by Tory MP and journalist Julian Critchley, who had asked to visit me at Broughton and explained his and Michael's past there.

Back in the 1940s Broughton was used to house two schools, one in the west wing, one in the east wing. These schools were huge rivals and Julian was a pupil in one and Michael a pupil in the other.

On returning early after a school holiday, Michael and his fellow pupils (aided and abetted by the headmaster) led a revolt on the other school, turfing all desks, books, blackboards and equipment onto the lawn.

This ended – bizarrely enough – in a legal battle between the headmasters with the young Michael appearing as a witness for the prosecution. He was nicknamed at the time 'the pink-eyed ferret'.

So, after Michael and myself were seated on the plane next to each other and we had we spent a few minutes on small talk and politics, I ventured: 'I believe you were a pupil at Broughton Hall where I now live.' The bonhomie between us immediately evaporated. 'I have work to do,' he said, immediately cutting off any further communication.

But as stand-offish as he was throughout the rest of the trip, I have to say I have rarely witnessed a more accomplished orator. In the days that followed, up he'd get after a dinner or a meeting and give the most compelling speeches – without any notes at all. I could see exactly why Mrs Thatcher considered him a great ally – well, until 1990 that is...

Once I arrived back home, I refocused my efforts on Kate. We had been referred to a trail-blazing psychiatrist, Professor John Cox at the North Staffordshire Hospital Centre. He was an older guy, in his sixties, but one of those Oxford-educated Establishment men, who made you feel he knew exactly what he was talking about. We both desperately wanted to believe he would really be able to help Kate.

Professor Cox, who had done much of his research in Uganda, was one of the leading specialists in perinatal psychiatric disorders in the country. Several years earlier, in 1986, he'd been awarded a Merce Medal for his pioneering clinical work in Perinatal Psychiatry.

Just a few days before Rufus was due, the professor asked Kate and

I to go and see him. I was hopeful about the meeting, and felt sure that he would have a positive plan.

'Let's just see what he has to say,' I told Kate, as I steered her into the car. She looked exhausted but her expression was completely blank. My heart broke for this beautiful girl who was suffering so much. Professor Cox was waiting for us in his office, along with several other male psychiatrists who were part of his team, holding Kate's files.

'I believe the best thing for Kate,' he said. 'Is that she begins a series of ECT treatments almost immediately after she gives birth,' he said.

I was completely taken aback. I knew what ECT was – electroconvulsive therapy – more commonly known as electric shock treatment.

'Absolutely not,' I said. 'I do not believe that is the best course of action.'

Professor Cox looked at us both very intently. 'This situation is extremely serious, John,' he continued as his team nodded their assent. 'It's not just the best option for Kate, but in the short and long term it's the best option for your baby. Prenatal depression can worsen post birth, and we need to take drastic measures.'

Kate said nothing. I continued to ask questions, suggest options and push for explanations. Not a single member of his team believed there was another way. Professor Cox asked Kate if she would agree. She had been sitting in silence as if she hadn't even been listening. Years later she told me she felt totally insignificant, with her fate being decided by a group of men. I only wish I had known what was going on in her head, but I was persuaded to believe this was a real, significant hope, and I was desperate for something to make her well again.

'Kate?' said Professor Cox.

'Whatever you think is best,' she answered quietly.

ICARUS MELTS

LOOKING BACK NOW, that period of my life was unutterably sad. I'd fancied Kate from the moment I saw her in The Thurston pub – probably well before that actually, because I'd known who she was for months before we even spoke. She was the one I loved and wanted to be with for the rest of my life. The mother of my children, a funny, clever, warm woman who was loved like a daughter by my mother. She was the girl who had changed my life.

People talk about prenatal depression or more commonly postnatal depression, and in many cases it can be just a temporary hormonal shift resulting in the 'baby blues' which can disappear as fast as it came. With Rebekah, it had lasted a matter of months. With Libby, it lasted a few months longer. But with Rufus, our world fell apart as Kate, my Kate, seemed to fade away in front of my eyes.

She was given ECT within 24 hours of our beautiful, angelic baby boy, Rufus being born. She was taken to a room where she was sedated, and then a metal helmet was put onto her head. A mouth guard was placed between her upper and lower teeth. Then electric currents were sent through her brain, intentionally triggering a brief seizure, which Dr Cox believed could reverse her symptoms of depression.

To experience the joy of Rufus's birth and, simultaneously, endure this extreme pain, was almost unbearable. She underwent eight or nine sessions, and at one point she went into a truly terrifying seizure. Neither of us could stand it any longer, so the ECT stopped. Kate was put on heavy doses of the anti-psychotic drug Largactil, also called Thorazine, which now I know often reduces patients in prisons and care homes into sad shuffling creatures whose expressionless faces would contort with twitches and gurns. My Kate slipped further and further into a catatonic state of depression.

I would come home from work and she'd be sitting at the table, and her depression took on a physical aspect. Her anxiety was such that her face looked permanently haunted, her hands were clawed with tension. I'd try and act as if everything was completely normal. 'You'll never guess what happened today?'

No reply.

'Anything special you want to eat, Kate?'

No response.

'Have you heard from your mum or your sister?'

Nothing.

I think that I went into grieving mode. Grieving for the loss of the love of my life. I believed she was still in there, but I just couldn't reach her. Nor could the psychiatrists. Nor could her lovely mother, Jean, who dropped by the office to see me. I was – as usual – in the midst of some huge multi-million battle but as soon as I saw Jean, I dropped everything and sat her down. 'I'm so worried about Kate,' she said.

I nodded.

'I think we've lost her.'

I looked at Jean. I felt tears pricking at my eyes. But I hadn't given up.

I thought of my baby son and the future we all could have. My business was the house of cards, not my family. I believed my home and my family to be solid enough to withstand anything. I never wanted it to fall apart.

Chapter 18

BROUGHTON

I FIRST SAW Broughton Hall as Kate and I were driving through the pretty Staffordshire town of Eccleshall.

It was the dawn of the '80s, a time when Wham! were in the charts, perms, neon colours and shoulder pads were all the rage and, after years of strikes, pit closures and economic gloom, Britain was booming. Margaret Thatcher was the nation's leader, at the helm of government, and millions of us were looking forward to a bright new modern future.

And there it was, behind big, old, wooden gates, and walls of ancient rhododendrons. This beautiful, vast, black-and-white timbered Jacobean manor house, rising majestically from the dip of a shallow hill at the end of a long driveway. A spectacular reminder of our country's past, built in one of Britain's most fascinating periods, when Charles I ruled the country and the country was on the brink of civil war. 'Kate, look at that!' I said.

'It's stunning,' she said. 'It's the motherhouse of the Franciscan nuns.'

'Do you think they'll ever sell it?' I wondered out loud.

She looked at me and laughed. 'John, it belongs to the Catholic church. The nuns live there. They will never sell it.'

More than a decade later, I discovered that Broughton Hall was up for sale. The nuns – whose order was rapidly diminishing – could no longer afford to keep this vast house going. Gradually, this historic place was falling into an ever-worsening state of disrepair.

In business and in finance I am always logical, but this historical masterpiece of a building spoke to me. I have no idea why but Broughton felt like a calling for me. The idea of buying it was – for once – an emotional decision. To me, at that moment with everything that was going on in my life, Broughton represented legacy, stability, beauty and Staffordshire. Probably the last thing I needed was yet another challenge, but it did represent a different sort of challenge: to restore an institutionalised neglected mansion to its former glory, and in so doing create the perfect place for my family. I had to have it.

*****

'MR CAUDWELL, I'M afraid we have a problem.' It was the estate agent on the phone. 'Sister Mary Mark has died. So you will not be able to see the property.'

We were about a week from the final date on which sealed bids needed to be lodged for Broughton. I had still not been able to look around the property but I had found out everything I could about the house and its inhabitants. As sad as I felt for Sister Mary Mark, I knew she was in her nineties and had been unwell for quite some time. In fact, I'd discovered that the motherhouse of the Franciscan order of St Joseph was the place where elderly and ill nuns from convents all over the country came to spend their final days.

'Please pass on my condolences,' I said. 'And can we please make a new arrangement? If we can work out a new date, but I can only come out of normal office hours, very early morning or in the late evening.'

The estate agent gulped. Fixing an appointment had proved almost impossible and required trying to plan around my very complex schedule. There was barely any space in my diary during the day to breathe, let alone to view a place with around 50 rooms, 28 acres and innumerable outbuildings. I don't think he relished the idea of having to set his alarm clock for a 5am viewing, but this was the '80s and even most of the estate agents in Stoke had aspirations to become a Gordon Gekko of the property market. 'Absolutely,' he said. 'Get your PA to call me, and we'll hammer out a time.'

Less than a week away, the nuns had agreed I could come over for a couple of hours early morning. The night before I got a call from the agent. 'John, I have more bad news,' he said. 'I'm afraid Sister Mary Henry passed away a few hours ago. So they've had to cancel the visit.'

I shook my head as he spoke wondering if someone up there was playing games with me. 'Please pass on my deepest sympathy, and ask them to let me know a more convenient time for them,' I said. Despite being a lifelong atheist I was thinking at this point that I might actually need to start praying myself. I really did not want any more nuns going to meet their maker.

The estate agent and my PA jumped through more hoops with my diary and incredibly, at the eleventh hour we managed to arrange a viewing. It was a memorable – and rather surreal – moment. All the nuns stood outside the house, smiling and clapping as I got out of my car. I took it as a good omen. After all, the bible says, 'All things come to those who wait', and Lord knows I had waited. An Irish nun, who I later saw boiling up cabbage in the kitchen to make vats of soup, cornered me and she said, 'When we heard it was you, we were all worried about who was next!' That really made me laugh.

I stood outside and chatted to the nuns, paid my respects to the Reverend Mother, then looked up at the date – 1636 – engraved in the stone above the front door. This was it. I stepped through the doorway and into the past, to what I hoped would be a wonderful future.

Broughton wasn't anything like I had imagined. Inside was a mess. In fact, for any lover of history it was a travesty. Beautiful, old wood-panelled rooms had been cut into smaller rooms, with hideous plywood dividers. Big, ugly metal pipes ran through the house like Meccano, as part of some Heath Robinson-style heating system that at some stage had been rigged up. Gorgeous, leaded windows were covered in. Cables were stapled to the walls everywhere. Although the nuns had done their best to look after it, they had piled polish onto the beautiful wooden panelled rooms, endlessly trapping layers of dust into the polish, which gave the woodwork a miserably dull and grey feel.

As I walked through the fifty or so rooms, I knew this place was an absolute money pit. Everywhere I turned, I saw more and more horrors, but I also saw significant areas of restorable beauty. I had almost hoped that a lot of the original features had been ripped out, knowing that it would put me off buying the place. But this was the best and worst of all worlds. I could see beauty and heritage everywhere and I could also see that the cost of restoring that splendour was mind blowing – especially given my financial circumstances at the time.

A lot of people would have walked away, shaking their heads. But I was like a moth to a flame. I had to have it even though I knew it could potentially ruin me financially. I just didn't have the money at that time in my life to do everything I needed to do to transform this dusty, broken diamond back into a glorious, gleaming jewel.

The house and gardens needed so much doing to them if I was going to restore Broughton to its former glory. I tried to talk myself out of even considering it but at the same time I could not let it crumble or be ruined by a developer, or turned into a hotel or health spa by a corporate group. I saw what it could be. I saw my family there, my life there. Broughton – and all its unique, hand-made contents – had to be mine. Unless someone else made the nuns a better offer.

Before I left, I walked back through the grounds. There was a private graveyard marked by gravestones engraved with the names of the nuns who died there. I saw the graves of Sister Mary Mark and Sister Mary Henry and bowed my head in respect. I felt more connected than ever to this land.

*****

I LABOURED FOR some time on what offer to put into my sealed bid. I sat in my office, away from the magical spell of Broughton, and tried to think as logically as possible about a very illogical decision. On the one hand I could not bear to lose it, and on the other hand I was frightened to death of owning it.

I decided to make a bid that reflected those conflicting emotions – an offer that if accepted would be a good deal, but not an offer so low as to give me no hope. The best bid would win. The number I came up with was £800,000 and with that I put it to the back of my mind as best I could.

Three weeks later my assistant put through a call from the estate agent. I really don't know to this day what I wanted him to say. I felt I was damned if it was mine, but damned if it wasn't. 'John,' he said. 'It's yours.' I don't think I even replied for a few seconds. Broughton – and all its history – was mine. That house I'd fallen in love with more than a decade ago with Kate, was going to be my home.

*****

SOME WEEKS LATER, just before I took ownership, I drove over with a few bottles of champagne for a celebration with the nuns. As unorthodox as that sounds, they loved it and there was a lot of laughter and fun. Most had just a few sips but my Irish friend, whose domain was the back kitchen, commandeered the remaining bubbly and gave me her blessing for Broughton which I found both touching and felicitous.

As soon as contracts were signed and the nuns had relocated, I moved in with a sleeping bag and a shotgun. Maybe it wasn't in keeping with the holy spirit but the house had no alarm and no security. It was stuffed with Jacobean furniture and I couldn't bear the thought of squatters or looters hearing it was empty and raiding the place. With Broughton added to my list of duties, I was tearing myself in three between my business, my family and our new home. But this was all about creating our perfect future and I was ready.

I don't think I slept more than a few hours a night in those months before I was able to get the home fixed with adequate locks and security fixtures. It was a strange time but I did feel the sense of the house got right into my bones. Broughton had its own tales of ghosts from the past and every inch of those walls had a story to tell.

The house had been originally built in 1631 by Thomas Broughton, the High Sheriff of Staffordshire. He was a loyal subject of Charles I and shared his Catholic sympathies, regardless of the anti-papist feeling that had swept the country since Britain had cut ties with Rome a century earlier. When Civil War broke out 11 years later, Thomas sided with the King, and he was arrested and imprisoned.

The hall and estate were sequestered by Oliver Cromwell's army, which remained billeted there. Six years later, after Charles I surrendered to Cromwell's new regime, Thomas paid what was then the huge sum of £3,500 for his freedom and to be able to return to Broughton Hall. Thomas died in 1648 and a year later his king was executed.

But the Broughton family's loyal ties to the monarchy remained as firm as ever. In the midst of Cromwell's revolution, Thomas's son, Brian, fled Britain for France, alongside the young prince who would later become Charles II. For four years the pair travelled together, accompanied by other royal sympathisers, moving from France to Holland and the Spanish Netherlands, until the monarchy was restored in 1660 and the heir apparent to the British throne made king. The following year – as thanks for his loyalty – Brian was made a baronet and High Sheriff of Staffordshire. Like his father before him, Brian lived at the hall until his death.

Local gossip had it that in those troubled times of civil rebellion, a young boy in the Broughton household had run at Cromwell's soldiers as they stormed the building, shouting, 'We are for the King.' He was shot with a musket, crawled into one of the bedrooms off the Long Gallery and there he bled to death. It was said that sometimes blood would seep from the stairs, and that in the room where he died the bed would shake at night (some female guests have claimed they have felt their bed shaking, but I have never been witness to this). Every ancient house supposedly has its ghosts and spirits and although I personally have never seen or felt one, I am very sensitive to the unique atmosphere of Broughton.

But it was not, however, the cries and sobs of a 17th century loyalist boy that kept me awake at night in those early months of ownership. Instead it was the shrieks, bangs and ear-splitting gasps that came from the old Robin Hood boiler that was valiantly – and very inefficiently – trying to cope with the spaghetti junction system of large pipes that criss-crossed the building. It was like listening to a very, very bad novice orchestra attempting to tune up a host of broken instruments for hours on end. Absolute torture.

I would think about the hours I'd spent earlier, cuddling up on the sofa with my little Libby tickling her and then watching Coronation Street with her, laughing at our favourite character, Curly Watts (marvellously played by the actor, Kevin Kennedy) and his ill-fated engagement to the shop assistant Kimberley. Coronation Street with all its up and down dramas was the ultimate relaxation for me. But now I had a new routine, I'd go home to be with Kate, put Libby to bed (Rebekah was at boarding school) and then leave for Broughton. Inevitably, due to my sleep-deprived nights with the Robin Hood boiler, I'd be the one falling asleep in Libby's arms instead of the other way round.

'Daddy,' I'd vaguely hear her whisper as I nodded off to the *Coronation Street* theme tune. 'You're falling asleep again.'

*****

I HAD HUGE ambitions for Broughton but, given the delicate nature of the work and the fact that I was a custodian for the future with a very limited budget, I knew it was going to take decades to fully restore. That said, I knew it would only take me a few months to get it to a point where we could move in. The immense amount of work which needed to be undertaken could wait – getting it to be fit for a family was a priority.

At Woodlands, things weren't brilliant. With Kate still struggling through the ever-deepening fog of her postnatal depression and treatment, the house keeper stepped up to become a full-time nanny, which gave me peace of mind. And having a son, a golden-haired, blue-eyed boy, was an endless source of pride and joy for me.

As a dad of two girls, I'd often been chided by Kate (in happier days) for rough-housing far too much with them. I'd be the one encouraging them to jump from sofa to sofa in the sitting room, telling them not to worry about it if they fell and bumped themselves, instead of racing over in a panic. I wanted them to be tougher than they looked. When I'd put Libby or Rebekah to bed at night I'd jump up and down on the mattress, shouting, 'There's a rat in the bed, there's a rat in the bed', and making them collapse into giggles. Kate would appear at the door shouting, 'John, stop wilding the girls!'

And now we had a boy to add to our fun. I'd teach him to ski, to ride a bike, to swim and join in the crazy games I'd play with the girls.

We'd explore the grounds in Broughton, we'd build treehouses, slides and dens in the grounds and get to know every nook and cranny in the house. All of this was to come. For now, home at Woodlands was not a cheery place. I couldn't reach Kate. But I had to keep going, keep pushing, keep believing that everything would turn out right...

Chapter 19

POLITICS AND POETRY

FEW THINGS IN my life have remained constant – but my love affair with Broughton has never altered.

Broughton itself has been restored and developed with offices in the grounds, an indoor swimming pool, a gym, a train that takes visitors around the land and an army of staff who keep everything shipshape. The house itself has been returned to its former glory with massive amounts of time, energy and money spent on making sure everything is in keeping with its Jacobean heritage.

This house has a character of its own. It makes its own stand against modern life. It doesn't really like the high tech WiFi that has been installed and refuses to give anything but sporadic service, the bedrooms prefer the 17th century method of ventilation with wind still whistling between the old stone and the ancient glass. Yet those four poster beds with the best mattresses, feather duvets, pillows, cotton sheets and blankets I can find have given so many of my guests the best night's sleep they have ever experienced.

Broughton is not my only home. I have a house in London which is worth about thirty times as much as Broughton. It is much bigger and far more lavish inside with giant crystal chandeliers, an indoor river and a perfectly engineered car stacker that takes eight cars. With a £65 million renovation, it is known to be one of the most expensive houses in London and has been the subject of its own Channel Four documentary called Britain's Most Expensive Home. The WiFi there works perfectly.

Yet Broughton is my home. During the Covid-19 lockdown, I – like everyone else in this country – had to spend months in one place and that place for me was Broughton. Lockdown was a time for many things but for me was a lot to do with reflection and appreciation.

My eldest child Rebekah will say that the happiest she has ever known me was a period of time in the early days of Woodlands when I decided to make two large ponds – complete with islands in the acres surrounding the house. I bought a JCB digger and got up early every single morning to spend hours on that digger.

At weekends, Rebekah would be my helper, shifting stones out of the way and running back and forwards with cups of tea and sandwiches. I had very little experience with a JCB digger (none at all in fact) but I went at the task hell for leather.

At one point she remembers me managing to turn the whole digger over – pouring oil, diesel and battery acid out at a phenomenal rate – as I battled with the rocks and the land. I managed to rescue it double quick and Rebekah tells me, 'You were so happy being outdoors, making these huge ponds you could envision in your head despite any dramas.'

Rebekah has always been truly perceptive. In lockdown I spent many hours in the grounds of Broughton working away very happily or organising my team of gardeners. I feel connected to this land, which is not many miles from where I grew up in Wellesley Street. Yet at the same time it's a world away. I think back to that house with its dusty, dismal, joyless atmosphere and perhaps realise why Broughton means so much to me, with its fascinating loyalist history.

Yes, there has been sadness too but the walls and gardens of this house have been layered with great memories which somehow still resonate today. Even if you are on your own in Broughton, this place never feels empty. I have hundreds of photographs in frames scattered throughout the house and more photographs and paintings throughout.

Each one holds a smile or a memory which is dear to me and for all its bloody history I have had the pleasure of hearing so much laughter in its halls, corridors and galleries and that is what I choose to live with.

Broughton has witnessed many incredible events, seen some truly memorable moments and also hosted some very remarkable people...

*****

'MR CAUDWELL, WE have a favour to ask,' it was the leader of my local Conservative Association. 'Mrs Thatcher is coming to visit and we wanted to ask if you would host a banquet for her at Broughton Hall.'

This was the autumn of 1995, the year I moved into Broughton. At the time, I was pretty much a nobody outside the mobile phone world so the thought of having Margaret Thatcher as a guest in my home was an absolute honour to me. A shopkeeper's daughter from Grantham (about 80 miles from Stoke) who turned around the economic fortunes of Britain, to my mind, she remains the greatest politician this country has ever had. I could not say 'yes' fast enough.

Weeks before, security checked the entire estate and all its occupants and regular visitors. The day dawned. The police and security combed the grounds and the house. As cars came in and out, they were swept underneath for bombs or explosives. The sheer importance of the occasion could not be underestimated.

In person, she was everything and more than I hoped she would be. From her immaculately coiffed hair to her tailored cobalt blue tweed skirt suit to her pearl earrings and the subtle scent of Penhaligon's

Bluebell perfume which hung in the air around her. Her charisma entered the room even before she had set foot in it, such was the magnetism of her personality.

I have no idea what we ate that night. I cannot remember eating even a mouthful of food. What I do remember is our conversation. I sat next to her and we did not stop talking for hours. I called her 'Maggie'; she called me 'John' and it felt like we were the only two people in the room. With most people I will generally disagree with them on some subjects, even those I hugely admire, but with Mrs Thatcher there was nothing. All our opinions seemed to be in tandem.

We discussed business, we discussed economics and politics. Everything I said and thought she agreed with and everything she said and thought, I agreed with. No-one else interrupted us for the duration of the meal.

I confess I did feel completely star-struck. I have met dozens of famous people from Whitney Houston to Tina Turner to Kylie Minogue and none of them have given me that feeling of being in the presence of someone truly exceptional – except those few people who really have changed the world.

Some years later on a trip with Elton John I met Nelson Mandela and again I had that feeling of being completely overawed as I was that night with Mrs Thatcher.

As the evening began to draw to a close, I asked her a few personal questions about her family, her life, her hobbies but each time she merely returned to politics.

'Maggie,' I said. 'Do you have any hobbies?' 'Politics, John, they are my only hobby,' she replied. 'And what about your children,' I persevered. 'We both want to make a better world for our children, everyone's children,' she'd answer deftly, switching back to our talk of work hours, work ethic, privatisation. Try as I did, I could not get her to talk about anything else. But that train-track mind of hers was very probably the reason she was such a great politician.

I did however surprise her by reading out a poem I had written in her honour. She was genuinely flattered and pleased by that poem. Before she left for the evening with her husband, Denis, she said to me, 'Well we know who is going to be the next Poet Laureate don't we?' We all laughed although Ted Hughes remained in the role until Andrew Motion took over in 1999. Political forecasts were definitely more her forte.

Since that night, Broughton has been home to many a wonderful event and many an honorary guest – including the legendary Diana Ross and the late great Meatloaf – but few have been so perfectly suited to the legacy and history of this great British house as Baroness Thatcher. That her memory lives within these walls remains something I will be eternally proud of. In lockdown I often found myself wondering how she would have dealt with the Covid-19 pandemic and in recent months how she would have dealt with this crushing recession. I have conversations in my head with her, knowing, as ever, our opinions would be in tandem.

We both believed that if you keep borrowing there has to be a day of reckoning. Rather than give hand-outs, the only way to get through is to work hard, work efficiently and work long hours. These are not popular things to say but I am a realist and Maggie was the greatest realist. A great woman, a great politician and the greatest ever Prime Minister of this country.

And so I will forever treasure my memories of that night and – in an identical silver frame as the one I gave her – I still have a copy of that poem.

Chapter 20

ENDINGS

LIFE MOVES in cycles. By the time Rufus had reached his fifth birthday in 2000, my life had shifted and changed faster and more exponentially than even I could ever have imagined.

I was no longer that unhappy child in the gloomy house, or the ambitious trainee engineer desperately scrabbling to get a foothold in the world of business. I wasn't the small-time entrepreneur selling second-hand cars and doing deals on the mobile phones that were stacked in my boot. I was John Caudwell and, alongside my brother, I was owner of the phenomenally successful Caudwell Group.

For two successive years, 1996 and 1997, the Caudwell Group was named the UK's fastest-growing company. This was an ever-expanding enterprise, which incorporated the service provider, Singlepoint, and now the mobile phone retail shops, Phones 4u, which were springing up on every British high street.

One of Rufus's earliest memories is of standing with Kate as she pointed to the highly-distinctive red, white and blue logo of Phones 4u and saying, 'Look, that's Daddy's shop.' Although at the time he thought I worked behind the counter!

Libby also remembers when she'd walk into town from school with her friends, and would see that very same logo. 'I'd never say anything to anyone,' she told me later. 'But I'd always smile to myself and think, 'That's Dad'.' She recalled, too, how she and her cousins would visit Kate's lovely mum, Jean, who lived near Port Vale's football ground, Vale Park. On match days, and in Jean's living

191

room, Libby and the others would stand on her sofas so they'd be able to look in to the ground and see the name 'Caudwell' across a sponsor banner. They'd then all leap around happily, and cheer, as Jean's poor sofas got a battering from their little feet.

A century earlier my great, great, great grandfather, John Caudwell, had made the family name legendary throughout the East Midlands with his mills. Now I was making it known throughout Europe, China and America. A few years later in 2005, I'd feature in *The Sunday Times* Rich List, and *Forbes* would be writing about me. Hearing myself being spoken about, seeing the Caudwell name in print, never made me jump up and down with pure, unadulterated excitement. However, thinking of where I came from, there are times – usually when it comes to my charity, Caudwell Children – when I do feel that I have made my mark on the world, and that I have done something good. If only there wasn't so much more that I feel I still need to achieve.

But back to the difficult truth of the past.

I loved Broughton. In the early years, it was very much a work-in-progress as every inch of wood, brick, paint and plaster was carefully restored by experts to its former glory. With my engineer's training, and with all the work I'd done around the house when I was growing up, I knew the basics of most things, from plumbing to gardening and electrics, as well as basic building. Due to its age, however, and as it is a Grade I listed building which must be cared for with love, a high level of attention to detail was required. The right plasterwork, the perfect mortar, the perfect soil levels required to nourish those ancient rhododendrons – this was to be a learning curve I relished climbing.

As you know by now, I am all about the detail. If it took weeks to get the finest wood oil for damage to floorboards in the library, then so be it. I wanted it to be simply perfect, the place we would all come home to. But in the two years it took for the initial work to be completed, we were still living in Woodlands.

Looking back, it's strange to see that, by 1995, two very unhappy endings were set in motion and they would collide five years later, causing utter personal devastation, which struck at the very heart of everything that really mattered to me, my family.

As Broughton was lovingly put back together piece by piece, Kate and I fell further and further apart as the hell of her postnatal depression continued, and our relationship slowly but steadily disintegrated.

The medication we believed would help her only pushed her further into a decline. All I could see in her face was the ghost of the woman I loved, behind a tortured mask of fear and anxiety which I can still recall with absolute stomach-wrenching clarity to this day.

We pushed on, as you do when you want to keep believing everything is going to be alright. We'd been through this twice before, I kept telling myself, even though I knew this was nothing like the postnatal depression she'd been through with Rebekah and Libby.

I'd come home from work and we would exchange a few words. The distance between us grew. We looked after the children with the help of our house keeper turned nanny. We ate, we slept, I oversaw the Broughton project, I went to work and threw myself into the endless challenges of my ever-growing business. In the hours I spent in the office, I rarely had a minute to think as my new companies brought with them a new layer of problems.

When I think back to those times, I think of a line of people outside my office door, all of them coming to me with their issues, and a secretary putting through calls from other managers and staff. They'd all 'desperately need a word' about one thing or another. It was like being a doctor in A&E, as multiple crash victims are being stretchered in, trying to work out which crisis to deal with first and never, ever having a second to spare. And still I worked on, adding more and more companies, more and more levels of management and staff to deal with. This, I could always cope with.

I am not a man who brings his work problems home. None of my children ever recall me talking about catastrophes with staff, or about a problem with a supplier, or the daily financial wrangling. However hard things were in the office (or offices, as we grew and grew, with warehouses taking over half of Stoke), it was nothing compared with home.

And then I did something I swore I would never do. I had an affair. I can make excuses, such as saying I was lonely, or that I felt starved of affection and was grieving for my wife. Really, they are just that; they are excuses, and I am not proud of what I did.

But I am brutally honest and I cannot gloss over my actions.

I think that somewhere inside of me I knew my marriage was over. I didn't want it to be but it was. Kate was the woman I wanted to be with forever, but Kate had disappeared before my eyes and I didn't know where to find her. I was lost. And so I began a relationship with another woman. I was looking for comfort and affection. I couldn't stop myself.

*****

KATE AND I carried on, living this strange, unhappy life and now with a secret between us and a layer of guilt filtering through everything. We moved into Broughton. It didn't change anything – in fact, the gap between us widened, my affair continued and the running waters of our past began to freeze over. We didn't laugh together. We didn't cry together (although I know there were times when we both individually shed tears). We developed a civilised way of co-existing, where only those who really knew us could tell there was something very wrong. My affair remained secret. On the surface, it all seemed fine.

What we went through in those five years has made me far less judgemental of others. I was a man who would never cheat yet I had an affair which lasted far too long. There were reasons. Kate never cheated on me but she too did things she never thought she would do. And there were other reasons. We were both in pain. And as people we were changing – moving in different directions.

What I am proud of – and very grateful for – is that while we were not able to talk about everything at the time, we have done since, and we retained a wonderful and profoundly deep friendship. I have nothing but love, compassion and respect for Kate, and it was many years before we really talked about what she had gone through.

She recalls how, in the midst of her depression, she also began rebelling. She was 39 when she had Rufus, and she realised she was about to turn 40 and had never actually discovered who she was.

She'd started off as a daughter to Jean and Denis, and spent much of her childhood looking after her sister, Claire, who suffered from diabetes. She loved them all dearly and never begrudged a moment of caring for Claire. Yet she'd gone from being a daughter to steady girlfriend at the age of 14, and she was a wife at the age of 17 – the same age Rebekah would be when Kate turned 40. As my wife, and then as a mother at 23, her world had been built around us.

She had not known what it was like to have no responsibilities, to choose what she wanted to do that day, to find out what her own dreams were. I'd always known that Kate was a woman who would have blossomed at university. Both Rebekah and Libby thrived there and studied English Literature, something Kate would have loved and been more than capable of herself. But it had never been a path open to her and so, on the cusp of her 40th year, she started her own personal mutiny.

She started to drink, to smoke, to be less concerned about the way she dressed, and to show little interest in what I was doing or saying. At the time, we were no longer in a place where we shared our thoughts and feelings. I had no idea how she felt, or what was going on, except that she was becoming less and less the Kate I knew.

When we moved to Broughton, she felt lost. Rufus was in a nursery which was three floors away from our bedroom. And although she thought the house was beautiful, she never felt it was hers. At Woodlands, she'd put her mark on the place, with her style, decor, choice of paintings, colours and soft furnishings; Broughton with its fifty-odd rooms, giant ballrooms and galleries was overwhelming and very much its own historic character.

Kate told me later, 'One day I invited a woman I'd met with Rufus at baby classes to come over to the house. I told her we lived near St Peter's Church, which she knew, and I gave her the address. I was looking out of the window when her car drew up at the gates. And I watched her come down the drive. As I was about to go to the door, her car stopped half-way down the drive. I waited at the window, and saw her staring at the house for a few minutes. Then she turned the car around, and she drove away. My heart stopped but I knew exactly what she'd been thinking when she looked at the house. She'd been thinking, 'I don't belong there.' I knew it because I felt it, too.'

'It wasn't completely clear to me in that moment,' Kate added. 'Because it was then more of a feeling than a realisation. But I knew that what you wanted was so much bigger than what I wanted, and I was shrinking and losing who I was.'

It makes me so sad to know that, but that was Kate's truth. Deep down maybe I was aware of it because she wasn't the only one who knew that she could not continue by my side for what I saw as an incredible journey. She needed to go on a journey of her own, which I'm happy to say she did. After her few years of internal rebellion, she worked with an incredible psychiatrist, Jennifer Crisp, and grew into the even more wonderful mother and woman she is today.

In 1995, Brian had also told me he wanted out of the business. The bigger it got, the more corporate it had become. Brian, like me, is a down-the-line, straight-talking man, and he wasn't happy. Our pace, which had always been relentless, had increased to unbelievable levels as we grew. He felt torn between his family and his work.

'It's going to be fine, Brian,' I'd say whenever he broached the subject. 'Tell me what you need to make things easier.' Honestly, I didn't want to hear it because couldn't bear the idea of the Caudwell Group not being Brian and me.

Over the next few years he would tell me he wanted to go, but I would always persuade him to stay. Brian was far more than a brother to me. He was my anchor, the one I wanted by my side because I trusted him, I knew him and he knew me. He was the little brother who had been my companion from the moment he could walk, the one I took with me on boyhood exploits and adventures around Stoke, the one who aged seven and eight would help me work on a second-hand car I'd bought to sell. He was a teenager when we started our business together, but now he was a father-of-four.

I couldn't be without him but I knew he wanted out. Like Kate, he'd realised my dreams and ambitions were endless and far bigger than he'd ever imagined or wanted for himself. He was satisfied with everything he had achieved so far and his dream was an early retirement after an incredibly hard and successful career. I wasn't satisfied. I didn't want to stop. I wanted more. But I wanted it for us, the Caudwell brothers. For me, that was what this whole empire was about. But as the years went by and Brian kept trying to make me see that this no longer suited him, I realised I was never going to change his mind. Eventually I knew that because I loved him, I had to listen to him. 'John, I really do need to leave,' he said.

*****

THERE'S A LOT you can do with a house that is falling apart. You can treat dry rot, and replace or restore wood-wormed floorboards. You can find the perfect lime mortars and lime washes. You can agonise over the benefits of air-dried timbers, and make tired soil healthy again with the addition of manure and fertilisers. You can, I discovered, bring in experts to track down pieces of 16th century metal work to replace turnbuckle window casement handles, lead latticework and stone mullions. You can bring an ancient, crumbling building back to life.

But there are times with relationships when you just have to accept that they have come to an end. Whether it's a marriage or a partnership. What is it that Sting says? 'If you love someone set them free.'

And so, in 2000, Kate and I separated. In the same year Brian left the business. I remember months earlier, Kate and I telling our children. There really was no drama to our ending, no crunch moment, it ended not with a bang but with acceptance, resignation and – I am glad to say – a deep and lasting friendship. We both knew it was over – the question was, how we would both move on?

We stood in the library at Broughton and told our children we loved them and we loved each other and always would – which was the absolute truth, then and now. The children were incredible. They accepted what we were saying, they asked questions and we answered every one. I think – I hope – we did everything as painlessly as we could.

I worried about money. My empire soaked up cash like a giant amorphous sponge. I had to see Brian right by giving him what he was due as my partner, and I had to see Kate right. They were both my responsibility and I would go to bed anxious as I played out all sorts of financial scenarios in my head even though I knew that whatever we were going through, the trust and respect remained and everything would always be okay

I have no memory of the day Brian left our company. I know that I was happy for him but I know how deeply it affected me. He wanted to do his own thing business-wise, focus on his family, spend more time with Paula, and enjoy the things he loved, like racing cars (he is formidable on the race track, even now). But I can't remember the send-off we gave him. I can't remember the date, and I only know that it was 2000, both for my separation and for Brian leaving, because it is somewhere on record.

It is not fixed in my mind because, quite frankly, it was all too painful.

So much had happened in those years. I'd seen a future for myself and my empire that I had never thought possible a decade earlier, but I was excited by it and knew I could make it a reality. But huge, fundamental pieces of my past and my core had fallen away from me.

In the Millenium year, life was going to be very different. Even though Kate and I, and Brian and I, were no longer together, we were still family and we were all going to make it work.

Chapter 21

WHO'S THAT GUY?

NONE OF US ever get absolutely everything we want. But you cannot live a life of regrets. It gets you nowhere. When things change, you have to change with them, keep moving, embrace the next cycle.

I had to accept that for the past few years I had been unhappy in my personal life. I was now a single man. I hadn't been single since I was 17, and now I was two years shy of my 50th birthday. And the world viewed me very differently indeed.

I was moving in new, interesting circles; the streets of Stoke were no longer my only domain and my name was no longer confined to the inner wheels of the mobile phone world. I was now getting calls from all the national newspapers, TV and radio, who all became very interested in what I had to say.

'We can see you are a very successful businessman, but we want to know about you – who is John Caudwell?' I was asked on numerous occasions by reporters. Clearly, they were intrigued by what they saw as a classic 'rags-to-riches' story. They were tickled by the idea that I had a business valued at around £1 billion, yet still wore suits from Marks & Spencer, regularly cycled to work at 5.30am and cut my own hair.

'It saves me a £10 trip to the barbers,' I told one journalist. Gleefully, he wrote it down and then used it – very appropriately I guess – as the headline. I took it all with a pinch of salt.

In the mid-nineties I'd been asked to sponsor a cricket match to raise money for the National Society for the Prevention of Cruelty to

Children. Regardless of what was going on in my personal and work life, I'd made a commitment to a cause in which I firmly believed, and I made it my business to attend a couple of meetings.

Imagine, running an empire focused on maximum profit, turnover and customer satisfaction and then stumbling across a committee meeting at a local cricket club where a 30-minute debate could take place about how much money they might make from a bake sale on the green. I felt like a giant fire-breathing dragon stumbling across a group of mild-mannered Stone Age men and women who were trying to get a spark from a flint and a wet stone.

It took me a matter of hours to bulldoze my way into the situation to run it my way. 'I think we could tackle this a bit differently,' I said. And that was it. I took over and – as I did in my day job – looked at every angle to make money. God knows what some of the older, more traditional members thought of me, though within a matter of months, huge amounts of cash were being donated from all sorts of businesses and events. I was made President of the North Staffordshire branch of the NSPCC and then I became the regional representative for the Full Stop campaign, which entailed having meetings with Prince Andrew at Buckingham Palace.

Now very few things make me feel special. Wherever I am, whoever I am with – whether it is Elton John, Elizabeth Hurley, the actress Eva Longoria, or the endless list of celebrities that are or have been involved with Caudwell Children – I don't get sucked into the glitz and the glamour or the gossip. I see it for what it is, I see them for who they are and I remain very much myself. But I have to confess that when I drove through those wrought iron gates – the ones embossed with the lion and the unicorn herald – and into the courtyard of Buckingham Palace, I was pretty overwhelmed.

As a liveried footman made his way towards me to open my car door, it was impossible not to be affected by the thought going through my mind – this kid from Stoke is on his way to sit down with a Prince of England albeit one who – years later – would be disgraced.

I was led through the corridors to take my seat at the meeting and I took that time to focus on the reason I was there. To help children. For the first meeting, I watched and took in everything. I could tell a lot of the people there were just pleased to be invited, and rather over-awed by the whole thing. Prince Andrew was, I felt, very committed, if a little aloof. But I could see that he was actually trying to do as much as he could to help.

After a few more of these meetings, I realised that not very much was going on in terms of getting things done. It was a very grand version of those meetings at the cricket club, a lot of talk and not much focus on results. Many of the people there were – like me – very busy individuals. Creating ways of raising money for charity takes time, and most of us in the room were money rich, time poor. So, I thought I'd do something about that. I was getting fed up with initiatives being discussed at length and no clear results. I stood up. 'I haven't had time to do anything substantial about the campaign,' I said. 'But I've decided to donate £500,000.'

Prince Andrew and the room were delighted. 'That's fantastic John,' he said, completely taken aback. From that moment on our relationship became slightly less formal, he would direct a lot of his conversation towards me and look to me for ideas. He liked the way I was so straightforward and happy to put my money where my mouth was.

Years later, in 2012, I had a message from one of his charities, The Outward Bound Trust. 'Have you got the guts, the balls, whatever you like to call it, to step over the edge at 1,000ft?' He knew by then I could not resist a challenge so, after weeks of training with the Royal Marines, donating £100,000 of my own money, I abseiled down the Shard with Prince Andrew (along with a few others including the

A cuddle with my youngest daughter, Scarly

Bonding time on the ski slopes with my little boy, Jacobi

After the hot tub comes the challenge of rolling in the snow, outside my house in Vail

Not quite Eddie the Eagle, but one of my best jumps. Skiing with family and friends has given me such enormous pleasure over the years, as well as the odd bump and bruise

Money is only one of my motivational levers, but an important one

A typical Phones 4u store. There was barely a high street in Britain that did not have one of our stores

Meeting Nelson Mandela along with Claire and Elton John. What a remarkable and humbling occasion

The exact moment I signed on the dotted line and sold the whole Caudwell group of companies in 2006. It was a signature worth £1.46 billion and changed my life forever

Prince Charles and I share a humorous moment as we take a tour around Middleport Pottery in Burslem, Stoke-on-Trent. I had donated a significant sum to a project run by The Prince's Regeneration Trust which helped to transform Middleport into a fascinating visitor destination that celebrates the unique industrial heritage of Staffordshire

This was such a special day. My wonderful eldest daughter Rebekah's wedding day was an occasion of great joy and celebration

Outside the home I fell in love with 20 years before. Broughton Hall is a home and a place that has brought me such incredible pleasure over the years. It is one of the finest houses in England, not just Staffordshire, and hosting guests and functions there has become a massive part of my life

A day of cycling with the very fit Richard Branson on Necker Island during Rebekah's 40th birthday week

With my wonderful and long suffering son, Rufus

A tough but amazing bike ride in the Alps. I first met Modesta when I saw her cycling and the rest is history...

With **Modesta and** her eldest son Leo
at our Monaco Butterfly Ball

Another one of our wonderful children,
Susanna Petersburska, my beautiful daughter
Scarlett and my gorgeous partner Modesta,
in a dress I designed for her, in Monaco

Fun on Titania with Libby, Modesta, Alexis, Francesca, and Rebekah

Modesta, our beautiful hostess at the Monaco Butterfly Ball

Me, terrified of heights, abseiling down The Shard in a Spiderman outfit for Prince Andrew and The Outward Bound Trust

Kylie and I with one of the children my charity helps, Abigail Bolt

Sports motorbikes have always been one of my biggest passions

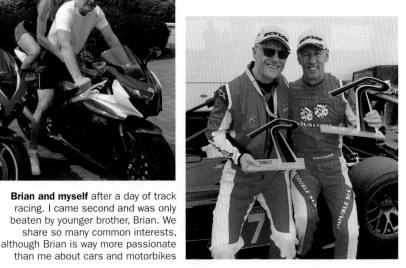

Brian and myself after a day of track racing. I came second and was only beaten by younger brother, Brian. We share so many common interests, although Brian is way more passionate than me about cars and motorbikes

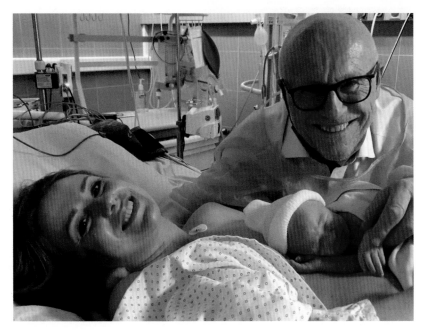

A joyous moment as Modesta holds our newborn son, William John. Becoming a dad again at the age of 68 was a fantastic gift and something I am very thankful for

My 1902 Westfield, strangely named Walter (my dad's name) by the previous owner, became the wedding carriage to take my daughter Libby to the aisle

Modesta, myself and old Walter on Regent Street before the London to Brighton Veteran Car Run

Our last Christmas with Mum. This book is dedicated to Mum for a very good reason. She was the most fantastic and inspirational woman I've ever known and Brian and myself consider it a privilege to have been her sons

then-Foreign Secretary's wife, Ffion Hague). We raised £1 million for the Prince's Charity.

Over the years, Sarah, Duchess of York, has become a good friend, and she and her daughters, Princesses Beatrice and Eugenie, have been guests on my yacht or my home. Sarah has a good heart, works tirelessly for charity, she is great fun and I like her a lot. It upsets me when she is often given a bad rap in the press, because she always tries her best and only wants to help people.

One of the things I love about Sarah is how very open and down-to-earth she is. It was on my yacht that I introduced her to Robbie Williams who I'd invited to join us on a cruise round the Caribbean in 2010. Robbie, a working class pop star from Stoke, immediately bonded with Sarah.

Robbie, who loved to sit smoking and chatting, would spend hours talking to Sarah on deck. Both of them had been through hard times, both of them had been through media trials and both of them were believers in spirituality – not my thing but definitely something they had in common.

By the end of a few days they were like old mates and both her girls completely fell in love with him as a big brother figure. Before dinner one night, Robbie got up and sang – a capella – something he had written (with Gary Barlow) which he felt suited the laid back islands we were sailing by. It was his song, Candy, which had this Caribbean vibe to it.

'That's a definite hit,' I told him afterwards as all of us clapped and cheered. 'Not sure yet,' he said. Two years later he released it as the lead single from his ninth studio album, Take the Crown. It went straight to number one and made me smile because it reminded me of his friendship with Sarah and later how he ended up as godfather to Princess Eugenie's daughter, Sienna. He really did win over the Crown!

*****

BY 2000, I decided to set up my own charity, Caudwell Children, because I wanted to do more, and I wanted to do it properly, with every penny raised being put to best use and spent on children who needed it. By this point I knew enough to know I could do things differently and more efficiently.

Because I pledged to pay all the operating and administrative expenses, I was able to guarantee that 100 percent of the donations went directly to the children in desperate need. I wanted to target those children whose parents had reached the end of the line with doctors and were desperately looking for a way to improve the life of their child, whatever their illness or disability. Those kids and parents who had fallen between the cracks and couldn't find anyone to help them – the charity underdogs.

This was the cause I'd been waiting for, ever since, as a seven-year-old child, I'd had that astonishingly vivid dream of myself sitting in a Rolls-Royce, handing out £5 notes to people in the run-down streets of Stoke. Only now, there was clarity and purpose to that dream. Finally, I was in a position to do something about it.

*****

ON A PERSONAL front I too needed help. I simply wanted to be happy. I knew that I wanted and needed female companionship. For years I'd been one half of John and Kate, and now I was just John, on my own. I'd spent years grieving my relationship with Kate before we finally split but the time had come for me to see if I could find someone to share my life.

I regretted having an affair, but it had woken me up to that fact that women – like everyone else – now viewed me differently.

It wasn't so much about me being a successful businessman. I was different. As a teenager, I had low self-esteem and lacked confidence when it came to women. But at the age of 48, I was extremely confident, knew who I was, knew my own mind, my priorities. I knew exactly what I wanted.

I began going on dates. I'd spent most of my life surviving on four hours of sleep, so working hard and playing hard was not a problem for me. It was an interesting time. I dated a lady from a council estate who soon told me how much she 'loathed' rich people. We met in a nightclub called Maxine's which is now, funnily enough, a care home. She bore more than a passing resemblance to a young Kate, and I was rather smitten for a few months because I liked her wit and feistiness. But, she had a chip on her shoulder about well-to-do people which was a constant barrier between us. She was also very flaky in many ways. Finally, she kept Mum and I waiting for an hour when we had arranged to go to a restaurant. She did not feel it necessary to offer any reason or excuse. I couldn't deal with anyone being so disrespectful to my mother, so I knew things were never going to work out.

I kept my options open. One day at the gym I saw a stunningly beautiful blonde girl. I'd seen her a year or so before at a charity event and thought she was extraordinary looking. 'I'm going to date her,' I told my training partner. He laughed. 'As if!'

He watched me walk over to her – I was in my bright-red gym vest, muscles bulging (in those days I had some), as she worked out on a machine. 'You know you're doing this all wrong,' I said to her, and grinned. She looked up. Huge, blue eyes and this big smile. I went to the gym most days and, whenever she was there, I'd do an hour or so training with her.

I found out she was called Claire Johnson. She'd grown up in Stoke, been to a local convent school, worked as a model and then worked in a boutique on a cruise ship. She had just turned 30 years old.

We talked. I'd tell her about the girl I was seeing. She told me about the guy she was with. Neither relationship was working. I asked her out for dinner. We got to know each other better. To me, she didn't have that hard edge that many beautiful women have. She was vulnerable, kind and chatted to everyone in the same warm, friendly manner. I liked her a lot but she was with someone else. We went out for more meals together. I put my cards on the table. 'I've ended my relationship.' She nodded but said nothing. I waited. Then I said, 'So, I'm going to date other girls.'

She smiled. 'Good luck.'

I felt that together we really could have something. I could see Claire Johnson was a very special woman, one of those people who lights up a room when she walks in. But I also knew that after what I'd been through with my marriage break-up, I wasn't going to rush into anything. I had my family to think of, Kate to consider and, of course, I had work, which was, as ever, in that constant state of build and break.

A huge extra stress was placed on me with Brian's decision to retire and the money I had to find to enable him to do so. As always, I was stressed to the eyeballs in every direction and constantly working flat out, and Brian leaving the business added to that practically, but also emotionally. We had customer service issues with our service provider company, Singlepoint. These took huge amounts of time to solve and that upset and frustrated me beyond measure because my aim with every single thing I'd ever done, from my Belstaff jackets to our cars to the phones – even those blasted mushrooms – was to provide a quality service for customers that I could be proud of.

There was a point when I sat down in my office and wrote a personal letter apologising to every single customer, whether they had made a complaint or not. There was such an enormous amount to be done and now, along with my wife, I had lost the other closest person in my life, my brother. But, I had to agree because it is what he wanted and I loved him and wanted him to be happy.

Almost a decade earlier, I'd stopped the growth of our business in its tracks. I remember the looks on the faces of my sales team when I told them that we were going to focus on consolidation. I remember my finance director having to spend hours sorting through mountains of boxes in the stockroom, like some sort of Rumpelstiltskin of the mobile phone world, trying to spin the chaos into ordered gold.

But now I knew I had found a way to consolidate and grow simultaneously. In order to achieve one, I didn't have to press the pause button on the other as I had back in 1991 when business was growing so rapidly, our lack of foundations, systems and order could have made the very floor of the empire collapse under our feet.

So many things had been out of our control, problems with external production, distribution, staff poaching, especially the logistics of warehouse operation. My solution was to do all those things myself. Create my own distribution set up, have my own company which sourced the best staff.

It meant spreading myself across all areas of the industry but in reality it was the same vertical integration path my Caudwell ancestors took when they went from being mill owners to having their own farms growing wheat, oats, barley and millet and setting up their own bakery – at the bottom of the road I grew up in – to sell their produce.

The boy with the Lego didn't want to just have a few pieces to play with, he wanted the whole box. It gave me a huge set of other issues to deal with but it also gave me more control.

Within the next few years I would have more than 20 companies within the Caudwell Group, each working both independently and symbiotically with the other companies.

The most important companies broke down like this. Phones 4u, the chain of shops selling phones on every high street; Dextra Solutions, which became the largest distributor of mobile phone accessories servicing the high street, supermarkets and 33 countries worldwide; 20:20 Logistics was the biggest distributor of mobile phones, annually distributing six million units to the UK and 53 other countries; PAS, the world's largest insurer of mobile phones, Cornerstone Recruitment and Singlepoint, the UK's biggest service provider by a long way.

In order to find the high quality people needed for our exponential growth I had set up Cornerstone Recruiting, servicing my own operations and head-hunting and advertising for other talent within the industry.

There was also our Mobile Phone Repair Company – which had gone from strength to strength since those early days with our sexually experimental tech guy. By 2006, we were dealing with 3,000 broken handsets every day, as well as doing repairs and diagnostics for customers from other companies such as Argos, Comet and Orange.

Caudwell Logistics, which I set up in 2003, dealt with high-value supply chains, warehouse storage and the distribution of 17 million goods every year to 40 countries, and 4uBusiness became the most successful independent provider of business-to-business mobile solutions.

At the top of all this was me, the 24-hour on-call doctor in the A&E of the business world. That is why I had to work, on average, more than 12 hours a day, at massive intensity. Of course it was exhausting, maddening, frustrating, difficult. But it was also as challenging and as exhilarating as standing at the top of one of the toughest black runs on a snow-covered mountain, then pushing myself off on my skis, knowing I might fall and break a leg but that, more likely, I would reach the bottom in one piece, with my heart racing, feeling completely and utterly alive.

Maybe I have just described the rush that makes a man or woman a workaholic. I was good at it. I loved it. I had the perfect mind and character for it. Business for me was an enormous headache, but it was also an addiction. Sadly, it still is though I am trying to learn, like my brother has, how to balance my life better.

*****

WOMEN WERE ALSO becoming something of an addiction. During that period all sorts of pretty girls came my way. But I never forgot myself and I never forgot the girl in the gym who every now and again would go out on a date with me. In the meantime, I had several flings but the benefits of having a late bloom in the romance department is that you are far less likely to lose your head. You might occasionally lose your heart, but never, in my case, my head.

I thought Claire could play a bigger part in my life, but she had a lot of things to deal with. Things had got to a point when we were seeing each other regularly but not completely exclusively. I wasn't sure whether things could work out and she wasn't sure so we kept things initially quite casual. And like the businessman I am, I kept my mind open to any other opportunities that came along.

I was with Claire, flying back to Broughton from a football match in the helicopter when I saw, from my bird's eye view, a very attractive, well-dressed blonde lady standing outside my house. As we got out of the helicopter, she watched us, waving and smiling. By coincidence, Claire knew exactly who she was because she had gone to the very same convent school, but Claire had been in the year above her. Her name was Jane Burgess, and she was a professional violinist and she moved in the upwardly mobile echelons of Staffordshire society.

'I'd like to introduce myself,' she said, smiling at us. 'I'm Jane. I'm a violinist, I've just come back from a tour of Australia and New Zealand and I'd like to discuss a charity idea with you.'

That was, I admit, back then, absolute music to my ears.

Chapter 22

MEA CULPA

RUTHLESS. It's a word that's been used or – in my opinion – misused to describe me. As a businessman, I am exacting. I have high standards, I demand loyalty, hard work and honesty. If you look at the dictionary definition of ruthless, I most certainly am not. The reality is, I always tell people what I want and what I expect. I am true to my word and expect others to be so, and I am always, always looking for perfection.

But few things in life are perfect, and I find it particularly hard when someone or something doesn't live up to my expectations – including myself. There is no-one more tough on me than myself. If I have done something wrong, I will punish myself for it.

At times this can be very painful, and other times comical. My children – who know exactly how inflexible I can be – relish an incident that takes place at Christmas every year without fail, when after a wonderful day, with some lavish gifts, exquisite food and great wine flowing, I fall victim to a 90 pence (the large version) Milky Bar that one of my children accidentally leaves in my path. They know white chocolate – the cheapest, lowest grade, fattiest and sugariest of all chocolates – is my Achilles heel.

At which point the inevitable happens. A white chocolate mist takes over me. Then I, the pious, nutritionally-obsessed man who preaches about the evils of sugar, who packs down more than 20 vitamins and supplements a day, won't eat dairy, limits carbs, avoids meat and has eaten the same non-toxic, fully organic salad with herbs, beetroot and avocado every day for lunch for the past three years... becomes some sort of crazed, sugar-guzzling monster.

I march about my house, hunting down any remaining sweet or chocolatey treat, shovelling it into my mouth at a rate that would embarrass even the gluttonous Augustus Gloop from Roald Dahl's Charlie and The Chocolate Factory. Rebekah, Libby, Rufus, Scarlett and Jacobi witness all this with the greatest glee. The wilful fall of their father into a chocolate mess. What makes them laugh most is that in between gulps, I berate myself, genuinely horrified by my own actions. As I'm tearing through chocolate wrappers, I'm shouting at myself. All my rules go out of the window, including my dislike of swearing and there I am screaming at myself: 'You big, fat bastard!' 'What are you doing, you idiot?' and 'Disgusting'.

Then comes the backlash. I spend Boxing Day, punishing myself with a massively restricted diet, alongside the treat of extra hours of exercise. My penance for my chocolate binge. It can be the same if I come back from a particularly epicurean holiday. In spite of everything I know about what you should eat and what you shouldn't eat, I do adore great food, I love good beer and wines and I have an insatiable greed within me that I am constantly trying to curb.

If ever I put on weight – and I often do – I will eat the bare minimum until that extra stone has disappeared. My housekeepers, Carol and Sarah, are constantly puzzled by my quest to remain slim. They see me as normal, or even trim when in my mind, I see a button on my shirt straining over a newly emerged roll of fat. As they prepare yet another beetroot, herb, lettuce, avocado and goat's cheese salad they are probably wondering why on earth I've been eating this same lunch for years and years, when in reality I could have anything I want. I eat it because it's good for me, it's delicious and I despise my natural propensity for over-indulgence.

I exercise every day that I am able, pushing myself as hard as I can.

I view myself objectively. I don't buy bigger trousers or tell myself I still look fine; I will not lie to myself – or anyone else – or cheat my standards in any way.

And so yes, I can be harsh. I've had to be to build my business. But I also recognise that the behaviour that makes a person succeed in business can, on occasion, make him or her seem harsh as a human being. I can make mistakes by being too harsh. I can let that harshness spill over. As time passes, I examine myself as a man who ultimately lives for his family. I reconsider my actions, look at how they have affected others and I can be filled with remorse.

None more so than with regard to my sweet, wonderful, darling daughter, Scarlett.

*****

SO FOR ONE month in 2001, I was torn between two very, beautiful women. Claire was vivacious, loving and kind, but Jane was exciting, talented and artistic. I believed both of them knew of the existence of the other. I had been clear that I was in the process of 'dating' as opposed to committing to a relationship. However, before Jane arrived on the scene, Claire and I had been slowly getting more and more serious. She wasn't happy about Jane but very graciously, she never gave me an ultimatum, although later she told me that she had come very close to walking away and calling things a day.

What I knew – and what they presumably knew – was that after my period of running around, I did want to have a proper relationship and settle down with one of them. But I wanted to give myself time and opportunity to discover more about these two very special women and work out who would be best as a life partner. Maybe to some people this sounds rather business-like, but it's the way that I am and it still makes sense to me. A relationship is a commitment and, as long as you are honest to all concerned I think that it is acceptable though not entirely desirable.

*****

PEOPLE, TO ME, are like jigsaw puzzles. It takes many years, lots of analysis and some crisis events in order to complete the full picture, to make the decision that you really do value that person and you want them to remain in your life as long as possible. Over the space of that month, I was finding out about Jane and discovering more and more about Claire.

Jane was an intriguing woman but there were things about her that irritated me. Little things. She was very scatty. I know this often comes with the territory with musicians, and perhaps it's a fault of mine that I have limited patience with a scatty disposition, but it's the truth. I was in awe of her ability to play the violin. She was cultured and smart, which I liked. We had several things in common, but I did come to the conclusion that it wasn't going to work.

Regardless I did, however, enjoy her company. We did some memorable and romantic things together. I flew her to Dinard, the pretty seaside resort in Brittany and, on a whim, we spent an afternoon busking – her playing the violin and me drumming up support and holding out a hat to the folk who stopped to hear this beautiful woman play. She was a marvellous violinist.

But my doubts about Jane were as persistent as my initial infatuation. We went away for other romantic weekends but after three months I knew it wasn't going to work. We were cut from very different cloth and, as much as I admired her talent, I just felt like we were not quite right for each other.

I had other big things on my mind that were preoccupying me. I could see that with more and more people owning mobile phones, the service provider business could become less and less profitable. It wasn't something many other people were worrying about but I knew it was there on the far horizon, and I'd made a decision to sell my service provider arm, Singlepoint. I was also in the midst of buying a boat, a dream I'd had for many years. I had a trip planned, to sail from Poole to Barcelona during the first four days of which I would learn from a professional captain how to handle and manage the boat.

I called the 64-foot Sunseeker Manhattan, 'Rubekian', which is a combination of all my children's names, Rufus, Rebekah and Rhiannon – which is actually the name Libby was christened by, but rarely used. I couldn't wait for my first adventure but I was also trying to picture myself with one of these two women by my side on the boat. I'd seen Jane a few more times since our weekend away, but it was becoming clearer to me that we had no future together.

I knew I wanted to take Claire on my maiden voyage. All my children were coming along with two other friends, and I wanted to see how well Claire bonded with everyone. I had a good feeling about the trip and was really excited to shadow the guy who'd been employed to captain the boat, in order to hand over to me during the first three or four days of the epic three-week trip. I wanted to know about everything, from the engineering of the boat to the mysteries of navigating the ocean itself and how to keep everything clean, controlled and shipshape.

*****

'JOHN, I NEED to see you.' It was 11pm, the night before the voyage, and Jane was on the telephone.

'It's not a good time. I'm going on the boat tomorrow and I've still got a lot of things to do,' I replied.

'It's important,' she insisted. 'Really important.'

We met in a pub car park. I could tell she was nervous behind her beguiling smile and she must have been able to tell that I wasn't exactly thrilled by this late-night encounter. She began, 'I need to tell you something but I'm in such turmoil and I want you to promise me not to be angry...'

My stomach sank. 'I can't make a blind promise, Jane,' I answered, wondering what was going to come next. My head was spinning with the various possibilities that had caused her to call me to a meeting so late at night.

'I can't believe it but I'm pregnant and I don't know what to do.'

I stared at her in complete disbelief. She was holding in her hand a card wishing me luck for my maiden voyage. I took the card and told her I would call her from the boat. I needed to try and make sense of this situation. I still couldn't quite get my head around what she had told me.

It took me ten days to call Jane. I needed time to think. By now my mind had cleared, the shock had subsided and I just wanted clarity on where we stood. I asked her what the options were.

'I'm having the baby. I'm a Christian. I want this child.'

As I write these words I feel an awful lot of pain, not just for me but for my little girl Scarlett. All I knew then was that this was not the way I wanted to be a father. I felt my world turning upside down and I felt a massive decision about my life had been made by Jane. It didn't feel right and I was angry. I'm not proud of how I felt or of what I said publicly about the situation at the time. But I have to be honest about this because of the consequences it had on my relationship with Scarlett.

*****

I WAS THEN faced with the job of telling Claire. I knew it would be devastating but at the same time, I knew it was the right thing to do.

Claire, of course, was extremely upset and I am sure must have contemplated the future of our relationship, but she does have an amazing ability to take things in her stride and cope with the situation. She did exactly that with great dignity and kindness.

The trip was not uneventful. If you've ever seen Perfect Storm, the disaster-at-sea movie with George Clooney, it will give you an idea of how the voyage went. On the third night we arrived at the French port of Brest and, despite our 'captain' giving a full explanation on the perfect way to moor a boat, we ended up late to dock and tied up on the outside of a pontoon, which he assured us would be fine. I had already asked him to leave earlier that evening because of a catalogue of mistakes, so we were now entirely on our own.

In the middle of the night, there was a sound of crashing and splintering. Wearing only my boxers, I ran outside and into a storm. The boat was going up and down like a toy, smashing into the concrete pontoon each time it fell. I leapt off the boat and, in a state of superhuman strength (no doubt inspired by the threat of my brand new boat sinking with my family on board), managed to lift a huge tractor tyre out of the water from the adjacent quay side, roll it along to my boat and lodge it between the bow and the concrete pontoon.

The next day, I surveyed the damage, did some fibreglass repairs to the hull of the boat and took over the voyage myself.

Claire, along with my kids and my friends, Mark and Kim Ryan, became the crew, with me, a total novice, as captain. Did I know what I was doing? No. Did I believe I could get the boat from France to Barcelona? Absolutely. Did I think there'd be a few more adventures? Probably.

Leaving Brest, the sea rapidly increased in choppiness and the bow of Rubekian was smashing through the waves, at times quite violently, and I must say that my lack of experience left me very nervous, even though I had been told that the captain will give up a long time before the boat does.

Mark went down below to go to the loo when the bow of the boat hit a giant wave and there was a huge crash. Mark, who was in the toilet, had been thrown up in the air, hit his head on the roof and landed badly injuring his leg. He was in a lot of pain, but we did not know it was broken at the time.

I slowed the boat and continued the journey, tossed about by the sea, but somewhat more comfortable as a result of the slower speed. Mark was clearly in some degree of pain whilst Claire – whose experience working in boutiques on luxury cruise ships enabled her to quickly step up – became first mate. She, helped also by the children, was brilliant. All of us were in it together.

We now started our crossing of the challenging Bay of Biscay, some 300 miles of notoriously difficult water. My boat did not have the fuel range to do this at speed, so we went very slowly at first – around about 12 knots – to get as much distance under the belt as possible for the least amount of fuel burnt.

Finally, 20 hours later we arrived at a little Spanish port at the southern end of the Bay. We decided to celebrate by going into the little town to eat. But in order to get to the town we all had to make our way up a long metal harbour ladder which got us on to solid ground.

Mark eyed the ladder and looked at his swollen leg sorrowfully.

'I'm never going to make it up that,' he said. 'I don't think I could even get on the first rung of the ladder.'

I looked at the ladder and looked at him. He was right. There was no way he was going to get up there. The kids were already climbing up, limber as little monkeys. There was no way Mark could miss this celebration.

I bent down next to him. 'Ok, so I'm going to get you up there,' I said. 'I'll carry you on my back.'

Claire clapped her hand over her mouth as I then hauled Mark – who was around 15 stone at the time – onto my back and made my way very slowly up the ladder with her just a few feet ahead of us, constantly looking back to check we were alright. When we got to the top it was clear he couldn't even walk so we wandered round the town with Mark still on my back and me stumbling somewhat under his not inconsiderable weight. We finally found a little restaurant and sat down to eat and then all of us returned to the boat, still with Mark on my back.

The next day, Claire and I were up at 3am to try and get a really big day in. It was a beautiful summer's morning, clear skies, warm and very calm seas. We were effortlessly cruising at 26 knots as the boat glided along the glassy surface. Everyone else got up at about 8am and around 10am Claire and I decided to go back to bed for a couple of hours and leave our crew in charge. We had only been in bed an hour when Rebekah came running down the stairs and said, 'Daddy, we are in thick fog'.

I rushed up on top and could barely see the bow of the boat. I switched the radar on for the first time ever but was completely confused by what I saw. I radioed for help but received no intelligible answer. I had my crew using mobile phones to ring ports ahead of us, to try and ascertain the level of fog. All to no avail. And all the time we were careering forward into the abyss.

My brain felt as misted as the air, but I needed an absolutely clear course of action, so I chose a port about an hour to the south, called Figueira da Foz, slowed the boat down and used my chart plotter to aim for our destination. As we approached the invisible entrance I had two people on the bow of the boat trying to spot the port entrance. Suddenly, a shout went up –'harbour wall!' – and we knew then that the chart plotter had done its job amazingly.

We were dead centre of the harbour mouth and we could now just about see the safety wall either side of us. As we berthed up, safe and sound, it was one of those moments that you kiss the ground (I have had a few of those from my flying experiences as well).

Unbeknown to me there were going to be many more of these ground-kiss moments in the remaining 1,000 mile journey.

Claire coped incredibly. She was unflappable in every storm and by my side whenever I needed her. She was cleaning the toilets, scrubbing down the deck, reassuring Mark (who finally went to hospital in this foggy city) that everything would be okay, and never once expressed any doubt in my abilities as novice captain. 'I trust you 100 percent to make it alright,' she told me.

When, eventually, we sailed into Barcelona, we sailed into a perfect sunset. Claire got all dressed up and brought out the champagne. As I steered neatly towards a clear space in the dock, I heard Frank Sinatra booming My Way from a sound system that Claire had rigged up. The kids all adored her. And if I had any doubt who I wanted by my side for the rest of my life, that voyage gave me the answer.

When we arrived back home in Broughton, I watched as she began to pack her clothes, ready to leave. 'What are you doing, Claire?' I asked.

'Getting ready to go home,' she said.

'Why don't you just stay?'

She did.

*****

I AM SO thankful Claire made the decision to stay with me. She told me later that, as stunned as she had been by my revelation, she had fallen for me, especially after our time together on the Rubekian. She also told me that the situation with Jane didn't change anything between us, and that if a baby came into my life then she would welcome it.

If only I had seen the situation in the way Claire saw it. But I was too angry with Jane and I couldn't bring myself to engage with her however much she and her family tried to connect with me to sort things out. Then she employed lawyers who told me she was going to have the baby at the Portland Hospital in London, and wanted me to provide a house in London for her and the child.

This infuriated me even more and left me feeling very negative towards her.

Today it is hard for me to justify the way I felt back then. I am deeply ashamed that I spoke openly of my anger towards Jane, and my initial refusal to accept our baby daughter, Scarlett Coco Caudwell Burgess, who was born on 21st March, 2002.

The Times newspaper approached Jane when Scarlett was born and a birth announcement appeared. Again, I was enraged and I held that rage against Jane and, as a consequence, felt I shouldn't or couldn't see my little daughter.

It is complicated to explain. I felt because of the circumstances I might not be the father she would need me to be, that my feelings about Jane were so raw they would leak out to my child, in spite of myself. I know many parents will find this impossible to understand, but I just felt a huge sense of injustice and hurt, and this was my way of dealing with it. My view was, and still is, that children should be brought into the world by two loving parents who have made a commitment to each other and the baby. But knowing what I know now, however much you try and convince yourself, nothing can stop a parent loving a child.

*****

A YEAR LATER, Claire was pregnant. I was delighted, and very much in love with Claire. Jacobi was born on 20th March, almost two years to the day after the birth of Scarlett. I pride myself on being a good and loving father. I adored my little boy. But I knew that I also had a little girl who was 150 miles away in London, and who I could not bring myself to acknowledge for reasons that I had started to struggle to understand myself. I pushed down all my conflicted emotions and, as always, my work, and the sale of Singlepoint diverted me with huge amounts of stress and tension.

I never stopped thinking about Scarlett but it took me five years before I knew I could no longer deal with the situation as it then was. The first person I spoke to was Rebekah.

'I've been having second thoughts about Scarlett,' I told her. She nodded, like she'd been waiting for this moment, hugged me, and told me she understood any decision I was going to make, but I could tell which way her heart lay. Then I spoke with Libby. 'Dad, I think it would be the best thing to welcome her into the family,' Libby told me, looking tearful. Claire and Kate said exactly the same. All of them knew that behind the hard stance I'd taken, I was desperately unhappy about not having a relationship with my daughter.

It was March, a few days before Jacobi's fifth birthday when I knew I couldn't put this off any longer. Scarlett was my child. It upset me to think that my little boy had a sister just two years older than him, but that he knew nothing about her. I spoke to Jane and asked her if Scarlett could come to Jacobi's party. We were having a little family celebration in the pool house and I'd like it if she and Scarlett could join us.

On the morning of the party, I sat down with Jacobi and Claire. 'Jacobi, you're going to meet your sister today,' I told him. He looked confused.

'I know Libby and Rebekah are coming,' he said.

'No, this is your sister Scarlett. You've never met her before and her birthday is the day after yours. She's just two years older than you.' He looked excited.

'Scarlett,' he said. 'That's great.'

My daughter was seven years old when I first saw her. I cannot forget that moment. She walked into the pool house wearing a pretty pink dress. She was so beautiful, with long, red-brown hair and the most delicate features. My little girl. I walked over and gave her a huge hug. I knew she'd be feeling confused and probably overwhelmed, though she didn't show it.

'I'm so pleased to see you, Scarlett,' I said, hugging her again. I didn't want to let her go. She was the missing piece of my heart and I felt wretched about how I'd behaved towards her and so very grateful to her – and to Jane – now that she was finally in my life. She was so shy she barely said anything. We had a little chat and I introduced her to her siblings, and Kate and Claire were wonderful with her.

Ours was an evolution of love. Kate developed a good relationship with Jane which really helped and, slowly but surely, Scarlett would come to more and more family events. Jane and her family were also invited and I have to say I am really impressed at what a good job she has done bringing up this polite, kind young woman.

Scarlett was a bridesmaid at Libby's wedding (Jane was there too) and she happily attends events, including Caudwell Children charity functions. She is a Burberry model, intelligent and a lovely young lady. I talk to her about being a little bit more assertive and she listens to me but she remains her sweet, shy self. I am so very grateful that she is my daughter because I am incredibly proud of her and immensely sorry for all my early years of hurt and anger.

All I know is that I am very lucky to have this special child in my life, and as part of my family.

Chapter 23

MUM

THERE ARE MANY good things about having money. I don't drive clapped-out cars that threaten to break down any minute. I don't spend time on my hands and knees, looking for loose coppers to pay for petrol as I used to in my twenties. I can eat in fabulous restaurants, and enjoy holidays in the sort of incredible locations I never knew existed as a child. I have houses all over the world. I own a beautiful and historic home in Staffordshire, and it takes my breath away every time the huge, wrought iron gates open, welcoming my return from my travels.

Yet if you really want to know the best thing about having money, then, for me, it's about being able to make someone else's life better. It's the reason I founded Caudwell Children. Those children who didn't otherwise have a voice, and whose parents have not been able to find help from doctors, or other charities, can now be listened to. We help them in any way we can.

There is also one other thing that makes me feel so privileged to have money and resources, and something that gives me one of the greatest feelings of love and satisfaction. That was being able to give back to my mum, who deserved so much and who, for much of her life, had to struggle and suffer through lack of finances and because of her marriage to a difficult man. I loved my mother completely and utterly, and always have done.

In the later years of her life, her health was very poor. She suffered from innumerable ailments, couldn't really talk and spent her days in bed. Mum was watched over by her marvellous carer Pam Clarke, who's a real character, and she also became a treasured member of the family. But whatever her aches and pains, Mum was always happy and smiling. She never complained, never felt sorry for herself and of all the amazing people I have met in my life, it is my mother who makes me feel humbled because she was such a good, inspirational and genuine human being.

Until she passed away this year, I would visit her every week without fail, as did Brian. 'So what are we watching today, Mum?' I'd ask. 'Inspector Morse, Heartbeat or Midsomer Murders? Take your pick?' She would point at the image of John Thaw and Kevin Whately on the TV screen, I would press play and she would smile. She loved those shows, and watched them again and again. I'd groan because I could practically repeat word for word what each character was about to say as I'd seen each episode so many times.

I would cook for her, take her food up on a tray, and Brian and I would talk to her about the old days and joke – 'How many more times do we have to watch Inspector Morse?' She'd just laugh, or pretend to complain to Pam about her naughty boys. And we would sit and laugh with her. Pam would often join in the fun, scolding us loudly for being cheeky. Sometimes we would sit quietly, checking our emails, Brian scrolling through endless adverts for cars as he is an absolute motoring fanatic. It was just the three of us; Mum and her boys, like it was half a century ago, when all that we now have was a seemingly impossible dream in my head.

Over the years, people have told me that I should take up meditation as a way to keep myself in the present, to ground myself and still my mind. I've never done it because I had that sense of peace thanks to being with my mum, sitting there, just the three of us in the simple, cosy home that we bought her years ago, stuffed with photos of all her grandchildren and all her favourite musical icons. I dreaded losing her but when the end came I just felt incredibly privileged to have had her in my life for so long.

I think that subliminally I knew something was going to happen when we were together for the last time, me talking, her smiling, me showing her photos of all my children. When we came to say goodbye, I held her for a long time in my arms, told her I loved her and how much she meant to me. I knew she was deteriorating and I knew her little world of that cosy bedroom was getting smaller and smaller with her less able to communicate in any other way except her beautiful smile.

One day later I got a call from Pam. 'John, I think you need to come now,' she said. Both Brian and I arrived. Her two boys. We sat together, each holding one of her hands, telling her again how much we loved her but this time she couldn't respond. We stayed by her side for 48 hours as she slipped peacefully from this life.

I didn't cry. I felt a sense of relief that she was out of any pain and discomfort and I felt glad that at the end it was the three of us together. It was her time. We were just lucky to have her love for as long as we did. And she will always remain at the very centre of my heart.

*****

BERYL JOAN WALSH was a natural-born lady despite the fact she came from a very humble, working class background in industrial Birmingham. She could sing, she could dance, she could play the piano, and she absolutely loved anything musical, and all aspects of the arts and culture. She was also very well-mannered, extremely stylish, the sort of woman who could make a cheap dress look expensive simply with a few nifty alterations on her sewing machine. All her dresses were cut to subtly show off her tiny 23-inch waist and hourglass figure.

Ironically, for such a feminine woman, Mum always lived in a house full of men. Between myself, Brian and Dad, there was little thought for things like vases of flowers; a newly-mended piece of machinery or motorcycle magazine was far more likely to ornament our kitchen table.

Mum had grown up the only girl in a family of four, and her dad, Harry, was a no-nonsense, old-school patriarch who had fought for his country in the First World War. My earliest memory is of Grandad Harry, when we went to visit my grandparents in Perry Bar, where mum was brought up. I was about three and for some reason I decided to test out my new teeth on Grandad. His reaction was to bite me back – hard. I must have howled for a good hour, and those teeth marks are still embedded – only in my mind – to this day. I never made that mistake again. Once bitten by Grandad, twice shy.

Mum's mother, my maternal grandma, was called Beatrice Fanny Onions. She came from Malvern, where the Onions family still lived. She was a bit like Patricia Routledge's character Hyacinth Bucket in Keeping up Appearances and her maiden name was, she said, pronounced 'O'Nions'. That used to make my dad chortle and – probably to wind up my mum – he'd refer to Grandma as 'Beetroot Fanny Onions'. This would get a giggle from me and a small sigh from mum as we drove back to Stoke.

As much as she loved her family and was extremely close to her mum, the Second World War opened up a whole new life for Mum. She got a job with the Air Ministry, working as a secretary in charge of wages, and made lifelong friends with two other girls called Olive and Vivienne. She thrived in the busy, exciting – and often incredibly tense – atmosphere at RAF Defford, the wartime airbase in Worcester. (Actually, it was the main station for the development of airborne radar during and after the war.)

Every Friday, Mum, Olive and Vivienne would go to a dance at the base which was regularly flooded with handsome American pilots whose well-cut uniforms, sharp haircuts and easy access to cigarettes, chocolate and nylon stockings put them several notches above most British servicemen.

Some 40 years later, while treating my mum to a cruise – along with Vivienne and her partner, John, and Olive and her husband Derek – I was regaled with several stories about my mum and the girls, who called themselves 'The Three Musketeers'. 'John, your mum never had a spare moment on the dance floor,' Vivienne told me. 'She was a marvellous dancer, always beautifully turned out and a real head-turner.' Then, she said, 'Your mum also scandalised the whole of RAF Defford.'

'Why?' I asked, utterly intrigued.

'Well, at one dance a black American pilot turned up. Very few people had seen a black man before and he asked your mum to dance. She danced with him for hours. Lots of people there could not believe she would dance with a black man but your mum didn't have any of that sort of prejudice. To her, he was just another brave pilot. In her eyes, he was no different to anyone else. She didn't care if people were shocked,' added Vivienne. 'She wanted him to know that she valued him as much as anyone else in the room.'

That story makes me so proud of my mum, especially as she was a woman who never liked any form of confrontation, yet she had her principles. Years later, after she'd married my dad and moved to Stoke, a Jamaican family moved into our road – the first black people I had ever seen and who were shamefully pretty much shunned by the rest of the road. My parents were probably the only people who were pleasant and friendly towards them – nothing more than a 'Good morning' or 'Good evening' and a smile, but enough to show they were on their side.

And when a girl turned up at school who everyone started viciously taunting, calling her 'Jew girl', I went home and asked my mum what that meant and why everyone was being mean to her. The next day I sat beside her in class and made friends with her, glowering warningly at anyone who called her names, because Mum had said to me, 'The war was fought to make sure everyone was treated exactly the same.'

*****

IN THE SPRING of 2003 my mother first died just a few days after her 80th birthday. It happened in front of me, in my kitchen at Broughton Hall. It was at the end of what had probably been one of the best weeks of her life. Myself and Brian had thrown a fabulous surprise birthday party for her at the Malvern Theatre, inviting along all her friends and the family. They all appeared on stage together singing 'Happy Birthday' while she stood in the upper circle with me. She cried tears of joy, completely taken aback – I'd pretended we were there just to do a little private tour of the theatre that she loved so much.

After her party, she went to Abergavenny where she spent a wonderful time with her old friend Vivienne and then she'd arrived at Broughton Hall, exhausted but happy. She settled herself at the kitchen table and we chatted as I stood at the stove, cooking, and Claire flitted around the kitchen making sure Mum had everything she needed.

And then mid-conversation, it went quiet. I looked up from my cooking and saw Mum looking blankly at me, and then I watched as her eyes rolled back in her head. 'Mum,' I cried, and rushed over to her as she slid to the floor. 'Mum. Mum. Mum.' I panicked, my mind whirling as I tried to work out if she'd had a fit, if it was a stroke and what the hell I had to do.

Behind me, I heard Claire shouting for her step-father, Dr John, who fortuitously had been invited for dinner and was in the sitting room. I knew I had to give Mum the kiss of life, which I had been trained to do years ago as part of my Michelin apprenticeship and more recently as part of the training to be a yacht captain and pilot.

'Move over John. Claire's called an ambulance.' Dr John's calm voice suddenly took over and immediately he bent down and gave my mother the kiss of life. Again, the memory blurs, but it seemed within minutes the ambulance arrived. Dr John managed to revive her and then she was immediately given oxygen and taken away in the ambulance. 'It's a stroke,' Dr John told me. 'Serious, I'm afraid.' He didn't need to tell me that. I knew already, by the fact she'd stopped breathing, how devastating it was.

Despite the shock and trauma, in hospital I moved almost into business mode. 'Don't sugar-coat anything. I want to know exactly what we are dealing with,' I told the doctor a few hours later, as he began to talk to me about 'an uncertain prognosis'. 'I want you to give me the exact statistical facts.'

They were pretty grim. 'Fifty percent of these cases die within a month. Forty-five percent live but will remain totally dependent, and may die within three months to a year. Four to five percent may live longer, and a smaller percentage may gain some form of independence,' he told me.

And then I cried. I could not stop crying. A whirl of images went through my head... My mum laughing and crying as we all sang 'Happy Birthday'... Mum dancing to the Glen Miller Band that Brian and I had hired for the night... Mum on her knees, endlessly scrubbing Grandma's gritty, dull encaustic Minton Hollins tiles in Wellesley Street... Mum lying there, kind of lifeless, on the kitchen floor, and then the flashing lights of the ambulance.

For the first time in my life, I didn't recognise myself. It was like I was split in two. One half of me predictably jumped into action.

Brian was on his way, and I called Uncle Doug, her favourite brother.

Like Mum, he was a culture vulture and he spent so much time with her. A list was building in my head – I had to find the best doctors, research the optimum ways of dealing with this, and make sure Mum had everything to make her comfortable.

The next day, having had no sleep, I had to host our Annual Summer Ball for Caudwell Children, entertaining 2,000 guests and acting as auctioneer for the night. I could not let the children down or the guests who had paid money for tickets. I am sure a lot of people there could tell that I was not really myself but I did my best and battled through to make the evening a great success, smiling for the cameras, all the time wondering what was happening to Mum.

I would try to get on with life. But then I would cry. Tears would drop unbidden from my eyes at any time of the day or night. Even when I knew Mum was in the best hands, getting the best care, I would be in a meeting at work and suddenly I'd feel the tears coming. I am not a man who easily cries. I have broken bones in my body through motorbike accidents and horrendous skiing accidents, or taking one dare too far, and never the slightest tear on those occasions. One word universally used to describe me in business was 'tough'. I was tough. I was so driven to pursue this dream of building an empire, I worked on the armour I'd begun to develop as a child and hardened myself so as to be able to fend off all attacks and constantly battle forward. I never broke. Like my dad, I never cried. Until then.

I have no idea what my staff and colleagues thought of me during that time. They knew, of course, my mother was unwell, but few realised exactly how much my mother meant to me. Grief, they say, is the price you pay for love, and my grief felt as bottomless as my love. I hadn't lost her but I had known what it was to lose her, and I had no idea where Mum would fall on the grim scale of the doctor's statistics. I tried to feel at peace with the idea of her dying, knowing the possibilities of living in a coma, or as a permanent invalid, would be just another kind of death sentence. I thought of the hell my dad went through, stuck in his armchair, unable even to make himself a cup of tea. But I didn't want to lose my mum. And so for six weeks, I cried.

*****

'MUM, BRIAN AND I have a proposition for you.' It was 1975. The three of us were standing in the small kitchen of the Dividy Road, the only house she'd ever owned. For months, I'd been turning over a plan in my head which I saw as the first real chance of my dream of expanding my business becoming a reality. I'd discussed it with Brian, and he was with me all the way. The only problem was we needed something from Mum.

Kate and I were living in Ash Bank, the £18,000 property which gave me real collateral with the bank. I'd finished my apprenticeship at Michelin and was now on staff, earning more money and still doing every extra shift I could get in the dreaded 'Black', and Brian was into his first few years as a trainee. Thanks to my own little garage and driveway at Ash Bank, I'd been doing a steady turnover in buying and selling cars, anything I could do to try to succeed.

Brian, like me, always had an interest in cars. Occasionally, he'd accompany me to the car auctions in Birmingham and watch what I was looking out for, just like I had with Dad. He was a natural with engines, spray paints and machinery, and he knew a good bargain when he saw one, but he was also very straightforward in his dealings with people. In Brian, I saw a great car salesman in the bud just waiting to bloom.

We'd both talked about the idea of setting up a car salesroom. I'd found a site less than a mile from our old house at Wellesley Street

– all we needed was a cash injection to get the show on the road. And that's where the equity in Ash Bank came in. Two years later we had an ambition to expand that required substantially more cash. That's where Mum came in. It would require a huge leap of faith on her behalf.

'We want to expand,' I said, trying to keep it as simple and straightforward as possible. Mum, would you consider mortgaging your house so we could have an extra cash input? We'd make sure everything was paid back and all mortgage payments upheld. And we absolutely will not let you down... What do you think, Mum?'

She looked at me. She looked at Brian. Then she smiled, and just said, 'Yes.' We did put her mind at rest and offer to answer any questions, but she had already made up her mind. Mum put her whole security on the line – the house that had been bought with Grandma's money – for her two boys. People think it was myself and Brian who built the Caudwell Empire, but it was my mother too. Without her trust, without her selfless gift of the only thing in the world she actually possessed, the dream may never have become a reality. That was how much my mum loved and believed in her boys.

I was in my twenties then, old enough to see my mum for the woman she was and the life she'd had. As a child, I never felt loved enough. There were no big kisses and cuddles, no open demonstration of how much I was loved. My mum was always busy, constantly working away or cooking and cleaning. Years of her life were spent under Grandma's thumb, being put down, and then years more, dealing with Dad and his misery.

On top of that, she had two boys who were a handful – myself, especially. When I was little, she must have had a very different idea about what sort of boy I was going to be. Her favourite outfit to dress me in was a pair of smart lime-green shorts and a bright yellow buttoned-up shirt. I hated it with a passion. I was always more of a Dennis the Menace than Lord Snooty.

I was barely out of nappies when I caused my first uproar with the neighbours. I'd toddled over to an intriguing mosaic on a near-by front porch and with the aid of a large sharp stick, I'd patiently managed to dig up a half the tiny little mosaic tiles which – after a stressful complaint from the house owner – Mum had to painstakingly set back into the original pattern. On my first day at nursery, I watched as the teacher pulled out little camp beds for 'Nap Time' and stared in disbelief at my fellow infants curling up under a blanket, closing their eyes. I just couldn't comprehend why we were meant to sleep when all I wanted to do was have fun.

I progressed from mischievous schoolboy to motorbike-mad teenager, riding to school over the slag heaps on a Royal Enfield 350 Bullet motorbike when I was 14, smoking my Woodbines and Park Drive cigarettes, wearing leathers, listening to rock music, swearing like a trooper and desperately trying to grow my pathetically thin hair as long as possible. God knows how she coped with me, and God knows how she managed to keep everything going when Dad could no longer work. She was fully responsible for an invalid husband, a seven-year-old child and a teenage tear-away. So it's understandable that hugs, kisses and birthday presents wrapped with big red bows didn't get much of a look-in throughout my growing up.

But knowing that your mother believes in you – when no-one else does – and loves you enough to trust you with their home; that meant everything to me. And through all my tears in those six weeks came an absolute steady determination to believe that – despite the odds – we were going to get my mother through this stroke. She was going to be the one percent who would defy all the statistics. My mission now was to get Mum back.

*****

'BRIAN, HAVE YOU got the HP sauce?'

'Yes, John.'

'And the bacon and eggs?'

'Yes.'

'Right, let's go.'

We were standing in the car park of Bucknall Isolation Hospital. Mum had been moved there as she recuperated from her stroke. Brian and I had been at her bedside every day, living from one diagnosis to the next, celebrating when she opened her eyes after a couple of weeks, and no doubt exhausting the doctors with our constant questioning and suggestions. We were months in, which was good news, but Mum was in a wheelchair, her movement was terribly limited and she couldn't really speak.

But Brian and I had not given up hope.

'Afternoon,' I said to the staff nurse, as I wheeled Mum out of her room, followed by Brian carrying various blankets and large carrier bags.

'Have a lovely walk round the grounds, Mrs Caudwell,' she chirped back. 'It's a lovely day for a walk.'

We weren't going for a walk. We were going for a picnic, and carrying out the first stages in our alternative plan to rehabilitate Mum. She'd always said her happiest moments were when we all used to drive down with the caravan and visit our relatives, the Onions, in Malvern. If you ever asked what her favourite dish would be, she'd say, 'The lovely fry-up breakfasts we had on the campsite.' And they were wonderful times, all of us gathered around the fire for hours cooking and eating a (semi) full English, with our aunties and cousins, passing around the sausages and bacon. I tried to cram in as much as I possibly could before the clearing-up and washing-up started.

So we came up with the idea of every afternoon, finding a place in the grounds of the hospital for our own little mini camping fry-up.

Of course, it wasn't any form of traditional medicine or conventional treatment, but it was a memory – her memory – of happy times, a reminder of who she was and who we were. The three of us. Brian would bring the bacon, eggs and bread. I'd bring a petrol camping stove and frying pan, and we'd huddle up and cook up a feast, hoping that the unforgettably-delicious smell of the bacon sizzling in the pan would bring back another level of consciousness. A reminder of the good things in Mum's life.

'Just a small bite, Mum,' Brian would say, patiently feeding her bird-size cuts of a bacon and HP sauce sandwich, which she'd take in tiny mouthfuls. We had those camping picnics for months at Bucknall. We ate enough breakfasts to keep us going for decades. I have no idea whether the staff knew, whether they approved or disapproved or turned a blind eye, but day after day we would cook and eat the same meal together, and incrementally Mum would take a little bit more, stir a little bit more, enough to make me convinced we could all get through this. We did.

After Bucknall, Mum was moved to a live-in physio unit in Malvern. Five or six months in, she was walking around the care home with a four-pronged stick and slowly starting to say words. A few months later she had improved enough to move back to her own bungalow that we had bought for her, which she loved, and all of us – Kate, Claire, the children and Brian and his wife Paula and their children – would visit, filling the house with pictures, laughter and love.

The last thing to return was her speech – but just a few words. But I decided I would make our communication as fun as possible. 'What do you want to talk about today, Mum?' Together we'd work out what that was. 'Family?' I'd ask, and often she'd say, 'No,' which actually meant, 'Yes.' And we'd laugh and treat it as one big guessing game, until finally we got little sentences and a lot more smiles and laughter. Through patience, determination and a hell of a lot of love we beat those impossible odds and although she never regained any meaningful speech, we got Mum back.

The thing is, I knew we would. I had faith in her that she could achieve the impossible, just like she had the belief in me that I could achieve my impossible dream of building an empire. My mum had a will to live then which came from her joy in life, a joy and happiness from the simplest of things, as well as her love of her family.

I was lucky enough to make a lot of her dreams come true – I took her to wonderful operas and performances by her favourite stars, such as Alfie Boe who also sang at her 90th birthday. We went on cruises, holidays with the children, and Brian and I did everything possible in the second half of her life to treat her like a queen and to make up for the hardship of her life in Stoke. Covid-19 made things harder for all of us, as it has for everyone – and especially those with elderly parents – but we did everything we could to make it work and make her know we were there for her.

But whatever I was able to give my mum, she always gave me more. I don't think words exist which truly express how much she meant to me. I would not be the man I am without her love, her belief, her spirit and her resilience.

I am proud to be my mother's son.

Chapter 24

CHAMPAGNE, STARS AND CLAIRE

'SO… IF YOU are a multi-millionaire, John Caudwell, why, may I ask, are you wearing that cheap dinner suit I've seen you in a hundred times before?'

I couldn't help but chuckle. This was the great musician, Elton John, having a go at me in jest. We were in South Africa, and in his hotel suite. Claire was doubled over, almost crying with laughter, and Elton's husband, David Furnish, was joining in, telling me that my suit looked like a rental outfit.

It was all a bit of fun. We'd all become quite close ever since I'd bid a large amount of money at his White Tie and Tiara Ball, to go to South Africa with them, and see how Elton's Aids charities were working in action; something that fascinated me.

And yes, my suit came from Marks & Spencer. So what? It was perfectly serviceable and extremely good value. In reality, Elton was tickled by my very un-millionaire ways. We got on really well as we travelled round South Africa, going from one project to another sponsored by his Foundation. The work that they were doing with the poor HIV sufferers of South Africa was inspirational and compelling and further committed me to being a big supporter of his work. On the fun side we went backstage with Elton and all the cast of Lion King. We chased through the streets of Johannesburg, with a multiple police car escort and Elton's own security cars in convoy, breaking all the speed limits and going through all the red lights. They say celebrities live in the fast lane and it is true. It was like something out of the movies.

Through Elton and his charity, we were invited to meet Nelson Mandela. That was both a profound and magical experience. He is one of the people who I admire most in the world, having suffered appallingly in apartheid times, serving that dreadful jail sentence, and then going on to become a wonderful and balanced leader of South Africa. Just being in his presence felt transformative and truly emotional.

I have to admit there was also an unexpected side to the man I'd always viewed as rather saintly. The day we first met him, there he was with that big smile, dressed in this rather spectacular African print long shirt in white and blue. 'It's an honour to meet you, Mr Mandela,' I said. He smiled and nodded but I could see he wasn't really looking at me, he was focused completely on Claire who was looking particularly fetching in a pure white suit and blue blouse.

Within minutes of the introduction, he put his arm around Claire and began to chat to her. And when I say 'chat' what I actually mean is 'flirt'. 'You cheeky man,' I thought to myself, although I was actually rather impressed by his gall.

'I would like to show you some wonderful things we have in South Africa,' I heard him say. 'I bet you would,' I thought. But I was also chuckling to myself. I decided to take it all as a compliment. I mean, if Nelson Mandela flirts with your girlfriend you can't really take offence can you. Claire of course was completely oblivious. 'He was just being friendly,' she said when I teased her about it later. I can't blame him. Underneath everything, he was also very much a red blooded man.

But how did I get here, suddenly hanging out with people I'd only ever seen before on the television or in movies? Now I was sitting having dinner with Elton and he was offering to perform free of charge at one of my charitable events. There were no agents, no publicists, just me, Elton, Claire and David having a wonderful time. The answer was Claire. It was pretty much all down to Claire's fabulous personality along with the large donations I had made to Elton's own charity.

Being friends with people like Elton was very much new territory for me. It was also often rather surprising. The first time I met Elton after his ball, he was a little under the weather but he didn't make excuses or sit in silence. He was totally engaged and in less than an hour he promised to perform at my ball. 'And please, I don't want a fee,' he said. 'I'm doing this for your charity.'

Elton has a huge heart but he is also one of the most switched on men I've ever met. Politics, football, fashion, art, culture – he has an opinion on everything. A few months later he invited Claire and I to dinner at his beautiful home in the south of France. Claire was on a table with David Furnish and I was on a table with Elton, Hugh Grant and Liz Hurley.

That dinner was one of the few times in my life where I felt out of my depth. It was nothing to do with the fact I was sitting on a table with three hugely famous people. It was the conversation. The three of them were discussing Middle Eastern politics. Each of them knew huge amounts about the Arab Spring, the different religions and cultures and back and forth they debated while I sat thinking, 'These people are seriously smart. I'm just going to shut up and listen.' It was not exactly what I was expecting. But then again, never judge.

I have never courted fame. In the first years of our life together, Claire was very much a homebody. We spent the majority of our time in Broughton with little Jacobi. We were really happy. Everything revolved around family. Kate and Claire developed a good friendship and when Jacobi was born she asked Kate to be his godmother. I felt moved when she suggested her idea to me, but it was typical of

Claire – she's just a particularly thoughtful, lovely lady who wants everyone to be included and feel loved, valued and respected. She finds it very difficult to think badly about anybody, no matter what – a lovely attribute, although sometimes a weakness.

Claire was – still is – absolutely gorgeous. People often looked at us together and assumed she was a gold-digger, just as they assume my current partner, Modesta is. I can spot a gold-digger a mile off. Of course I've had women coming on to me in the most inappropriate way, but I'm not a fool. I can tell very quickly what their agenda is and I know exactly what I'm doing.

I make a point of never buying expensive gifts in the early stages of a relationship because I believe it sends out the wrong message – a transactional message. In those early years, the most that I ever bought Claire was a £20 dress from Topshop. I love to spoil my family, I loved to spoil Claire, but all that came later, once we'd established a real togetherness and stability.

Falling in love with Claire was easy. Her outlook on life was so sunny and positive and she was at her best when surrounded by family – hers and mine.

She'd been well brought-up and was extremely close to her mum, Alma, and sister, Toni, as well as her late father, Peter, and step-mum, Karen. Her life hadn't been easy. She'd done four years of modelling and winning beauty contests after she left school.

She could easily have had a career on the stage but she married young; she was just 21 as she walked down the aisle. When, a few years later, that marriage failed she supported herself by getting a job with a medical supply company.

The year after Jacobi's birth, Kate was going to turn 50. I wanted to do something really special for her. She remained one of the most important people to me and, whatever we'd been through, I still loved her as the mother of my children and as a wonderful woman who was a huge part of my life. 'Why don't we throw a huge party for her here at Broughton?' suggested Claire. 'Let's do a surprise party.' I've never seen someone go to such great pains to make someone else so happy. Claire – with the help of Kathy, our housekeeper – got busy sorting out the caterers, the invitations, the music, the florists and party designers. She was in cahoots with Rebekah and Libby, giggling on the phone and making sure their mum suspected nothing.

You'd think there'd be a bit of jealousy from Claire towards Kate, but she saw my ex-wife for the funny, kind person she was. And to Kate's great credit, throughout our divorce and since, she prioritised family unity above everything and did her utmost to keep life smooth for me, our children and my new partner. So much so that Claire came to think of Kate as a good friend. Lucky me.

But then that was Claire, who'd also accepted Jane and Scarli with open arms. On the day itself I'd told Kate that I wanted her to come to the house. 'I've had the garden completely transformed,' I said. 'I know you love gardens and I'd really value your opinion.' It was true, Kate adores beautiful gardens and she was more than happy to come along and see what I'd done.

I led Kate through the kitchen and into the Great Hall, where there is a small side door leading to the sunken garden. As she stepped through, we had arranged all of Kate's friends – some she hadn't seen for years – to be lined up in front of the box hedges singing 'Happy Birthday'. Kate watched, with tears running down her cheeks and the biggest smile I'd seen on her face for a long time. There was a marquee, dancing, music, a huge cake and Claire, in a stunning dress and huge high heels, never stopped running around making sure everyone was having fun and that Kate was having the most fabulous time.

I will always remember the speech Kate made on that night. It was so moving and she cried as she shouted out, 'Life will never get better than this.' I looked over at Claire, who was also moved to tears, and I felt incredibly happy. I also knew I had another surprise to come.

The next morning Kate came over to Broughton for a post-party brunch. She brought her new partner, Michael, who has been a big part of our family since they met a few years after we separated. There was something for Kate that I felt I needed to do. In that very painful time when we were going through a divorce, Kate never once demanded vast amounts of money from me. We both agreed to a settlement, and she never brought in lawyers to 'take me to the cleaners' which many women – and men – do. Not Kate. 'I hope you trust me to be fair and reasonable,' I'd said at the time, and she did.

But as the years passed, my financial position – including the sale of my service provider Singlepoint for £405 million in 2003 – had massively improved. After the brunch, I gave her an envelope containing a certificate. She opened it and read it out. 'I, John Caudwell, will buy you, Kate Caudwell, a beautiful villa in the south of France to the value of £10 million.'

'John,' she gasped. 'You don't need to do that.'

'Yes, Kate, I do,' I answered. 'It's your favourite place in the world, and I want to find the perfect place for you.'

And of course it was Claire who helped me to find that perfect place. We spent our two-week holiday in the south of France, researching villas, visiting every single place we could find that suited the requirements I'd stipulated. I don't think Claire got to sunbathe once but, never for a moment, did she complain. She was as delighted as me when, finally, we found the perfect house. 'John,' she said to me, looking out onto the stunning view of the islands of Cannes, from this beautiful sunset facing waterfront villa. 'Kate is going to love this place.'

It was moments like that which made me realise how lucky I was to have this woman by my side.

*****

BY 2006 I had sold my business, and turned my focus to my charity, Caudwell Children. I was a billionaire, but what does that mean? I couldn't possibly spend – and wouldn't want to spend – all that money. I wasn't going to leave fortunes in big trusts for my children. I don't think it is healthy or desirable for children to have such vast amounts of wealth left to them. My philosophy is very much to encourage my children to forge their own success and happiness, and to be part of the process of understanding that money needs to help society, to help others who need it more. So I decided to pledge half my wealth to my foundation, the purpose of which was to change as many people's lives as possible, during and after my lifetime. Of course, Caudwell Children would always be a very important part of this.

I wanted my charity to succeed beyond all possibilities, to make a difference to the many sad, damaged, disabled children living in discomfort and pain through no fault of their own. That vision I had as a child – of handing out money from a Rolls-Royce – provided a direction and purpose in helping these children in need.

But, after years of supporting various causes – I'd been officially part of the charity sector for seven years since I got involved with the NSPCC –I understood the way things often worked, and wanted my charity to work differently. It had to be sustainable and efficient. I used my money to personally pay the annual administration and management overheads, so that 100 percent of donations went directly to the children and families who needed the support.

But charities are basically businesses. You are in the business of asking people for money. You do this by inviting them to balls with celebrity performers, and having wonderful auctions to raise money for your cause.

In charity, there are two sides of the coin: there is the harsh reality of the people you want to help, children who are suffering every single day; then there are these high-octane, glamorous events that you put on in order to attract wealthy people to give to those individuals. Nothing attracts people to an event like a celebrity. These individuals are the magic fairy dust you need to sprinkle onto your charity event because they have a power to get people through your door. Then it's down to you to educate your audience and to persuade them – in their fine gowns, eating their Michelin-starred cuisines, and enjoying first-class entertainment – to put their hands in their pockets for others less fortunate.

I've had huge names all giving up their time to come to my events, from Elton to Sarah, Duchess of York and Princesses Beatrice and Eugenie, Rod Stewart, Robbie Williams, Chrissie Hynde, Robin Gibb, Kylie Minogue, Joan Collins, the wonderful late Sir Bruce Forsyth, Elizabeth Hurley, Whitney Houston, Peter Andre and Tamara Ecclestone. I am always very grateful.

The late Robin Gibb was a gentleman. He was ill with cancer when he agreed to perform and I worried it was too much for him. 'I'll be there, John.' he said. And he was. A real star. Rod too is wonderfully reliable, funny and completely professional, he knows exactly how to get a party started.

Robbie came up with a strange idea. He is very much a Stoke boy, born and bred. 'John, we need to set up a shop selling oatcakes,' he told me when we first met. Oatcakes are a local delicacy. 'We can call it Williams and Caudwell Oatcakes,' he said. It's a conversation he would return to every time I saw him. But I'm not sure it's the best business idea so it's never become a reality.

However, there are some performers who come and who don't engage in the mission of the charity. What they want to do is get on stage and get out as fast as possible. At one of my events, we had a legendary Motown performer who was clearly getting more and more annoyed that the auction – the part that actually raises money for the charity – was taking too long.

She (who shall be nameless) and her entourage decided they would crash the stage despite the fact there were several lots to go. Luckily they were stopped as they tried to make an entrance on the right hand side of the stage. Blow me, the woman and her crew simply marched backstage to the left hand side of the stage, got up as the auctioneer was talking and immediately plugged in their gear, drowning him out in seconds. The auctioneer had to vacate his post and we lost four or five valuable lots but she got to be back in her hotel by 10.30pm. Lesson learnt.

Sometimes the celebrity act can make me rather sad, which was the case with Whitney Houston when she performed the year she got out of rehab in 2008. I met her the day before in London where she had agreed to meet some of the children. The beautiful Whitney of all those memorable videos was a thin, haunted looking woman in a black suit whose eyes were blank as she turned to greet me. 'Hello,' is pretty much all she said. She didn't seem that interested in meeting the excited youngsters and I was worried what was going to happen the next night at the Butterfly Ball.

But, like a butterfly herself, she was absolutely transformed. She looked incredible in a black slinky dress, cinched in at the waist, her make up was perfect and her eyes were sparkling. On stage she came alive, lighting up the room, belting out: I Wanna Dance With Somebody (Who Loves Me) and I Have Nothing. The atmosphere in the room was electric.

Her voice wasn't perfect but Whitney Houston at 95 percent is still magical. I actually think it was her last great performance as her European tour later that year bombed and within four more years she sadly succumbed to her addictions and died. I choose, however, to remember her on that wonderful night and how happy she looked to be doing what she loved.

I am not a natural socialite. I do enjoy a party and pride myself on throwing some of the best events in my homes in Mayfair and Broughton. I love to be with my friends and family, celebrating into the small hours. But I'm not great with celebrities; I don't always recognise them or know who they are because – particularly back then – they weren't part of my everyday world. I don't necessarily know the names of their songs, television shows or movies.

I am, however, a businessman. I know that to really attract the first-class celebrity bees you need the best honey. I watched Claire glow at our parties at Broughton. I saw her light up rooms and get everyone enjoying themselves and I knew she would be a huge asset to my charity. She was wonderful fun, could dance like a professional, and charm and personality dripped from her fingertips.

'Claire,' I said one day when we were at home together in Broughton. 'I really think you could help me with Caudwell Children. You could be a great ambassador for the charity.'

'Do you really think so?' she answered.

'Yes,' I know you'd be perfect.'

*****

CLAIRE WAS A natural. (I was right.) We bought a small apartment in Imperial Wharf, and she hosted a few little parties, largely with the ladies-who-lunch crowd. Claire was amazing. I'd turn round to find her chatting with any number of celebrities. She made friends with everyone, everywhere. Every day there seemed to be a new friend she'd added to the list.

She went to Chiltern Firehouse one night and sat next to the rock star, Chrissie Hynde. Chrissie, the former punk from Akron, Ohio, got on famously with Claire, the former beauty queen from Stoke. Claire told her all about our charity, how we didn't blow money on huge administration fees, everything went to the children. Chrissie was impressed and came along to sing Brass in Pocket. 'That was for Claire,' she shouted as the song ended. What an incredible and unexpected performer, and a huge coup for Caudwell Children.

Everyone loved Claire. She met the late, lovely Stephen Gately and his husband Andrew Cowles. They didn't become friends, they became family. Stephen even came along with me one night to a little pub in Stoke where a friend was having a 50th birthday party

She made Elton laugh, and she bonded with David in a bid to get me to change my wardrobe, which I did, eventually. The late Cilla Black – a wonderful lady – used to call her 'Cleur with the eur' (Claire with the hair) because Claire's Titian blonde hair was her crowning glory.

But it wasn't just celebrities who gravitated towards her. I'd check into a hotel to meet her and the receptionist would look at me with awe. 'I've just met your wife,' they'd say. (Everyone referred to her as my 'wife', and I never corrected anyone. Indeed, she was known as Claire Caudwell.) 'Not only is she one of the most beautiful women I've ever seen she's also so charming. She helped me pick out a present for my daughter... What a kind lady.' I got used to everyone telling me how remarkable she was. It made me feel very proud.

But things were changing.

As Claire now says, 'There were three of us in the relationship. Me, John and the charity.' Socialising and raising awareness for Caudwell Children began to take over Claire's life.

Our days of domesticity and Topshop dresses were a distant memory. Now there were frequent parties, fuelled by champagne and glittering outfits. In order to be the perfect ambassador, Claire needed to look the part. There was a part of her, she admitted, that felt intimidated. A part of her that still felt like the shop girl on the cruise ship, an imposter. To get over that feeling, she needed armour – designer armour. Mixing with the wealthy London ladies-who-lunch set, she had to have the right Chanel handbag, the Tom Ford dress, flowers by Rob Van Helden (Elton's florist) and, of course, designer shoes by the rackload.

Shopping with Claire became an experience in itself. In Nice, Monte Carlo or in Sloane Street, she was like an Exocet missile aimed at the most glamorous items in designer shops. And then there was her hair. Her hair is extraordinarily beautiful, but she was in and out of the salon on a daily basis – exactly the right shade of golden blonde had to be used and the blow drying, the shampooing and the fluffing took forever. She also needed to go to a specific salon in London. The bills were eye-watering.

Of course, life and relationships are never plain sailing. Like on our first ever boat trip, Claire and I suffered a few storms together. In 2006, I discovered what felt like cysts in her left breast and insisted she see a doctor. All tests came back clear. Two years later, they were still there. More tests showed it was ductal carcinoma in situ, a pre-cancerous condition with a 50/50 chance of turning into breast cancer.

I did my research and took her to two top surgeons, both of whom told me they had never been quizzed so extensively by anyone about a procedure. Elton, genuinely concerned for Claire, waded in with advice.

'John,' he said over the phone. 'I'm putting together a list of specialists for you to speak to. Anything you need, anyone you need help getting hold of, anything at all, just let me know. Call me, text me. I'm here for you both.'

We took a decision for her to have a full mastectomy with the highly-skilled Professor Andrew Baildam, who we count as a close friend to this day. It was a really tough time for her, and I understood how difficult it was for her to come to terms with the surgery.

'You are even more beautiful now, Claire,' I would tell her. 'You need to wear your scars like a badge of honour and talk to other women about it. You can inspire other women with your story.' She did. She gave interviews to newspapers and on television to raise awareness for breast cancer. Two weeks after her surgery, she appeared at Elton's annual White Tie Ball, and she wore an asymmetric dress to hide her stitches. To me, she had never looked more radiant.

*****

CLAIRE AND I had our issues. She wanted to get married but I wasn't ready to make that commitment. Looking back, I don't blame her at all for wanting to make our relationship legal. As I say, I referred to her as my wife and in time I would have probably asked her to marry me but I don't like to be put under pressure and the subject of marriage disappeared.

Although I made mistakes with Claire, I always fought like fury for her health and the health of her family. There was a time in the south of France when I became certain I was going to lose her. We were on our boat in 2013 when she suddenly doubled over in pain. I thought it was gastroenteritis, so first gave her lots of antacids, which over the next few hours made no difference at all. The pain got worse so I immediately took her to the hospital in Cannes.

But the whole experience turned into a nightmare. I wasn't Claire's husband and the doctors kept refusing to see me or let me in to see Claire. I have never been in a situation like that and, after being told again and again that I wasn't able to see her, I threatened to call the police. Eventually, I was led into a dark room and informed that there were two swellings in her abdomen and a lot of fluid. They suspected cancer in multiple locations and that they were going to operate.

'No way,' I said. 'I want a second opinion. You must not operate.' I was desperate. They were talking about her needing a colostomy bag, and then how she might not survive. I couldn't believe what I was hearing. Based on their diagnosis Claire did not have long to live. I had no confidence in the hospital or the doctors, but given the apparent severity of what they were saying I really feared that I was about to lose the woman I loved. I thought about Jacobi and how I couldn't bear him to lose his mother. I knew it sounded hopeless, but I needed to do everything in my power to give Claire the best chance of survival.

I kept asking questions but I was being treated like some sort of irritant the doctors wanted to push out of the way. This felt completely wrong to me. In fact, it all felt wrong. The idea that Claire was about to be butchered without any second opinion could not happen so I went into the battle of my life to stop the operation. 'This is the mother of my child,' I kept saying. 'No operation now.' I pressured the hospital in every way possible then told them I was going to find my own doctor to give his opinion.

I contacted a specialist friend, Rob Kirby, who agreed to fly out, and later arranged an air ambulance to take Claire home. I was terrified but massively driven to save Claire's life. My instincts were right, it was the beginning of a case of severe endometriosis.

Within a year I had met with endless consultants and found a radical gynaecologist called Ashwini Trehan, in Huddersfield. The man was incredible, a genius in his field. He saved her from having to undergo a hysterectomy by his method of removing all cysts and scarring. It felt like a miracle and, after everything we had been through, I knew I wanted to be with Claire for the rest of my life.

*****

BUT I DID lose Claire.

I lost Claire within months of saving her from an operation that would have changed her life. It was my fault. I had very foolishly strayed with one woman, and Claire found out and took her revenge.

I desperately tried to win her back but there was no changing her mind. I wanted her to understand that I was sorry, that I had gone through hell to save her life, that the affair was over but there was no reaching her. She looked at me as if I was a stranger. It broke my heart and it also broke hers.

What I have learnt is never to give up, never to stop communicating if I don't want to lose a relationship. Claire and I went through a messy time but we had a wonderful son together and that was the most important thing. Whatever had happened, Claire was part of my family and I never wanted that to change. We had had great times together. Really funny moments from her taking me in my Marks & Spencer suit into a gay sex shop in Soho to get fitted out for a fancy dress party where I was dressed up to the nines in leathers (the man in the shop did a complete double take when he saw me in the dressing room in my leather chaps).

I'd arranged for Diana Ross to perform at her 40th birthday at Broughton. Diana is an absolute pro and a superstar, she'd arrived at Manchester airport the day before and rolled up to Broughton flanked by two female assistants and a couple of bodyguards. 'I'm ready,' she purred, holding out her hand for me to shake. A real Hollywood entrance.

I'd tried to keep her performance a surprise so when she appeared on stage in a black dress with huge sparkling earrings and an enormous white, bubbly cape which she wrapped around herself, everyone – especially Claire – went wild as she burst into her huge hit, I'm Coming Out. The performance ended with her singing happy birthday, dragging Claire on stage to cut a cake which was held by three semi-naked young men.

It was a fantastic night neither of us will ever forget and we had so many special moments with both our families.

When I think back on my times with Claire we just had so much fun together. Everything was an adventure, we became involved with people I never thought in a million years I would get to know and I saw sides to them many people don't see. An example of this is the actor Hugh Grant.

Geordie Greig, who was then the editor of the *Evening Standard* newspaper, invited us to a gala dinner to raise funds for the Raisa Gorbachev Foundation, which provides desperately needed medical equipment for cancer patients in Russia.

One of the auction pledges was dinner with President Mikhail Gorbachev in his dacha (country home) outside Moscow.

I had a word with the auctioneer and asked him if I could auction this Lot off. He was one of the 'Grand Daddy' auctioneers from one of the world's biggest auction houses and probably thought I was being highly impudent, but he graciously went along with it. 'I will leave that Lot to you, Mr Caudwell.'

When the moment for my Lot came up he handed me the microphone and I started the bidding. President Gorbachev was a guest of honour at the event and in the room there were also people like artist Tracy Emin, singer Bryan Ferry, the Duke of Marlborough, actress Vanessa Redgrave and the writer and comedian, David Walliams. I got the bidding to £80,000 and then no more hands were waving in the air.

But I had a rather daring (or possibly rather stupid) plan. 'I will put up £250,000 for this Lot if someone else matches my bid and if President Gorbachev agrees to entertain four of us.'

There were gasps then a ripple of laughter and the former Soviet leader got to his feet and waved, saying: 'I agree'.

Then there was a deathly silence. I stood at the podium dying a death. I could see Claire watching me smiling and turning round, willing someone to put up their hand. More seconds ticked by and the official auctioneer came up and asked if I would make the same offer for less money.

'No,' I said. He looked stricken. I was pretending to be as cool as a cucumber but on the inside I was on fire.

'Come on, this will be a historic occasion,' I said and then began to push and push the audience, sounding as confident as I could that I could make this work. More silence. I started to feel sweat at my hairline. This was about to be an epic failure. My brain was scrambling for some way to save face and then finally an elegant hand waved in the near distance and I saw a man stand with a charming smile on his face. It was Hugh Grant.

'I'll match your £250,000,' he shouted. 'Thank you Hugh,' I thought as I banged the gavel down.

A few months later, Hugh, Claire and I and his friend George spent a few days together in Moscow getting to know each other, and swapping highly entertaining stories. Hugh is very charismatic and has lots of fascinating experiences and he'd laugh in his cool way when I told him my tales of business or growing up in Stoke.

Every morning he would look at me with that well-known slightly-dazed expression, and say, 'How's Caudworld today?' Then he'd flash that charming Hollywood smile. But when we sat down for our dinner with Gorbachev, Hugh the Oxford University graduate with the incisive brain I'd witnessed in the south of France, came alive. He peppered him with all sorts of questions from, 'What did you think of Ronald Reagan?' to his opinion of politicians of the day. Hugh is also very cheeky. As the dinner neared its end, he put down his wine glass and said, 'So, was there chemistry between you and Maggie Thatcher?' with a devilish grin.

Gorbachev leant back in his chair and Hugh and I simultaneously leant forward. 'When we first met,' he said slowly, in his deeply accented voice as the room fell completely silent. 'We sat down together and as she sat, she folded one leg underneath the other and kicked off her shoe. In that moment I thought to myself: 'This is a woman I could do business with.' Hugh and I smiled at each other. It was clear what sort of chemistry he was talking about. That night was one of the most memorable experiences of my life and it was a huge piece of history I shared with Claire.

*****

IT TOOK MONTHS but we worked things out. I bought her a house a few miles from Broughton, so Jacobi would be with both of us. She is still a fabulous woman and both of us know how good we were together, but things happen.

My break-up with Claire occurred at a really terrible time in my life. It was in fact the worst time of my life. I was fighting a legal battle with someone I considered a close friend. On top of this, my eldest son Rufus had been diagnosed with Lyme Disease and was in a dreadful physical, mental and potentially suicidal state. It is the only time in my life that the idea of ending it all did – albeit momentarily – come into my mind. I was lost.

I look back now and still remember the devastation I felt. But you get through. I kept going. Claire and I are now great friends and she remains hugely important to all of my family. My fight with my former employee is over and my fight for my son's health will continue – for as long as it takes to get him better.

Life is like a voyage on the sea. Out of clear blue skies storms come, they threaten to upend you and destroy you but you have to fight, to keep a steady hand on the wheel, and believe you will get through. And finally you will hit calmer waters.

Chapter 25

MADNESS – A BUSINESS LESSON (PART I)

WHEN BRIAN LEFT the company in 2000, and my marriage to Kate had broken up, apart from the emotional devastation I went through, the situation also left me with a very practical business problem.

The money I had paid to Brian in a very fair and amicable settlement created a massive hole in my finances. I also had to continue to support Kate and the children. I was juggling more than 20 companies under the umbrella name of Caudwell Group, which meant I was dealing with, and feeding, a multi-headed monster. Cash flow was an issue all the way through my career. Now I was at my borrowing limit with the banks, trying to keep everything going.

As always, I had a solution that was going to resolve a huge amount of stress for me. My service provider company, Singlepoint, was the most cash-hungry of all my operations. I knew I needed to sell it as to do so would bring in money and also off-load a storm that I could see gathering on the horizon for that whole business model.

When the mobile phone industry started up, the service providers were extremely valuable. It was a business that relied entirely on getting customers. You would buy a phone for, say, £400, and sell it for £50, but you would get £500 from the service provider who hooked them up with a network. But now, with Singlepoint, I was the service provider. Which meant that this money that was paid out, was ultimately coming from me. My value became the number of customers I had, yet I was paying my mobile phone companies for those customers.

By the end of 2000, 47 percent of households had mobile phones, the following year 64 percent. By 2003 it had risen to 76 percent, and the numbers were rapidly going up. When I started out in 1987, only one in a thousand Brits had a mobile phone, and business was a landgrab. It was survival of the fastest, the fittest and the best. That rush for customers, however, was rapidly coming to an end as more and more people owned phones which, in turn, meant that profit margins were being squeezed.

On top of that, new legislation was coming in left, right and centre, reducing call charges and international roaming. And, with the increasingly fast uptake of mobile phone customers, I could see that at some stage in the near future all service provider companies like Singlepoint – whose leverage had historically been their customers – could be under massive threat from any future actions taken by the networks.

Technology, it seemed, was moving at the speed of light. I sensed how that could spell trouble for the mobile phone business. A thousand miles away in Scandinavia, two young entrepreneurs, Niklas Zennström and Janus Friis, were working on a revolutionary idea called Skype. It was founded in 2003 and would eventually offer free chat services to customers all around the globe. I knew the communications world was changing. In short, I wanted out before my still-hot property went stone cold.

*****

AS I AM a businessman, I want to explain in detail how this all worked out because it explains a lot about the way I operate. Making a deal to sell a business like this takes time. You need to plan ahead. You have to get every aspect of your business in the most seductive shape possible, in order to entice suitors. You must target all the potential purchasers, find out everything you can about the way they do business. You also need to have Plans A, B and C, accommodating all eventualities. And you need to know exactly the right time to get the word out that you are thinking of selling.

In my career, few deals are done in gentlemen's clubs, over a bottle of vintage claret and a handshake. This sort of deal is all about presentation of a quality business, intelligence (in both senses of the word) and brinksmanship. You have to be prepared to switch in a split second from Queensbury rules to a street fight.

I am a forward thinker. If I see a tiny plume of smoke on the horizon (like the rapid rise in customers and continuing legislation) I hone in on it. I focus on it and work out what consequences it could present. I never ignore it.

By 2002, I was ready to go into action. Singlepoint had around two million customers with a split between two networks: Vodafone, which had 1.2 million of those customers; and Cellnet, which had the other 800,000. At this point in time, the balance of power was still on my side and these customers were extremely valuable to the networks as a big influx of customers increased their share of the market.

Selling a business is complex.

You need to simultaneously build desire and sometimes fear in your prospective buyers. Desire to have what you possess, and the fear that it could go to someone else; they could lose it. You also have to keep your management team on your side.

They will be bought out with your business and your buyer could try and turn them 'native', which means they could end up fighting you from within, handing over information and generally undermining your position. You need your team – and I had a brilliant team – to be loyal to the very end, and you have to manage them shrewdly to achieve that objective.

I was under monster stress. In many ways it was a dress rehearsal for the big company sale to come in 2006, but I needed to do it right. I had to be sure of every move. I also had to keep all my other businesses buoyant, and not let any of the plates I was juggling slip and crash to the ground. I cut down the hours I slept so that I could constantly stay on top of everything.

I drove myself – and everyone else – hard. I have an unnatural capacity to handle stress, but it was incredibly tough. I was 50 years old. Over the years I'd seen brilliant, strong men buckle under pressure. I could not let that happen to me.

I knew Vodafone were the natural buyers. They were the biggest network and had a policy of buying up valuable operations like mine in order to increase their share of the market and become the biggest fish in this particular sea.

I knew it wasn't going to be easy. I'd watched Vodafone buy-outs from the sidelines before, consciously taking note of every move, every small detail. They were smart. But I knew their strategy. Go in high and then relentlessly start chipping down.

It's like when you are selling your house and you get this great offer, which you accept with a happy smile and reject all those other lesser offers. Then the surveys are done, insurers and builders flood through your property with clipboards and all sorts of equipment.

All seems good. So you put an offer in on that perfect house you want to buy and it's accepted. Then suddenly months down the line, the buyer of the house you are selling knocks down the price right, left and centre for possible dry rot, signs of boiler trouble, roof problems. The original price that you agreed now drops like a stone. You are left with poor choices. Drop the sale, put it back on the market – inevitably at a lower price – and risk losing your dream home. Or accept and take the hit.

I was not, however, planning on being the loser.

*****

AS I HAVE said already, I am not a ruthless man. I am tough, I am up-front and I stick to my word. I expect others to do exactly the same. If they don't, then I will go into action. I shall do whatever it takes to save my business.

The chief executive of Vodafone was Gavin Darby. Once it had become known on the grapevine that Singlepoint was up for sale, we met at his office in Newbury. I had two million customers. I had a management team at Singlepoint that was second to none. Everyone in the business knew – and I'd made sure they did – that Vodafone's main rival Cellnet had been sniffing round, as had several other smaller companies.

For the time being, power was in my hands. Desire was in the room. Now I just had to instill a hint of fear.

'I know the way it works at Vodafone, Gavin,' I said in my usual direct manner. 'You guys are notorious for trying to chip away the price after you put in the offer. But if the offer you make is right, then that is the offer I take. I want you to know I'm not going to be screwed around.'

I still think Gavin is a good guy, but just as I had a game to play, Vodafone also had a game to play. They made me a good offer, which was provisionally accepted. Then came their due diligence – the accountants, the lawyers, the merchant bankers, you name it came through the door – and then, as I predicted, the first hint of a chip to their offer was officially made known to me.

Fear could no longer be a hint. Fear was now my main player.

MADNESS – A BUSINESS LESSON (PART I)

I went to see Gavin. My mind was completely clear and focused. I knew exactly what I was going to do. Everything in my life had prepared me for battles like this, from way back, jumping off the highest roof as a kid, and watching the bigger boys back down from my dares. The endless fights with Motorola, and even the way I'd dealt with Belstaff when I was 19.

I knew what my reputation was in the mobile phone industry. I was one half of the Dangerous Brothers, the Caudwell men who raced the fastest and never turned down a chance – on those corporate jollies – to take on the toughest, most extreme challenges, even if it meant breaking the occasional bone. I was unpredictable. I wore Marks & Spencer suits, shoes that were only replaced once they were completely worn down and – regardless of my top-of-the-range cars – I rode a bike to work. I didn't fit in any mould. I said exactly what I thought. But it was to my advantage that I was viewed by most as a wild card.

I had previously warned Gavin that if he screwed me I would press the nuclear button of mutually assured destruction and sell the business to the highest bidder outside Vodafone. This would have been devastating for me but also immensely damaging to Vodafone's share price, and we both knew it.

I had been very clear. I had told them that if they tried to chip the price it would be terminal.

I was raging and, deliberately, I did not hide it. I wanted him to think I was capable of doing something insane. At times, in business, there is nothing more powerful than appearing like a mad man. And because it's a technique I've used, it's something I always wonder about Donald Trump. Is he insane or is it an act?

Whatever it is, the power play between him, a nuclear button and North Korea's leader Kim Jong-Un certainly forged an interesting relationship which is worth studying.

'John, it's just the process,' Gavin began, but I cut him off mid-sentence.

'That's it,' I said. 'I'm going to sell to Orange or 121. I'm done with Vodafone.'

'But that makes no sense at all,' said Gavin patiently. My management team sat impassively, making it clear they were all on my side. But every single person in the room knew it would be an insane move. The offer I had from Vodafone was more than £400 million. To sell to Orange or 121 was an act of insanity because I would only be able to do a low-grade deal, where I'd get paid for every customer I persuaded to migrate – nothing like the money I'd get from Vodafone.

'Gavin, I would rather do that than have any more dealings with Vodafone,' I said very calmly and decisively. 'It's over.'

*****

SO WHAT HAPPENS next? This is the psychology of negotiation. A dangerous game. You can't make empty threats; you have to stick to your plan, even if your real plan is to make Vodafone come crawling back with the original deal – no chips.

Gavin was not the only person who thought it was madness to set up deals with Orange or 121. The chief executives of Orange and 121 thought so, too. I could not be serious, they said. So I had to persuade them that I was. They were going to be my stalking horses. Vodafone had to believe that I was prepared to go through with it, prepared to blow myself up, rather than have anything more to do with them. And they had to believe that their smaller rivals, Cellnet, Orange or 121, were going to somehow get the deal of a lifetime.

I turned on the charm. I went to visit Orange, Cellnet and 121 and entered into preliminary discussions. Although they must have suspected they were stalking horses, they had to engage and bought my line that, 'I'd rather sell my customers to you, than have my business taken over by those guys.' That said maybe I would if Vodafone had not come back to the party? Of course, they had to engage, in case my insanity carried through. I still wonder to this day what would have happened if Vodafone had not come back to me.

I wanted to be seen in their offices. I was loud in my arrivals at the competitor networks, making my presence known, making sure my signature was very clear in the signing-in books at Reception – purely to inflame industry gossip. The occasional email to Orange, arranging yet another meeting, might be sent by mistake to Vodafone.

In the meantime, I refused to take calls from anyone at Vodafone. I knew some people did wonder whether I was feigning madness, or actually losing the plot, and that was something I had to address.

I assured my management team that I knew precisely what I was doing. I am not sure that they believed that. I had to appear to my managers that I might be totally irrational for fear they would be loose-lipped. You have to cover yourself for every eventuality. And so it was that Vodafone was completely shut out and if they weren't they were getting the message that I wanted them to receive.

As the weeks passed, Vodafone's fear and desire must have increased. For my part, I never, for one second, stopped courting the other networks, never took my eye off the ball with Singlepoint and carried on growing sales as fast as possible.

*****

A COUPLE OF months in, negotiations were moving forward with my stalking horses when Gavin called me and asked how Vodafone could get back into the process. Now Gavin and I were more than just business friends. We'd spent a day together with our families at Alton Towers and they'd all stayed over at Broughton.

That day everyone had screamed their way through rollercoaster rides but now we were on a very different – equally terrifying – ride and right now, I didn't exactly have my seatbelt fastened.

But I couldn't let him see that.

I played hard ball and told him I could not see any way that Vodafone could get back in on a trusted basis, since they had already broken that trust and that I was a long way down the road with other potential buyers.

Days passed and back Vodafone came, wanting to talk. 'No.' I said, politely, but softening my stance, by saying, 'I don't know how I could trust you,' giving them a little foot in the door. Each time they came back I rejected their advances, but I also always left them with a small amount of hope, an idea that they could still change my mind.

In reality, however, it was me reaching the highest point of the rollercoaster, about to go over the edge, with no idea if the carriage would hold. Selling customers off individually to Orange or 121 would have been ruinous. If Vodafone didn't buy my company, the damage would have meant any worth I had to any other network was seriously eroded. In addition, I also had my back against the wall with borrowing and cash flow.

I had to believe that my plan would work.

Looking back, I imagine I lost quite a few hundred hair follicles just waiting for the right moment for things to fall properly into place. But warfare is divided into three levels – strategic, operational, and tactical – and I had played all my cards.

Now it was about waiting it out.

I had no guarantees. The only real knowledge I had was that even though, to me, my company would in a few years be as worn-down as the shoes on my feet, right now it still looked, shiny, polished and very desirable to Vodafone. Indeed, it was a fantastic potential acquisition for them and I knew that. I have always been a long-term thinker, but a huge amount of people in business only have short-term strategies. I still knew that I was right at the top of their agenda but I wasn't backing down. I wasn't going to 'talk'. Talking would get me nowhere. Only a solid offer would do.

Months passed since my preliminary meeting with Gavin and then finally I got the call I had been waiting for. The call I was now desperate for. Vodafone pretty much guaranteed me the price they were going to pay.

In the summer of 2003 the deal was finally done for £405 million. I had the money that I needed but a second plan was forming in my head. The stress was getting too much and I didn't know how much longer I could take it, or, in truth, I should probably say wanted to take it.

I knew that I wanted to sell everything.

Chapter 26

MY WAY – A BUSINESS LESSON (PART II)

WHEN I FIRST came into her life, Kate's wonderful mum, Jean, had me down as a 'motorcycle hooligan'. In my black leather jacket and scruffy old trousers, I must have looked like a real loser to her.

Over the years she came to love me as a son, just as my mum loved Kate as a daughter. That never changed. I adored Jean and I still miss her very much.

Every so often, up until she passed away at the beginning of 2020, I would invite her to my home for a cup of tea and a chat, and she loved to take a ride around Broughton's beautiful grounds on the miniature railway. I smiled when I was told of the framed photo of me she kept in her hallway, the confirmed atheist sitting alongside a photograph of the revered head of the Roman Catholic church, Pope John Paul II. The two Johns. 'I'm so proud of you,' she'd often tell me, giving me her big, warm smile. I later heard how she used to talk to all her friends and neighbours about her 'genius businessman' son in law.

Jean had a lot of faith in the two Johns. Pope John Paul and me. I found this touching and amusing in equal measure.

But I also had faith in myself. I had to. I had faith when I was that teenager on the motorbike that I was going to ride into a better future. I had faith when I was working at Michelin, trading Belstaff jackets, selling cars on a freezing November morning, scraping ice

266

off windscreens and belting up and down motorways to find precious bargains at the auctions. I believed, even in the early days when I couldn't shift a single phone, that I would one day be a successful communications entrepreneur. And now I was.

Writing this book, I've had time to think about what motivated me. I remember the sensitive little boy in the dark, scruffy house in Wellesley Street who was told by his grandma that the family had once been successful and respected. I still recall that awful feeling of being pushed about by bullies, and having to toughen myself up and learn to deal with them.

I remember wishing I could change things, bring that wealth and security back to my mum, dad and grandma who worked so hard and struggled to get by. From childhood, I felt a huge weight of responsibility to change not just my life, but the lives of everyone around me.

And I'd done it.

I had wonderful, loving, intelligent children who would never want for anything, fabulous homes, a helicopter, incredible cars, a beautiful boat – all the trappings of wealth – but, more importantly, love and support.

'You're a lucky man, John,' I was constantly told.

*****

THIS MAY SURPRISE people, but I do not consider myself 'a lucky man'. The way I see it, luck has rarely been on my side. The dictionary defines luck as being, 'success brought about by chance, rather than one's own efforts'.

When I think back over my days of building my communications business, all I remember is constantly having to put in almighty, Herculean efforts to reverse unfortunate situations that I found myself in. And always I had to have absolute faith in my judgement – regardless of what anyone else thought.

I was always fighting, fighting, fighting – borrowing money, spinning plates, clearing up messes, strategising, endlessly trying to think long-term for my business but acting today to keep my staff happy, defending us against attackers, and growing the profitability whilst improving the quality of earnings. Years went by with me sleeping just three to five hours a night. Often there was no sleep at all. There were times when I made myself ill, but I couldn't afford to stop because I knew everything could come crashing down around my feet. I never really believed that I had built an empire – just a towering house of cards that permanently threatened to collapse if I stopped running to shore up everything.

If you've ever seen the brilliant, nail-biting movie Speed with Keanu Reeves and Sandra Bullock, that's what I felt like running my business. I had to keep everything going at a certain speed – whatever obstacles were thrown in my way – or else the whole thing would blow. Day in, day out, on top of anything and everything going on in my personal life that was the monstrous stress I lived with for two decades.

*****

AFTER I MADE the deal with Vodafone to sell Singlepoint, my mind was made up to sell. Again – as I explained in the previous chapter – you need to think of every angle, you need to strategise, gather intelligence, build desire and fear, but first, with a huge, multi-faceted company like mine, you need to keep your own counsel until you are ready to make a move and take a long, hard look at what you have.

First, you must know how you are going to position your crown jewels, the one irresistible piece to put in your shop window to dazzle buyers and build desire.

Phones 4u was my crown jewels. A phenomenal amount of cash had gone into the expansion of my shops all over the country. I was under pressure to get into the best, most profitable shape, a business model for the industry. I needed to trim any fat.

In business, I do things my way. Yes, I study figures and read reports and spend most of my life working furiously away behind a desk, but there comes a point when other methods are required. There are moments when you don't want reports from regional and area managers. You want to go and do things your way, see what is happening with your own eyes. And when the occasion requires it, I believe in a direct, feet-on-the-ground approach.

My journey towards selling everything began on an autumn morning in October 2003, a couple of months after the sale of Singlepoint. I woke up at 5am, spent half an hour in the gym and had a frugal-but-healthy breakfast of fresh fruits. Then I left the house on my bike at six, to cycle to Birmingham to visit a Phones 4u outlet. I arrived at 8.30am. It was closed. I waited with my bike and watched people walking past on their way to work, clocking the footfall in my head. At 9.30, I saw a guy in a suit – the manager – walking towards the shop.

'Morning,' I said. 'Why don't you open at 8am? I've seen lots of people walking past. They could be potential customers.'

He did a double-take. No doubt his heart sank when he realised it was me, John Caudwell, boss of the whole company, with his bike outside his shop.

'There's no trade,' he said. 'They are all on their way to work. It's not worth it.'

I said nothing. Now I fully understand I may be very intimidating, and it makes me chuckle now to think of the poor guy being faced with me, unannounced in my cycling gear, on a cold but sunny Monday morning. All I was concerned about then was getting answers, observing my business on the ground and finding out information. We went into the shop. The interrogation continued.

'How many mobile phones have you sold this month?' I asked.

'None,' he answered, trying not to look uncomfortable. 'I'm the manager. I manage the team. I don't sell.'

I was genuinely confused. 'How can you manage a team if you're not selling? How are you going to understand any issues with customers, questions about tariffs? How on earth can you get any feedback, or know what to get your staff to focus on, if you are not selling yourself?' To me this was basic common sense. He looked blank. The veritable rabbit caught in the headlights.

'You need to be one of the best salesman in the shop,' I continued, genuinely horrified by what I was hearing. 'You need to lead by example. Give the staff targets, show them how it's done. These shops are here to sell mobile phones not to manage staff.' The poor guy was flushed in the face but he gamely stood his ground and shook his head.

'But what about all the emails I have to answer from head office?' he stuttered, opening up his computer and showing me yards and yards of emails clogging up his inbox. 'There's four hours' worth of emails to answer here. I have to go through all of them and answer the relevant ones. That's what I do all day, unless there's a problem in the shop.'

I stared at the computer, looking at the massive amount of names in the distribution box of each email. There were names of people from head office, area managers, regional managers, directors. Most of the emails were completely irrelevant to the manager of the Birmingham office who hadn't had time to sell a single phone since he was given the job.

'Thanks very much,' I said. I shook his hand and left. He looked like he needed a stiff drink to get over the shock of that 15-minute meeting. But I'd had a bigger shock.

And I had a revolutionary solution.

I cycled back to the head office in Stoke-on-Trent, and as I pounded the pedals on the 40-mile journey, what had happened was turning over in my head. I arrived in the office and immediately gathered my directors. 'Right,' I said. 'From tomorrow I'm banning all company emails. No-one is to send emails from this office.'

They looked at me in horror. Possibly some of them believed I was still stuck in my 'feigned madness' routine from the previous year, but I was deadly serious.

'Emails are the cancer of business,' I announced. 'You're all sending out hundreds of huge group distribution emails. Most of them are completely irrelevant. I have managers who should be selling, but they're spending every hour answering emails to head office, and people here are spending yet more hours sending yet more emails back and forwards. Wasted time is wasted money and wasted opportunity. This has to stop.'

There was immediate uproar, with everyone telling me that the business would be plunged into chaos and confusion. I eventually agreed to set up a night shift, where one bulletin would go out every night for managers, area managers and regional managers to read the following day.

All of the directors were shaking their heads in disbelief as they left my office that day. I knew that even my very top team was dead against me. Evidently they thought I was on a kamikaze mission. But I knew that I was right. I had absolute faith in my decision. I had looked at those emails and approximately one in 100 had any relevance whatsoever to the recipient. Think of the time wasted. We were in the telecommunications business, if there was a serious problem just pick up the phone and call. Or even better, go and check out the high street shops. At the same time, I put in targets for every Shop Manager, Area Manager, Regional Manager and Sales Director in the business to sell phones.

This in itself made a huge difference, but there were half a dozen other equally dramatic key actions that transformed the business over a short space of time.

Within a year, our profits had risen by £100 million. I later worked out that the email Bermuda Triangle had been costing about £20 million a year. Since they had been banned, sales were going through the roof, managers were given better targets and incentives to open shops earlier if they believed it would increase trade. Now the Phones 4u brand was shining like a real jewel.

*****

A YEAR LATER, I am gearing up to sell. It's 2004 and I can tell a recession is on the horizon. No-one is talking about it, there's nothing on the news, nothing forecast in the financial papers. In Britain, the nation swings from news stories on the British and American war with Iraq to endless excitement about a new television show called The X Factor, which sucks up millions into a fever of excitement about who is going to win a £1 million record deal.

The Labour Prime Minister, Tony Blair, and a former record company executive, Simon Cowell, are the most talked about men in Britain. As far as the economy goes, life seems great for most people with plenty of distractions to keep the nation occupied. But I see those small plumes of smoke on the financial horizon and I know trouble is coming.

I did not feel a tell-tale chill in my bones and this was no gut feeling. The signs were there; you just had to look carefully to see them.

MY WAY – A BUSINESS LESSON (PART II)

Banks were lending huge amounts of money compared to peoples' salaries and there was a feeling of great euphoria in the economy under Blair's government. But the economy is like a balloon – if it gets too inflated too fast, the inevitable happens. It bursts.

Well before my prediction became a reality, I had to get a sale together. I knew it would be a logistical nightmare. My last sale had been one company, Singlepoint. Now I was selling a big collection of diverse companies – from insurance, to distribution, to recruitment, mobile phone sales and repairs, all under the name the Caudwell Group. Splitting them up might seem the obvious solution but colossal tax implications made that absolutely prohibitive for me. I wanted one buyer for the whole lot.

By 2006 we were at the height of the boom for private equity firms. We went into the market and had indicative offers, and from some groups there were no offers at all (possibly they could see what I could see coming). But two were in the frame to buy me out – Bain Capital and Doughty Hanson.

*****

NOW, WE ARE talking about more than a billion pounds. That's the sort of figure that makes people start to lose their heads, but not me. I was incredibly cautious. I felt exactly how I had with Vodafone. I was not there to be messed around.

This was a business that I had built through blood, sweat, tears and years of sacrifice, and no one was going to try and turn me over at the last minute.

'Bain,' announced my advisors at one of our preliminary meetings. 'Bain are the best option. They are our best chance.' Every single person around the table – merchant bankers, bankers, corporate bankers, lawyers and directors, nodded enthusiastically in agreement. Meetings went ahead. I took note of everything. Again, I don't believe in gut feelings, for me it's about constantly observing – it's always the small things that give people away.

It could be a limp handshake, a strange glance, a smile you feel is false or a chance remark that sounds a distant alarm in your head. Months in, I wasn't comfortable, movement was slow, a couple of low-level warning shots were fired across the bow.

In our last meeting with Bain I got extremely nervous. I felt that they were going to mess us about until they bought the business for nothing, or the deal fell through. I had no proof, nothing but faith in myself that I knew what I was doing. I decided to throw them out of the process, much to the horror of my entire team. My rationale was if they really wanted the business they would claw their way back in and, if they didn't as I suspected, they would have never fulfilled the deal but chipped away until we were all completely demoralised.

'I want out of Bain,' I announced to everyone. There was silence. By now everyone had mentally spent the huge sum of money that was coming their way. No-one wanted to jeopardise this deal. When you are talking more than a billion, a lot of people are prepared to look away from those little nuances, those slightly negative remarks and cynical smiles, and pretend they never happened.

'John, you're just nervous,' one of the lawyers said. 'Bain are the right buyers.'

'Tell them it's off,' I said decisively. 'My feeling is they are going to pull out in a few months and if they don't pull out they are going to knock us down so low it's not worth it.

'If they are serious they will come back. Let's leave it at that.'

I saw blood drain from the faces around me. But I felt sure this was the right call.

I had to come up with another plan. We needed more potential buyers and somehow we had to get them interested without it appearing that we were somewhat desperate. Whilst my advisors shrewdly made moves towards other potential parties in the market telling them they had an amazing opportunity for them, I contacted the brilliant businessman and former Tory politician, Archie Norman. Archie, who is now chairman of Marks & Spencer, was setting up his own private equity company and I entered into a lengthy negotiation with him. Things started to move in the right direction. After many weeks of massively high-pitched stress we had two credible buyers, both of whom seemed to genuinely want to perform and a deal was structured between Providence Equity Partners and Doughty Hanson.

I knew this could work. But I also knew – with my vast experience of dealing with crises – that one wrong move could see this all fall apart.

*****

BY NOW MY stress levels were stretched to breaking point. This was everything I had ever worked for. At home I rarely discussed work, but this time my family knew I was selling everything. My daughter, Libby, remembers casually saying to me, 'But Dad, what are you going to do with yourself when you sell the business? I can't believe you want to sell it.'

I practically self-combusted on the spot. 'Have you no idea what pressure I've been under? How tough things are?' I rounded on her. It wasn't exactly fair on poor Libby but all of a sudden she got a small dose of the torrent of frustration and anxiety that had been pent up in me for so many months. She was genuinely stunned.

'But I've never ever heard you say any of this before. I thought you loved it,' she answered. My anger dissolved as I looked at her face. I hugged her. 'Not any more,' I said.

I was as near to closing the deal as I could ever be but, as ever,

I felt nothing was guaranteed. Providence and Doughty Hanson were straightforward, and all transactions were clean and absolutely honourable. The combined figure came to £1.46 billion and virtually all the due diligence and negotiations were complete.

When the day came, and we were all ready to gather in a room to do the deal – and take more money than we could ever have possibly dreamed of – the whole thing unravelled.

'It's a tax issue,' Craig Bennett, my brilliant financial director and number two, explained anxiously, the stress writ large on his face. 'We need to resolve the tax issues or everyone is going to be penalised. It's going to take a few more days but I think we can solve it.'

Now I had to trust them. I signed papers in advance and told Claire we were going to take my new boat on a trip. I didn't want to wait around. On 26th September, 2006, a beautiful sunny day, I had my hands on the wheel of the boat when my phone rang. It was Craig. 'Congratulations John,' he said.

I don't think I even replied. I looked at the clear blue waters ahead and felt like Atlas with the weight of the world falling off my shoulders. Claire ran to get a bottle of champagne and we toasted the sale in the middle of the ocean.

Those dreams I had at seven didn't even come close. I was a billionaire. I didn't jump up and down, I didn't burst into tears. I just felt completely at peace for one perfect moment.

*****

THE TEARS DID come. But not for several months. The moment of peace lasted for only one moment. My immediate concern – because of my conviction there would be an impending financial disaster coming – was to split my money into five different banks to spread any risk. It would be two more years before certain banks did collapse, but I was already on overdrive, working out how to manage this vast amount of money. A First World problem.

There were other issues. Strange issues. I no longer owned my own email; I had no staff other than Michele my wonderful PA. The vast, sprawling infrastructure that I had built up over twenty years disappeared from beneath my feet. For once in my life I was in complete limbo. Michele and I now laugh over my words, 'There won't be much to do. You've worked really hard, so now you can put your feet up and file your nails.' I know she would tell you she's never once had a single moment in these past years to put her feet up or file her nails.

'I want to have a party for everyone who ever worked for us,' I said to Craig, who, along with Brian, had owned 15 percent of the Caudwell Group. This was a week or so after the deal had been done and I was – with Michele's help – slowly but steadily rebuilding a new team around myself.

'Great idea,' he said, immediately.

'It has to be really special,' I told him. 'This deal will change our lives and I want to give every long term member of staff a month's money for every year they have worked for us over five years. But that has to be a surprise.'

'That sounds brilliant, John,' said Craig. 'I can't think of a better way to say goodbye.'

We held the party at the back of the old offices in Stoke, in a giant marquee. We had bands, music, great food and 1,000 members of our former staff all on top form, out to enjoy themselves, drinking champagne and dancing up a storm. I went to the podium. I was incredibly excited about the big surprise in store for them which we'd all managed to keep secret.

First, I made a speech, themed around Sinatra's greatest song, My

Way, which had by then become an anthem of mine. Then, I called out, 'Ladies' and dozens of girls who had been hidden from view walked into the room bearing individual envelopes, each with the name of a member of staff, each envelope filled with money. The total amount we'd put in the envelopes was £3.5 million.

'And now,' I said. 'We want to personally thank you for all your hard work and loyalty, and give you all a token of our appreciation.'

The girls dashed round the room, handing out envelopes. There were screams, there were tears, there was laughter as each member of staff discovered the money inside. Some got £15,000, some half of that, but everyone was delighted at the unexpected gift.

It was a magical night. I had people coming up telling me what a difference that money would make to their lives – a dream holiday, paying the rent, a trip to see a long lost relative. 'John Caudwell, can I kiss you?' shouted one older lady, grabbing me in a bear hug. I had never felt so close or so happy to be with the people who I'd spent years working beside.

I was fully aware I was a man who had a reputation in business for being tough, and that made me the success that I was. But the greatest satisfaction I got in my career was not being tough, but being kind and generous. And that night, surrounded by people who'd worked as secretaries, in telesales, on the ground floor of the distribution plant – that was the moment when everything really hit home. The building of the business, all those years I'd worked, my staff, the sale, the money.

And it was then that I cried.

Chapter 27

ON MY FIRST SON…

BUSINESS WAS MY work life but my life has not all been about business. Far from it.

Rufus, my first-born son, was my golden child. From the moment he was born on 2nd April, 1995, he was one of those special babies that glowed.

On any given day when I was out and about with him, I was sure to be stopped by instantly besotted ladies. 'What a beautiful baby,' they'd say. And I'd agree. He had white blonde hair, big, blue eyes, and a huge infectious smile which he'd happily flash at any admirer.

Regardless of the painful break up which Kate and I were going through when he was very young, Rufus was a contented little soul. His sisters adored him. Rebekah was 16 when he was born, and Libby was seven. They both mothered him, endlessly playing games with him and making him laugh.

The older he got, the more I realised what a smart boy he was. He talked early and, like the girls, he loved books and he loved to draw. He was nothing like I was as a child. He was the little prince of the family; funny, sure of himself and charming. He developed an early talent for music. He has this incredible singing voice and wanted to learn to play instruments. As the years went by, he had hours where he would be totally lost in his music, and I'd listen to him marvelling at the way he could naturally deconstruct a song, emphasise the right phrase or add his own sweet, little twist to a recording.

My boy had bullet-proof confidence. And that amazed me.

But it also slightly alarmed me. He would chat away to anyone; however much older they were than him. I worried he might appear precocious, so every now and again I'd remind him how privileged he was, and how important it was to be aware of that and those less fortunate than him and to appreciate everything around him.

I didn't lavish gifts on him – or any of my children – but, even as a toddler, Rufus was used to skiing like a pro, sailing, visiting fine places and being driven in beautiful cars. So I'd emphasise the importance of humility, caring for others – and he took it all in, nodding seriously as we spoke. 'You've got a lovely boy there,' friends would tell me. I had, but I would always give the credit for that to Kate.

Rufus absolutely shone. I remember when he was maybe six years old, and Claire and I were in a restaurant in Juan-Les-Pins. It was a lovely night, a cosy family restaurant, and Rufus got chatting to various people on various tables and then he just got up and started singing. The whole restaurant applauded. Rufus took a bow like a little professional. Claire and I were on our feet clapping.

A year or so later, he came along with me to our Employee of the Year awards, a night I referred to as the Oscars of Caudwell Communications. He was all dressed up in a tuxedo and bow tie, and as we sat at the table I said, 'How do you fancy singing tonight?'

He grinned at me and said, 'Tell me when.' He jumped up on that stage, cool as a cucumber, burst into his version of Maroon 5's She Will Be Loved. His voice was fantastic, but it was his movements, mannerisms and his cute looks that completely wowed the audience. He sang the song like a 40-year-old veteran with real attitude, not like an eight-year-old kid.

On another occasion, when Rufus was a similar age, a group of us were in a Spanish restaurant, laughing and joking. A table a few metres away were in uproar, laughing much louder than us and much more continually. We looked over and there was Rufus holding court with a group of people telling them stories and entertaining them, to their huge delight.

Robbie Williams' dad, Pete, who was a friend of mine, came to dinner at my home and saw Rufus performing in the Great Hall. He leaned in towards me and said, 'I've only ever seen one kid like that before – and that was my Robbie.' I have to say I felt a little uncomfortable when he said that. Genius though Robbie is, he was also a very troubled soul for a while, and there was no way I ever wanted my beautiful boy to have those sorts of problems in his life. That, I told myself, was never going to happen.

*****

A DISASTER CAN come out of nowhere. A sink hole. You don't see it coming. And I, the man who in business prides himself on seeing the tiniest specks on the horizon, saw nothing to worry about with my son.

It was a Sunday night in Broughton in 2005. Rufus, who was then ten years old, had spent the weekend with Claire and me.

Back then, Kate had a beautiful house near Manchester, and Rufus – who was a border at the same school the girls had been to, Packwood Haugh – split his exeats between the two of us. Everything in my personal life seemed to be completely on track. We'd celebrated Kate's 50th birthday at my home a few weeks earlier, and the words of her speech – 'Life doesn't get better than this' – were ringing in my ears and making me smile.

'Come on Rufus, time to go,' I said to him, looking at the kitchen clock. It was 7pm. He had to be back at school by 8pm. We needed to leave within the next five minutes. Rufus looked at me. 'I don't want to go.'

I'd been through this before, especially with Libby, and I knew the routine. You stick to the plan, regardless of the inevitable tantrums. If you don't, then you are simply storing up problems. I reminded all my children, 'You chose to go to this school, this is not a debate.' And on the hour-long journey in the car, you talk things through. Find out if there are any issues, suggest solutions but always stick to the plan. I wanted my children to learn the lesson that if they made a decision to do something or go somewhere, they had to stand by their choice. And Rufus had been very keen to go to the same school as Libby and Rebekah.

'Get your things together. We've got to leave now.'

'No.'

'Come on Rufus.' Now I was exasperated.

'No, Dad. I can't go.'

We carried on like this for ten more minutes. I was getting nowhere. This wasn't like Rufus. I tried to hug him, reason with him, but when I pulled back and looked into his blue eyes, I saw something close to terror.

'What's wrong, Rufus?' I questioned him. 'Has something happened at school?'

He shook his head. 'I'm not going.' He was slowly becoming hysterical. Suddenly I felt very anxious indeed. It was as if the room had gone completely cold. Rufus and I were facing each other. I could see and feel genuine fear emanating from every pore of his body. And that made me terrified. This wasn't the usual Sunday night school blues; this was something entirely different. I didn't know what it was. But I felt our world had shifted.

*****

WHAT FOLLOWED WAS a slow descent into a nightmare. My

son, my beautiful, perfect, talented son, began to fall apart before our eyes. That night he stayed with me, and I called Kate to explain and waited for the morning. Nothing had changed. 'I'm not going to school,' he said, clutching the duvet around himself in his bed. We contacted the school to find out if there had been any issues, but no-one could come up with anything.

Claire's step-dad, Dr John, who had been with us when my mother had her stroke two years previously, suggested a good counsellor who Rufus could talk to. I arranged a meeting and Rufus sat with him, repeating over and over again that he wasn't leaving. The counsellor was equally baffled as to what the problem was. Weeks passed, months passed, and Kate finally persuaded him to go to a small local school. Rufus, however, refused to go unless she sat outside his classroom in case he needed to leave.

In the years that followed he became agoraphobic, emetophobic and increasingly anxious. Still there would be times he seemed like his old self, but it was clear that his confidence and shiny personality was getting subdued, and he was increasingly confined to the house.

We employed counsellors, doctors, specialists. None had any answers for us. I took matters into my own hands. I would fly to Kate's house, and then get him into my helicopter. It was pretty traumatic but I was desperate. Just getting him to sit in it was painful. Then I'd switch the blades on and he'd go rigid with fear, gripping a glass of water in his hand so hard that his knuckles turned white. Slowly, slowly I'd increase the time in the helicopter and after weeks we finally flew back to Broughton. He stayed for about 15 minutes and wanted to go home.

I didn't give up. I kept increasing the hours until finally he stayed the night. Then, miraculously, we went to France on holiday for three weeks and he seemed almost completely back to his old self, laughing, joking, water sports, singing and dancing. He even said that he felt able to come to Vail with me in the winter for a ski holiday.

It was amazing. Our boy was back after four years in the wilderness. And then like a bolt of lightning, he suddenly started regressing at a rapid rate and within a few months was entirely back to his previous condition.

We were desperate. Desperately sad, desperately anxious and desperately stressed. We had miraculously got our boy back, for a few months, only to see him completely snatched away again.

For the next few years, from ages 15 to 18, he continued to deteriorate slowly. We really hoped that with puberty behind him and the possibility of hormone disruption, he would naturally improve. This was not the case. Indeed, it was the opposite.

For the next year a deterioration turned into crisis and Rufus became terrified of everything, his heart, his pulse, his breathing, generally of life. His emetophobia combined with gut sensitivity and nausea restricted his eating, both in terms of quantity and variety, causing him to become increasingly emaciated. At one point he would eat just Walkers crisps. We were so concerned for his health, we had a private nutritionist, Angelette Muller, come in to cook his foods. But we were beginning to lose the physical battle as well as the mental. It felt like everything was collapsing.

Through my charity work I have come across many, many sick children. I talk to the parents about how they cope. I look to see what we at Caudwell Children can do to alleviate in any way the relentless suffering of both child and parent. I always had empathy with these families, but now I understood exactly how it felt to have a child in constant pain with nowhere to turn. I was spending a fortune trying to find a diagnosis but things were getting worse and worse, and still we were all stumbling around in the dark.

The pressure was getting to all of us. Life should have been perfect. After everything I'd been through, I was now a billionaire with money to buy everything I wanted yet I could do nothing to help my son, no matter how hard I tried, regardless of how many avenues I explored.

Every so often he would have these terrifying attacks. He'd fall to the floor, clutching his heart screaming, 'Help me.' Paramedics would come and tell us nothing was wrong. 'It's a panic attack,' some said.

Doctors also said the same. 'He just needs to snap out of it,' one man muttered before he left. It was probably his fifth visit and he assumed we were wasting his time. We were all at our wits' end. Kate and the girls were beside themselves. Rufus was trapped in his own hell. It was like we were all screaming for help, but no-one could hear us.

At the same time, other parts of my life were being ripped apart. Everyone goes through struggles and you never have any idea what people – successful or otherwise – are dealing with. In my case things could not get worse. My 13-year relationship with Claire was coming to a devastating end and I was embroiled in an ugly and distressing fight with a former partner from a new business I'd set up in a legal case which would take three more years to come to court. I felt my world caving in. No amount of money, boats, beautiful homes or fabulous cars mattered.

For a few months, everything went black and, finally, I understood those desperate moments in which people decide to end their lives. But I knew I had to fight on, I knew I had more to do in life and I knew I couldn't give up on Rufus.

*****

I WAS SITTING in my charity office in Stoke. We were interviewing doctors for our soon to be built, Caudwell International Children's

Centre. We were talking about our work with autistic children, as I probed their knowledge on this subject and what they thought caused autism or contributed to it, and what they thought we could do to further improve the work that we were carrying out.

During the course of these interviews we became quite embroiled in how the health of the gut can play a significant part in mental health and, of course, this caused me to relay to them what was always at the forefront in my mind, Rufus.

The conclusion was that gut trouble could be playing a part in Rufus's mental health, so I asked them, 'Can you see my son?'

They did and came to the conclusion that this was much more serious than just the gut. We were referred to another professor, Basant Puri, who was hugely knowledgeable in a wide range of physical and mental conditions. The doctors noticed significant stretch marks on Rufus's back. I am not sure why we – the family – had never particularly honed in on these, probably because they seemed so insignificant in the scheme of things. How wrong that assumption was.

Professor Puri innocently gave a potential diagnosis of Bartonella, a co-infection of Lyme Disease that comes through a tick bite, and can cause serious neurological conditions, similar to those of Rufus. Blood tests were done, and it was confirmed. His Bartonella was through the roof. I was in LA when I got the call. The whole family were jubilant, albeit with a degree of caution. After nearly 10 years we now had a diagnosis that Rufus's sudden and unexplained mental illness had been caused by an infection transmitted by a tiny tick. The treatment was to be antibiotics and anti-inflammatories to control the infection and reduce the inflammation, and we should see big improvements in Rufus within months.

*****

ON MY FIRST SON...

I CANNOT TELL you how relieved and happy I was on that sunny morning in LA. I felt like I was floating through air. I was going to have my handsome, talented, charismatic son back. Yes 10 years were lost, but it is all about the future. The only trouble was, all the doctors and specialists we needed were in the London area which made it very difficult for them to spend the time travelling to Manchester.

We knew we had to relocate Rufus to London, but he could barely come out of his bedroom and for him the terror of travelling to London was too much. It was achieved in a horribly traumatic way – with the help of family and friends we had to force him 'kicking and screaming' to leave and finally he arrived at his new home in Audley Square.

From there on in, Rufus started his treatment and as he did the family became experts in Lyme Disease, its co-infections, symptoms and treatment. We read about it constantly and consulted experts, not just about Lyme Disease, but about inflammation, infections and chronic illness in general. We became so knowledgeable that we diagnosed ourselves with potential Lyme Disease due to one or two symptoms that each one of us had. We did the blood tests and sure enough almost all my entire immediate family had Lyme Disease, and started our treatment in the same house as Rufus, at the same time.

It was a bizarre time. Prior to my diagnosis, I had, months earlier done a charity bike ride from Land's End to John O'Groats in 2012. During the ride, I suffered from unexplained bouts of fatigue after physical exercise. Before the ride I could cycle 12 hours a day and yes, of course, feel fatigued, but it was a healthy fatigue. After the ride if I did two or three days with only a couple of hours a day, I would start feeling medically fatigued, something I can only describe as like a mild flu.

But this illness had a far more dramatic and sinister effect on Rufus. The rest of us had it to a far lesser extent. The whole family spent weeks together in my house in Mayfair strapped to IV drips as they pumped intravenous potions through our systems. But unfortunately, despite our bevy of expert doctors, our treatment and our own medical knowledge, Rufus did not get better and nor did we.

Definitions of any illness are words on a page. I have read more, know more, understand more about these conditions than many doctors. My daughter Rebekah – who, along with her incredibly supportive husband Nick, has sacrificed so much to help care for her brother – could do a PhD on the subject. But it seems that the more we knew the more we realised how little we knew. For every step forward we make, we have learnt to brace ourselves for two steps backwards. It is an endless preoccupation and that preoccupation has often made us far more ill – physically and mentally – than any actual illness.

The reality of my son's condition is that, since the age of ten, he has lived with depression, suicidal thoughts, pain, agoraphobia and an eternal feeling of failure. In Audley Square, Rufus only continued to deteriorate.

I have in my mind the devastating crystal clear image of Rufus sitting up in his bed, rocking backwards and forwards, pulling his hair out, screaming and sobbing. He told me wanted to kill himself but said he never would because he knew how much we loved him and how devastated we would be. My beautiful son, saying these words to me as I held on to him, feeling him just skin and bones. I remain haunted by this. From that moment on, I made sure someone was with him 24/7.

How do you get through all this? You do because you have to. The months rolled on, doctors came and went, more theories progressed yet nothing made any difference. On top of his physical issues, Rufus was getting to the point of malnutrition. We considered every option from psychiatric hospitals to private rehab clinics, but his gut was so devastated that we knew they would not be able to create the specialised diet that was essential to keep him alive and he would slip away even further, then be on a drip. That, we thought, would be the point of no return.

We never gave up hope, we kept researching and eventually came across an illness called PANS/PANDAS, which we had Rufus tested for. It came out positive. We now had yet another avenue to look at. PANS/PANDAS or Pediatric Acute-onset Neuropsychiatric Syndrome is an infection induced autoimmune condition that affects the brain function and can lead to the most severe depression. The symptoms of PANS/PANDAS could be almost identical to neurological Lyme Disease, but the treatment somewhat different.

Rebekah tracked down one of the world's leading experts, Jennifer Frankovich, who was based at Stanford Hospital, in Palo Alto, California. Over a period of time we made a plan to transfer Rufus to California, a seemingly impossible logistic nightmare for my boy who was so anxious, frail and at times terrified.

Kate – who had been badly affected by Lyme and also the stress of Rufus's situation – was not well enough to continue as his primary carer. Rebekah, who had already devoted a huge amount of her life to Rufus, said she would take over. It was another deeply traumatic move – it was not to be the last – but again it is something we did as a family so he could be under the treatment supervision of PANS/PANDAS experts.

And, amazingly, thankfully, it seems to have made my son's life a lot, lot better.

*****

RUFUS HAS VERY largely returned to us.

After the treatment he received at Stanford, we then moved him to

Los Angeles where Rebekah was now living and commuting out to Northern California to spend time with him. Thankfully we did as, unbeknownst to us, Covid-19 was about to hit and this would have left Rufus very isolated with only his carer for company.

Now in Los Angeles, in the dawn of Covid-19, Rufus was still suffering and with enormous courage, given his terror of leaving home, he took himself to a rehab clinic under his brilliant psychiatrist Dr Schiffman. There, for a whole year, he dedicated himself to recovery from alcohol, prescription drugs and from the mental ravages of 15 years of the terrible illnesses he had suffered, and from the traumas he had endured.

Two years on, I see the light coming back to my not-so-little-boy's eyes.

He sings again, he laughs again and he is able to visit nearby places in Los Angeles. Whilst he has not yet been able to fully combat the agoraphobia, after living in its grip for so many years, his recovery feels nothing short of miraculous. We put enormous effort into giving him every chance but ultimately only Rufus could rebuild himself. The way and manner he has gone about doing that is something that fills me with great pride and admiration.

Rufus's illness has shaped all of us. I've watched Kate fall apart. I've seen my daughters on their knees as they give their lives to helping Rufus. And me, the man who built a business from nothing to a £1.46 billion empire... I have been helpless.

I am not used to being helpless. I am not used to being unable to find solutions, however impossible the situation seems.

Often, I have felt like old King Canute, hopelessly trying to turn back the tide with my son. An illness like this is a wrecking ball in a family. It changes you all. Yet, finally, we have been given an opportunity to believe that Rufus can and will battle through the illness that has taken such a toll on him.

ON MY FIRST SON...

*****

I WISH YOU knew my son Rufus. He remains my special child. In spite of everything that he goes through, he still keeps trying, he can still make me laugh, and still he is the only member of my family who will sit for hours arguing a point with me. He looks at me knowingly, as if to say, 'I'm the only one who can beat you, Dad'.

One day I hope you will know my son. And you will know his entire story. He has a voice which should be heard, both as a musician and a public speaker. I know he could do so much good in the world, sharing what he has been through, educating and inspiring others to understand more, not only about Lyme Disease but also the ravaging impact of PANS/PANDAS, which affects one in 200 children yet is largely unheard of.

The fact that all the money in the world couldn't alleviate his pain has never frustrated me. There would never have been a moment in my life – however busy I was building my business – when I would not have tried to do everything in my power to help my son.

I am his father. Our relationship is massively important to me because I wanted it to be everything my relationship with my father was not. I have always wanted him to know he is loved beyond measure and that I would go to the ends of the earth to try and help him – or any of my children.

I want to say I could not be more proud of you Rufus for the way you have persisted and battled through, for your spirit and resilience. And whatever your life turns out to be, whatever path you take, we are so grateful to have you now, here, the smile back on your face, just as you are.

I am also incredibly proud that you have agreed to share some of your thoughts in this book, as my story is your story and your story mine.

Chapter 28

RUFUS'S STORY

By Rufus Caudwell

I AM FULLY aware that there are those who view me as the poor little rich boy, unable to cope with life. The boy who couldn't cope with being in the shadow of his incredibly successful father.

This is not the truth. In so many ways, I am the shadow my father lives in. He does not define my life. His life is now defined by me. By my illness, by my pain, depression and anxiety.

I never felt under any pressure to be my father. I was always my own person, with my own thoughts, opinions and taste, often in opposition to his. That was OK, for both of us. Dad does like his own way but he also likes people to have their own mind. Of course, I knew that my dad was a really successful man. Thanks to Dad, we had – if we wanted it – a lifestyle few people could ever imagine. There were glamorous parties, huge houses, massive boats and always lots of people around doing things for us or doing things with us.

One of my earliest memories of him was when I was very little, and we all lived at Broughton. I was crawling along the vast landing, what's called the Long Gallery. I bumped my funny bone and started to cry. Dad appeared, knelt down next to me and told me he could make me better with his magic hands. He rubbed my elbow and soon I was laughing.

I also remember him gently tickling my arm to make me fall asleep.

Dad was always pretty strict with me. Mum was soft, my sisters were soft but Dad was old school. He didn't like food being left on plates and answering back was not tolerated. I was a really outgoing kid but I was, I think, also a bit obnoxious and often cheeky. I was so used to being around adults but once I started school I had to work out how to communicate with other kids and that was a struggle until I discovered later on that I could be the class clown.

There wasn't any reason to worry about me. In hindsight I know there were little physical signs of the tsunami to come. Seemingly insignificant, but not. I want to say exactly what they were in case this alerts any parent to an inexplicable change in their child.

Researchers estimate that there were 8,000 new cases of Lyme Disease in the UK as recently as 2019. If the disease is not treated it can affect the brain and the heart. I have also been diagnosed with Lyme Carditis and PANS/PANDAS, which could affect up to one in every 200 children.

So this, I believe, was my first indication. It's a small, irritating thing. I was five or six and I woke up with this feeling that I had swallowed a hair. I couldn't get it out. I became obsessed with a hair being stuck in my throat. Then I refused to eat eggs, yoghurt or soup. A year or so later, I felt I had a lump in my throat. I couldn't swallow properly. It was worse when I lay down. I had to sleep propped up on five pillows. Maybe people thought I was just a very fussy child. Who knew what was to come.

*****

I CAN'T REMEMBER if I was ten or eleven, but I remember that day in the kitchen at Broughton, refusing to go to school. None of us deliberately disobeyed Dad and dug our heels in. But that night I was gripped by this feeling I can only describe as fear. I could not go back to my boarding school. I just couldn't. I didn't know what I was so fearful of. It was something inside me. This awful subterranean feeling that was mixed with something else I didn't at the time even know the words for – complete despair.

It made me panic. I was consumed by the most awful emotions which then started to affect me physically. My world drained of everything I knew. In the kitchen everything went monochrome; Dad, the walls, the floors, anything I looked at. I couldn't move. I remember Dad staring into my eyes and I knew that he was frightened, too.

That made things a hundred times worse. My dad wasn't scared of anything. Giant waves, motor-cross bikes, skiing accidents, knife-edge drives across cliff roads with sheer drops. But for the first time in the kitchen at Broughton I saw the fear in him – and it wouldn't be the last time.

*****

LIKE EVERYONE IN my family, I can describe in the greatest detail every aspect of my condition. Except I can tell you what happened day by day. I know all the medical terms and can remember with clarity not just every medication I've ever been on, but the precise dosage and the exact effects – good and bad – each had on me. I have kept a diary. I can tell you that when my blood samples were tested for Borrelia (the bacteria which causes Lyme) in a German clinic where 40,000 tests had taken place, the threshold indicating that you are positive is 128. Out of all the people tested previously, two people had come up with a test of 256. These were their most chronic cases. Mine came up as 512. The record.

There have been times since that first episode when life has almost returned to a version of normal. I went back to school 18 months after that first incident (a local day school). I learned to drive a car. I had a girlfriend when I was 17. I got into gaming and was really good at it. Then I started up my own gaming YouTube channel and had 60,000 followers.

After I left school at 16, I became passionate about my music. Dad, always wanting to encourage me, brought Robbie Williams on the phone to have a chat and Elton John offered to be a mentor. They are both great musicians but my style of music is more indie. I love Damien Rice, Bon Iver, Dermot Kennedy. Indie, folk, soul and a bit of pop. I never wanted to ride on my dad's coat-tails, always wanted to go my own way. They understood and were very kind. I believed in myself.

My relationship with my girlfriend, the love of my life, ended. I can't blame her. Depressive agoraphobics are no fun, really. My plan to perform at little music venues never took off because I couldn't face the thought of trying to get to them. What was I thinking?

I also sabotaged a £50,000 sure-win for me and the gaming team I'd put together because it involved a trip to London. My attempt to take my driving test ended because obviously it would involve actually going out on open roads. My world was my bedroom, my laptop, my family and, of course, doctors, life coaches, counsellors, therapists, specialists, carers, professors and anyone else my desperate family found to try and help me.

*****

IT TAKES FORTITUDE to have a chronic illness. Inevitably a few years in, your mental health becomes affected and there are fewer reasons to want to be alive. It takes fortitude to be around that person – my mum became ill with stress, my sister Becky took over. But it was always up to my dad to make the tough decision to move me from Mum's house to London, from London to Portola Valley, then to Los

Angeles and finally to a rehabilitation clinic where I received a lot of help – help that has changed my life.

I had a routine there. Therapy, meds and exercise. I did my washing and watched TV shows like Schitt's Creek (I can still laugh, you see) with the staff and the other inmates. That's what we were. Maybe the word 'client' or 'patient' was used. It was hard when people left but I always made an effort with the new people, showed them the ropes, pointed out the good guys among the staff, trying to find that balance between making them feel they had a friend and giving them that space. I missed my family. Covid-19 meant I wasn't able to see Mum and Dad or my brother and sisters – apart from Becky – for some time. That hurt.

But I digress. I want to try to be specific for two reasons. I want people to be aware of these diseases, of the effects of ill-health. I also want those people who see my dad at big, glamorous charity functions, and who envy him when he's there with his arm wrapped around Modesta... I want them to see that whatever big smile he has on his face, a part of his mind is always preoccupied with me or worrying about Rebekah or my mum. I've seen his sadness because I'm part of it.

We have fallen out many, many times in the past 15 years. I've been angry with him for pushing me. His certainty that he knows what is best for me has led to some of the most vicious violent rows and awful physical fights. I've often refused to speak to him and pushed him away. But he's never left me. That sadness drives him to keep pushing and it also drives him to raise more and more money for his charity to help other children. More than anything he's ever done in business, that's the thing I respect most about Dad.

*****

IT WAS NEW Year when I was 20 that I first thought I would never have a life. I would never be happy. The treatment for Lyme flooded my system with toxins. I turned into something from The Exorcist, screaming, smashing up my room, self-harming. 'Somebody kill me,' I kept wailing. My dad was there. 'I'd give anything to swap places with you,' he said, tears in his eyes. I knew he meant it but I wouldn't want him or anyone to be me.

A new phase began which I could not control. I started making these awful animal sounds of catatonic grief. My noises filled the house for weeks. It was unbearable. Then I began to have panic attacks about my tears. I had to stop myself crying at all costs. The noises stopped because the fear of crying became so great, and so my emotions shut down.

Months before that moment, just after my first diagnosis for Lyme Disease, Dad had moved me from Mum's to London. I will never forget the fight we had. I ripped off his shirt, kicked him, yelled at him. I wouldn't listen to him as he tried to stay calm and told me I was going to die if I didn't get proper help. I was hysterical for three hours before he managed to get me into the car, along with a medic, a life coach and Rebekah, to drive down to London. I remember that he sat in the seat next to me and grabbed my hand. I didn't even react. I had no emotions left. His hand just felt like a piece of meat to me.

*****

AND YET, TODAY, life feels very different. I look back on the past few years and know that I am, if not a recovered man, then one very much in recovery.

All I want to do now, in whatever small way I can, is to give hope to anyone similarly suffering, and hope to their families. At one point I saw no possible future for myself. Now, slowly but surely, I am rebuilding. My mind is no longer such a cruel place to live, the fear is not constant and I am better equipped to help my mind if it starts to spiral. Now I have a future, and I have a present that is not relentless pain.

I'm living in the hills in a beautiful house in Los Angeles amongst eagles and hummingbirds with my ever-loyal beagle, Eddy. My sister Rebekah lives 5 minutes away and we can wave to each other over the canyon which makes us laugh.

I have found my way back to music, and singing along with my guitar is my greatest passion. It has helped see me through so much and I've started writing my own songs. I also have aspirations to jump into the world of fashion at some point. I have a few friends in LA, though friendship is still hard for me to maintain. I live with my best girlfriend Vicky who (along with my best friend George) has been there to see me through. A wonderful lady, Lorraine, helps manage the house for me.

Between therapy, working out and music I find my days have gently filled. I take trips down to Sunset Strip for a manicure (I'm taking LA in my stride!) or to the local sports bar to watch Liverpool play. I wouldn't say I'm a jet-setter yet. The thought of aeroplanes still fills me with horror but I am quietly, day by day, building a life of meaning. A life with love and laughter. The life that for so many years I never thought was possible.

If I could end my chapter on one thing, it's this: it is never over, so please never give up hope. I know that I am in an extraordinary minority of people with the resources available to me. But even so, with time all things change. Medicine, and understanding of the mind, are always advancing. And with enough grit and endurance and, luckily for me, the support of an incredible family, life truly can change for the better. In love and gratitude to all my family; especially to Becky and Libby, my amazing mum who gave everything, and the patriarch of them all who never gave up, Dad.

Chapter 29

A BLONDE PONYTAIL

BY THE LATE winter of 2014, it became clear that neither I nor Claire could win each other back. Both of us had issues and strong feelings that prevented us from putting the effort in, though I did give a year to the possibility. It was over.

In business I can move mountains by force of will and strategy. In my personal life, I am subject to the same emotional wheel of fortune as everybody else. We had many talks into the night; there were many tears. But our happy thirteen years together had come to an unhappy end. We both had to move on.

I knew I wasn't ready for another relationship. There was too much going on in my life with Rufus, my court case with a former employee and coming to terms with Claire leaving. However, I wanted to push myself out of the darkness that had been enveloping me. I thought the company of a good woman would be a nice distraction.

I'd become friendly with the Hollywood actress, Eva Longoria. I'd helped her with her charity and we'd got on extremely well, or at least I thought. She presented me with the Noble Gift Philanthropreneur Award at a ceremony in London. I would never know whether she would be romantically interested, but I was too late. She had met the Mexican businessman, Jose Baston, who she's now happily married to. I'd also always enjoyed the company of Liz Hurley, but then what man wouldn't? Liz was polite, but made it clear by text that she wasn't interested. 'You don't know what you're missing, Liz,' I laughed to myself at the brush-off.

I threw myself into other things. I was invited to join Prince Albert of Monaco on a charity cycle ride. I accepted, though I had no time to train for the ride from Saint-Tropez to Monte Carlo. My schedule was tight as my flight arrived in Nice at 2am and then I had to travel to Saint-Tropez. I got up after three hours sleep for an 80-mile ride that started at 7am.

'Good,' I thought to myself as I calculated my rather punishing schedule. It would leave me with little time to dwell on my emotional turmoil. I'd have to focus on making my flight connections, the race, my bike and the road. It was exactly what I needed.

Up at day break, and off with another hundred riders, and no lack of testosterone. It felt good to be breathing in the air, getting my muscles working and my legs moving like pistons as I gained ground through some of the slower riders.

About 15 miles in I started catching up with a group of riders sheltering in the slipstream of a Renault van. There were about a dozen fit young guys taking it really easy. As I caught up, I saw amidst the crowd, a little blonde ponytail peeping out from the mass of multi-coloured polycarbonate helmets. The little blonde ponytail was right at the head of the pack.

I cycled faster. My mission was to get up to Ponytail. Within seconds her slim, athletic figure was within my sights. I weaved through the crowd of men, squeezing them out of the way one by one, until we were parallel. She glanced over at me and I saw her young, smiling, pretty face. 'Hi, I'm John,' I said.

'Modesta,' she answered. Then she faced forward to the road, head down. She was polite, there was a little smile on her face but I wasn't sure whether my interruption was welcome. Undeterred, I carried on chatting but she was too young for me and in any event they were all going too slow, so after a few minutes I pulled away, passed the van and carried on. Thirty minutes later we stopped for breakfast and I settled down at a table with a friend. A few minutes later I spotted the ponytail come in with her friend, Inga. 'Ladies, would you like to join us?' I said standing up. I wasn't really giving them any option, but they seemed happy enough to accept my somewhat commanding invitation and sat down.

Now, at this point I was merely intrigued by this clearly gifted, pretty cyclist. You don't get many girls in the cycling world who look like Modesta; I wanted to know more. Talented people fascinate me, and there also was something about her that I couldn't quite work out.

I found out a lot of facts about Modesta Vzesniauskaite over that breakfast. She was Lithuanian, 30 years old, had represented her country at the Beijing Olympics in 2008, and had raced all over the world as one of the top five female riders. She was number one in her own country and had an incredibly impressive record as a competitive cyclist.

'Do you still compete?' I asked her.

'No,' she answered. 'I got pregnant a few years ago and I have a son called Leonado, so I'm just working in Monaco.'

I scanned her left hand for a wedding ring or an engagement ring. Nothing. We carried on talking and she explained how she was getting divorced and going through a terrible time. I nodded. I was listening to her as she spoke but I was also paying attention to the fact that she would bite her lip every now and again, and clench her hands together as she talked.

I knew what my heartbreak felt like, and I could see this woman was suffering. I felt very sorry for her. She was so young, so talented and cheerful, and yet the underlying sadness was all too obvious.

I left that ride with mixed emotions and actually a little bruised. In the last few minutes I fell from my bike. I looked up from my rather ignominious position in the road to see the blonde ponytail bobbing in the distance shouting back, 'Are you OK?' I bravely, but not truthfully, said, 'Yes I'm fine' – and she carried on cycling. She didn't look behind or wait for me. That night, all the cyclists were meant to meet at a bar. I had already said to Modesta I might see her there. However, for some reason I did not go. Years later she told me she had kept looking for me at the bar because I had managed to make an impression on her.

She told me, 'I thought who is this guy who pushed his way through all these other young men to talk to me and I was so disappointed not to see you. I thought that would be it.' So did I. I never imagined what was to come and how that blonde ponytail would change my life.

*****

I'D MET A few good people on that ride. One of them was a man named Richard Hadfield, who worked at Barclays in Monaco and he turned out to be a good friend of Modesta. We got on well and cycled together quite a bit on that ride, fixed punctures, swapped numbers and I told him that next time I was in the south of France I would invite him on the boat for dinner and we would do a ride together with Modesta and Inga.

Sometime later I invited Richard and the girls, but he was on his way to South Africa, so I asked him to pass on the invite to Modesta and Inga, whose contact details I did not have. And that was how Modesta and I got in touch with each other and she accepted my invitation on the boat. Before the dinner we did a couple of cycle trips together.

On one trip, Modesta and I had been cycling for a while, stopping for a coffee, which on her insistence she paid for.

After a few hours cycling and chatting we were getting on extremely well. She clearly liked me. I told myself this was only ever going to be a friendship. Both our situations were too complicated and we could just have a nice time as pals. 'Do you want to play bike wars?' I asked her as I spotted a suitable battlefield, which was actually just a car park. She looked confused.

'Bike wars?'

'Yes, it's a game I created where the sole objective is to cause the other opponents to have to put their foot down, by jamming them in a corner they can't get out of. The first person to put their foot down on the ground is the loser.'

'OK,' she said, clearly humouring me, and as I found out later, going easy on me. She was obviously thinking, 'This amateur must be kidding'.

Of course, I had an unfair advantage. This is a favourite game of mine, and I am quite good at it. I've played it with my brother and lots of my friends. But Modesta was up for the challenge. First go, I won. Second try, she lost balance in seconds. I saw her jaw clench and her fists grip the handlebars.

'Best of ten,' I said, and laughed.

Every game I won Modesta became less humouring and more competitive, though try as she might, it made no difference.

I hit a perfect ten within 20 minutes. Modesta had failed to score. I was laughing to myself, thinking a 61-year-old had beaten a 30-year-old Olympic cyclist at a playground scrap game. On the way back we stopped at the top of a hill and, in the gap between two blocks of apartments, there on the glistening Mediterranean ocean, I spotted my boat. We were side-by-side on our bikes. I put my arm on her shoulder. 'Look,' I said. 'That's my boat.'

Her eyes focused on my stunning Titania, and underneath my arm I felt her whole body clench. I knew instantly that she did not like my embrace. Though I did not know it at the time, and not that I was, but this girl didn't want some great big show-boating rich guy trying to impress her. This girl was different. And that was trouble. The more I knew her, the more her values impressed me and the more my thoughts turned to romance.

*****

OF COURSE I was being completely ridiculous. Modesta was less than half my age, even a few years younger than my eldest daughter. What was I thinking? On top of that, she was in the midst of a very messy and emotional divorce and custody battle, and I was still reeling from the end of my relationship with Claire. We had everything against us. Modesta didn't even speak fluent English while my French wasn't great, and my Lithuanian non-existent. She lived in Cap d'Ail and I lived hundreds of miles away in Staffordshire. Her life revolved around her little boy, Leonardo, and there was nothing tangible to suggest she had any romantic feelings for me at all. We were a world apart, very different people but, somehow, we seemed to have a mutually strong connection.

I'd learnt more and more about Modesta over the months we'd got to know each other. And, as unlikely as it seems, there was a strange similarity in certain aspects of our backgrounds.

Modesta had grown up under a strict communist Russian regime until Lithuania gained its independence in 1990. She understood what it was to have a tough upbringing. With two older brothers and a younger sister, her family had struggled financially. Her mum worked as a dressmaker and her father a skilled watch repairer, but when the country opened up and cheap watches from China became available, his business began to fail.

There was no room for even small luxuries in Modesta's childhood. Like my own family, it was all about working hard to live a frugal life.

Her mother was a strict Roman Catholic, so their moral upbringing was hugely important to the family.

Very sadly, Modesta's father fell into a depression after the failure of his business. As a young girl, she'd had a close relationship with her dad up until this point, but she struggled with the ways in which depression changed the man she loved. I knew exactly what it was like to have a difficult relationship with a father.

Like me, Modesta was born with a competitive grit inside her. One of her older brothers had a bike and she started cycling, beating other kids in her neighbourhood. She knew her mother's cousin was a medal-winning cyclist and – although she'd never seen him race – that was her inspiration.

When she was 11, her brother entered her name for a local bike competition. 'I beat everyone easily,' she told me with pride. 'There were sports coaches at the race, and they came to my family and said I had a chance to be very good if they agreed for me to go to a special school to be trained.'

I remember asking her what type of bike she had, and she replied, 'One of those little fold-up bikes with no gears. Some of the other competitors had proper racing bikes. I'd never even seen them before.'

She was sent to a boarding school for talented young athletes who coaches believed would one day represent their country. They all had to be extremely disciplined, eat the right food, get up early and push themselves harder and harder in training. She shared a dormitory with other girls and most of them cried every night because they were so homesick. Modesta, meanwhile, was determined to work as hard as she could to be the best. When she was 16, her parents divorced.

'Everything fell to pieces,' she told me. 'Things got harder for my mum and I felt it was up to me to earn money to support everyone.

So I had to do well with cycling. I felt responsible for everyone.' Again, as a child, I'd had similar feelings.

Her skill and determination were evident, and Modesta found herself in bidding wars between different cycling organisations and on the Olympic team for her country. But being an attractive woman in this environment was tough. Various people higher up the cycling chain would try and pressure her into having sex, and she was discriminated against for refusing. She was deliberately overlooked or given lesser quality bikes. She refused to use any performance enhancing drugs but was still a formidable cyclist who competed and won at the highest levels.

When she talked, I felt incredibly angry at the perpetrators and very protective towards her. It was despicable that a woman should be preyed upon and punished for refusing to compromise her morals, and even worse to be bullied into sexual submission. She told me how she'd had a chance to train in America.

America changed everything for Modesta. Years earlier she had been told by doctors it would be impossible for her to become pregnant. But after a few weeks in America her ex-boyfriend came out to her uninvited and they got back together for a few weeks. She knew he was not right for her, so finished the relationship and sent him back home.

Then she discovered she was pregnant. For the sake of her unborn child and her Catholic family, she married her boyfriend. They moved to Monaco, where he grew up, but very soon after the wedding she knew she'd made a huge mistake. The marriage fell apart in a pretty horrible way followed by a rather traumatic divorce.

Now she was dealing with the aftermath of that divorce and trying to make a life for herself and her son. All her aspirations of a life in professional cycling had been set aside and she moved to Cap d'Ail, on the border of Monaco and found a job working as a receptionist in a spa then in a small Kindergarten club. She never complained, never asked me for help, and I found myself opening up to her about what I'd been through. We were both, in our own ways, wounded.

And then something happened after a few weeks had passed. We got caught in torrential rain on another bike ride and ran to find shelter under a huge tree. The rain didn't stop, we were soaked and freezing. I saw her shivering and gently – conscious of what had happened last time – I put my arm around her and drew her towards me. She didn't flinch. I held her in a warm embrace, which she gradually reciprocated.

Once the rain stopped we rode towards the seafront in Nice. The sun came out and we laughed as we basked in the warmth. She was smiling at me and slowly I put one hand on her face, then the other, and kissed her on the lips. I no longer cared about the age difference, what other people thought, about the language difference or the complications. All I felt was attraction and warmth.

*****

I STOOD IN Modesta's kitchen, surveying the scene. There wasn't a great deal to look at, as the entire room was not much bigger than the size of an average breakfast table. The tiny sink was crammed with dishes, multiple extension plugs rammed in two small sockets, an oven and one or two cupboards filled with pans and crockery.

The whole flat was miniscule, around 600 square feet with no air conditioning and in the summer months it was unbearably hot. The whole space consisted of a bedroom, lounge and bathroom, and all of it would have fitted into just one room of my house in Broughton.

But Modesta didn't want me helping her out or moving her to somewhere more comfortable. It had been a struggle enough to persuade her to let me order a dishwasher for her, after I'd found a space under the sink one could fit into. I'd got the specifications and tracked down the exact model that could work, which would make life a little easier.

The deal was that if I came to stay with her in that tiny apartment in Cap d'Ail, I would stay there with her and Leonardo regardless of whether I had my luxurious boat with me or the fact I could afford for us all to stay in a grand house or a five-star hotel. And, if her mum, Danguole, was staying, Modesta and I would share the sofa bed in the living room, while Leonardo slept in the bedroom with his grandmother.

That was fine by me. In fact, it was more than fine. Bar the heat and the cramped space, I liked being part of this little family unit. I liked cooking, I liked sorting the tangle of wires and plugs in the kitchen into something that resembled a more streamlined solution. But that night, as I looked at the postage stamp-sized area where I always felt like a mighty giant attempting to cook with child-sized equipment, I had a better idea. I was going to take her out to a beautiful restaurant.

Kate's beautiful villa was not far from Modesta's home, and a wonderful guy called Jean-Paul worked, along with his lovely late wife Michele, as her gardener and housekeeper. Jean-Paul is a marvellous character with a great big beard, and an occasional scent of whiskey on his breath. He used to pick me up from the airport and regularly lent me his very scruffy old Renault Espace.

There's a fabulous hotel with a Michelin-starred restaurant, La Chèvre d'Or, in Eze on the Côte d'Azur. It's a beautiful rocky outcrop overlooking the blue Med with incredible gardens filled with jasmine, bougainvillea, roses, fountains and little waterfalls. The food is delicious, the view spectacular and the atmosphere incredibly old-school romantic. I wanted – just for one night – to spoil Modesta.

'I'm taking you out tonight,' I told her on the phone. 'Put on a nice dress and I'll pick you up after work.'

But, what was I going to do about the car? I knew Modesta was very easy going but this car really was disgusting. The seats were dog chewed, covered in straw and various other bits of gardening debris, and the footwells were filled with all sorts of things I didn't even want to imagine. I cleared what I could and put a cover over the front seat.

Modesta looked amazing in a black evening dress. It was the first time I'd seen her in anything other than cycling gear or a gym outfit. She took my breath away. I hastily threw a rug over the front passenger seat and we chuckled as the pair of us drove out to this stunning restaurant in our skip on wheels. We laughed even harder when I handed the keys to the parking valet outside the restaurant. The car was probably worth less than the smallest bill at this place so goodness knows what his thoughts were – probably that we would end up doing the dishes!

As the months went by, I continued to learn more and more about Modesta. After two years together, she eventually met my family and they all got to know each other. One of the first times she came over to London was when the whole family, including Kate, was in my house in Mayfair. All of us had just been diagnosed with Lyme Disease and were linked up to IV drips. Modesta just got on with everyone and fitted right in.

The more I got to know her, the more I loved and admired her. I also got to know that black dress well. Every time we went somewhere special, or she accompanied me to an event, out came the little black dress. It was, she then told me, the only dress she owned.

'I'm going to take you dress shopping,' I told her.

She rolled her eyes. 'No, John, it's fine. I hate shopping,' she said.

We went to the designer quarter of Nice. We had coffee, went in and out of shops but came home empty-handed. She was just not interested. On another occasion we ended up looking at art galleries instead of shops. I realised later that her whole life had been focused on training and racing, no social occasions, nothing to dress for. Then, after her split, she had to fight like fury just to survive so fancy clothes and fancy shops were an irrelevance to her. It took me three years and a Caudwell charity ball before I finally persuaded her to allow me to design and make a dress for her. 'It's a huge event, Modesta,' I explained. 'Everyone will be dressed up to the nines and I'd love to see you looking fabulous.'

'Okay John. If it makes you happy,' she said. It did. In fact, it gave me a mission to design a perfect dress for her. I consulted with the tailor who makes all my evening jackets and came up with a classic, figure-hugging nude voile dress, which accentuated her body shape, was super sexy but still modest enough for her to wear.

Over the years, I have persuaded her to be more glamorous and to enjoy getting dressed up and showing off what a beautiful young woman she is. She is still, however, most at home on her bike, in her cycling gear, conquering the mountains and enjoying the scenery, which is, again, something that makes me very happy.

She is also the mother of my sixth child, my beautiful son, William John Caudwell, and has put so much of her passion into her role as Charity Ambassador for Caudwell Children. She is the driving force behind our charity bike rides and the Monaco Butterfly Ball

And as for the black dress; well, it's still part of my happiest memories.

Chapter 30

A MODERN FAMILY

'DAD, I WANT you to stop giving me an allowance.'

It was the winter of 2012 and my daughter Libby had asked me if we could have a serious chat. At the time, she was not long out of university and was trying to work out what she wanted to do in life.

I knew she was finding her way. She was living in London, writing articles for newspapers and magazines. She'd also done a small amount of modelling and acting but hadn't found anything she felt that absolutely fitted her as a career. In order to give her a financial cushion I was providing her with £1,200-a-month and she was also living with Rebekah so she didn't have to pay any rent.

But Libby has always been a sensitive, exceptionally thoughtful girl, and I knew she had issues with her situation. Let's face it, on a lot of levels it cannot be easy being a child of mine. By that, I mean the child of a man who has made £1.46 billion by building a business, a man whose name is often linked to money in the press.

Although on paper Libby does belong to that rare group of 'billionaire daughters' whose members in this country includes Tamara Ecclestone and Chloe Green, she has very little in common with those ladies or that lifestyle (in fact she wrote a very good article published in a magazine on the subject). Libby, like Rebekah, is old enough to remember times when there wasn't much money in the Caudwell family. She's too young to remember the days of the used car sales lot where Kate and Rebekah would often come down to say hello but she still remembers our holidays in the south of France where we all slept in the car for a couple of nights in order to save money, and many of her clothes were hand-me-downs.

She'd had a good and pretty expensive education. We lived in an incredible house and she was 12 when I bought my first boat, the Rubekian – that was a rich man's toy but it was still a novelty and all of them had to pitch in as crew. Libby was 18-years-old – a young adult – when I sold my business. Then everything changed. My name was in *The Sunday Times* Rich List and *Forbes* magazine. Money, a lot of money, a hell of a lot of money was now part of our family and the Caudwell name. The result of a lifetime of hard work and ambition for me, but being the daughters of a billionaire was a strange thing for my eldest children to get used to.

Of course it was wonderful in so many ways. Leona Lewis came to perform for Libby's 21st birthday party and it was a spectacular night for her and all her friends. They would accompany me to fabulous balls, wearing exquisite dresses they picked out with Claire (who only bought the best of everything). They would be introduced to the likes of Elton and Hugh Grant, have wonderful holidays, and know – because it was all over the newspapers – that their dad could afford to pay any bill. But neither of them had been born into money and they were still conflicted because they'd grown up with a dad who hated waste, knew the price of a pint of milk in the Happy Shopper and who had worked like a demon to create this wealth.

But Libby, when we talked that day, told me she also felt a lot of guilt. She had done nothing to earn this money, she didn't even know exactly what she wanted to do. I was providing so much for her and – although she knew I never had and never would – she put a sense of expectation and pressure on herself.

'So Dad,' she said, 'I've decided to travel and work to pay my rent and my bills. I need to know I can support myself and give myself time to think about what I'm going to do in life.'

My own feelings were conflicted. I felt partly proud, partly anxious, partly sad but mainly I simply wanted my Libby to know that I would listen to her, support her, be there for her and just love her with every ounce of my being, no matter what she wanted to do.

I also felt guilt. As I listened to Libby, I understood exactly what she was saying. I'd seen children of friends of mine who had access to as much money as they wanted, spending thousands on clothes they'd wear just once, or on cars that would be damaged within weeks. I never wanted that for my children. I'd witnessed a sort of aimlessness among these very rich children. Lots of them did nothing week-in week-out, and I didn't want that life for my kids. Libby was given a First Class degree in English Literature at Bristol University and one of her tutors had told me how exceptionally gifted she was. That had made me unbelievably proud of her.

I wanted them to have enough to be safe, not to have to worry about hailing a cab in the middle of the night or buying groceries. I also wanted them to know the value of money and to have a sense of self. Lots of my friends thought I was terribly mean for giving my children a very modest allowance but now I was concerned that even this relatively small amount of money had caused Libby to feel the way she did.

'No Dad,' she said. 'I just feel I need to do this. For myself.' I told her I would do exactly as she asked, but – wherever she was, whatever time of day or night – to call me if she needed anything. 'Yes Dad,' she said, and smiled. 'But I have to learn to stand on my own two feet.' I look back on that conversation 10 years later and I feel humbled by Libby, by Kate because there is so much of Kate in Libby, and by the fact that I raised this girl who has such conscience, integrity and self-awareness.

She did go off. She went to Australia and worked in a beachside hotel organising activities. It changed her life. She met the man she later married, the skipper of one of the boats she took guests for tours in, Simon Morgan, who set up a thriving yacht charter company. She is now a mother to baby Moses and has a doctorate in clinical psychotherapy and she remains my kind, sensitive, wonderful daughter.

*****

THIS CONVERSATION WITH Libby only served to reinforce my decision not to leave all my money to my children. I am grateful to have more than enough money to provide for my family, but equally grateful that I can use my wealth to change the lives of ill and suffering people, especially children. I never wanted my own children to be spoilt with wealth and materialism.

There are many who think this is unfair. I am not one of them. I know what it is like to have nothing. And I also know what it is like to have enough money to buy anything. Money solves problems, like being able to put a roof over your head, and I can – and do – treat myself to some incredible cars, boats and motorbikes. But it doesn't change who you are on the inside. And I don't believe having huge amounts of money to spend on yourself is a good thing.

I never wanted my children to feel under pressure. There was no pressure to join my business and no thought in my head to keep it in the family. There was one occasion Rebekah remembers when she was nine or ten years old I asked her to do a little business negotiation for me. It was for something like ordering paper for the office and I asked her to get me the best deal. 'I was terrified,' she told me years later. 'But I did it and I think I got a reasonably good deal.' She did.

She was a natural but I knew the stress my business involved and I didn't want that for anyone else unless they really wanted it. Rebekah's heart lay elsewhere. Like Libby, she travelled, teaching English in

India and Art History in Italy for several years, before returning and setting up an interior design and property development company in London and then New York. This was joined and expanded by her husband Nicolas Dupart, who had migrated from a successful career in the Mad Men world of NYC Advertising.

I have never believed in trusts funds or limitless credit cards, but I have always believed in people finding their own way. My philosophy is very much to encourage my children to forge their own success and happiness, even though that will undoubtedly involve much more modest levels of wealth creation.

Money needs to serve a purpose. Apart from that one incident in my past when I was badly advised by accountants, I have never shirked my taxes. I have a home in Monaco but it is in Britain that I pay my taxes. I believe in Britain because it is an amazing country. It is where I made my money. I want it to remain great and have the best education system, the best health service, social services and to have the best economic success.

But I also feel that extremely wealthy individuals like myself should do more with their money. If you are worth a billion you can still leave millions to your children, but you can also leave huge amounts to charity to help transform the lives of people with traumatic health challenges.

I had long since pledged to give half of my wealth to charity, so in 2013 it was a simple decision to be the first Briton to sign up to Bill Gates and Warren Buffett's Giving Pledge, which calls on billionaires to commit at least half their wealth to charity during their lifetime. I went further than that. Seven years ago or so I met Bill Gates at a restaurant in London with other potential pledgers to see how we might work together to help encourage other wealthy British and European individuals to do the same and it's a drum I keep banging.

I was really impressed by Bill. He is unassuming, understated but he has a firm handshake, looks you in the eye and is intellectually rigorous and very well informed. The dinner was very straightforward, he talked, we listened. It wasn't about small talk or getting to know each other, it was purely about the pledge. When he had finished talking, he paid the bill and left. No nonsense, just business. I liked his approach.

In 2019, I upped the amount I was leaving from 50 percent to 70 percent. We've gone through the toughest year in decades thanks to Covid-19 and charities need all the help they can get.

I have made plans for my future. My children may not have been involved with my business but all of them have always been involved in my charity. When I die, they will become trustees of that charity and of the remains of my wealth and I have written a letter of wishes advising them how to use that money for the benefit of society. One thing I do know is that for me and many people like me, there is far more pleasure in giving than receiving.

*****

I AM OFTEN asked the question by interviewers, 'What is your proudest achievement?' I know the answer that is expected of me. 'Coming from nothing and making a business worth more than a billion.' It is an answer I never give because it is not true. Money makes you rich, but in my case it doesn't make me proud. Building a business made me proud because it was the fulfilment of a childhood dream. But it is not my proudest achievement.

There is only one answer to that question. My family. I have three daughters and three sons. My perfect half dozen. I cannot even claim full credit for this achievement. My children are incredible individuals in their own right. Rebekah is one of the most selfless women I know. Libby has extraordinary empathy. Scarlett has a natural, pure sweetness. Jacobi has great character. And my darling, talented Rufus has taught me again and again over these terrible years what it means to be a father. As for the baby boy I now hold in my arms, well, maybe one day he will win the Tour de France. I don't know. All I do know is that at 68, I was given the precious gift of another life.

I never expected to become a father again but over the years Modesta and I have talked. It was important to her and what is important to her is important to me. It wasn't an entirely straightforward process. Modesta was concerned she had fertility issues after years of competitive cycling and having a very low weight so we went to see an amazing guy called Dr Taranissi at the ARGC clinic in London.

All was well. Then one morning I woke up in Broughton and there was a little box on my pillow. Modesta was smiling. 'Open it John,' she said. Inside was a pregnancy stick with a blue line for positive. We both then laughed, she cried and that was it... baby number six was on his way.

It's definitely different being an older father. I'm more present in his life than I was with my others because I'm not so frantic with work. I saw his first steps, I see those little changes – new words – week by week and that is very precious to me. And he's my absolute Mini-Me. I tell people, 'Don't worry, he's got time for those looks to change.'

William will not be spoilt. None of my children are. I think spoiling a child with anything other than love is a sure route to a fiasco. I believe in love, discipline, clear rules and fairness – my own father was never fair with me and I never felt loved by him so it's hugely important for me to make my children feel they are each loved and valued equally.

But I am a logical man and the fact is that William has an older father. I've come to terms with this in my head. If something happens to me, then I know that he will be looked after, loved and cared for by a wonderful mother and he will have a large family who will all be there for him. Modesta and I have already asked Rebekah and her husband Nick if they will bring William up if anything happens to both of us. I know they would be amazing parents, I know I have many safe hands around me and around my son.

Next to my children are the three women who are pivotal in my life: Kate my beloved ex-wife; the wonderful Claire, Jacobi's mum; and my amazing and beautiful Modesta, whose eldest son, Leo, I also regard as my child. My eldest daughters have married wonderful men in Nick and Simon. Then I am lucky to have my loyal, brilliant brother Brian and his wife Paula, who has been part of the family since she was a teenager and they are parents to four great kids. And, of course, there was my Mum. I appreciated every single one of the days we had together, and those wonderful big smiles she gave me.

There are various times in my life when I feel proud but really these are mostly related to family or charity achievements. People find it hard to believe, but we are an incredibly close and unified family and that includes all my ex-partners. At Christmas all of us spend time together, swapping presents, laughing, eating together and catching up. Scarlett's mum, Jane, is also included in major family events, which makes me happy because it makes Scarlett happy.

When I hear Kate chatting to Modesta, or I discover that Libby has been on the phone to Claire for advice, or Jacobi shows me a photo Kate has sent him of her dog, that is when I do feel quietly proud. In themselves these things aren't earth-shatteringly important but they are the daily humdrum proof that my family – despite all our massive ups and downs – works.

If I spend an hour talking to Jacobi about a bad day at school, listening to him go through what one teacher said about an essay and why he fell out with a boy in his class, I will listen carefully and talk things through with him. When he then signals the end of our chat with a casual, 'Anyway Dad, I'm going to go on my Xbox now', I do feel grateful, not just because we've had a good chat and he's calmed down, but because he chose to tell me about his bad day. I never had those little conversations with my dad when I was 16 or 17. I would never have dreamt of it and he would never have listened.

And then there have been slightly more sinister incidents. I remember an occasion years ago when I was with Claire, and a tabloid reporter turned up on Kate's doorstep. He said his editor had heard she had been badly treated by me and they wanted to hear her side of the story. She sent the guy away with a flea in his ear and called me afterwards to tell me about it, laughing, 'Can you believe the cheek of it?'

Of course I could. I know plenty of high-profile friends who have ended up in the press due to their family rifts and fall-outs. I have many friends who don't speak to their ex-wives or who don't see various children from one month to the next and whose Christmases, Easters and summer holidays have to be organised with military precision so that partners and ex-partners' paths don't cross. It's always a huge source of anxiety, guilt and grief. I have had enough of that in my life. In business I could walk away from partnerships, betrayals and splits without so much as a backward glance. In my personal life, however traumatic my relationships have become, I have to try to resolve things.

I am never going to pretend this has been easy. When a massive relationship ends sadly – as it has done twice in my life – there is a process to recovery. You keep talking, you remember that together you have children – or a child – and that is what comes first. You both share a love and a history which neither of you will ever forget and you remain in your present and your future forever linked, so try to honour that and make it work.

Friends tell me I have been 'lucky' with the women I have had relationships with. Again, I will say I am not a lucky man. But I have always chosen well and known that Kate, Claire and Modesta do not have a petty or mean bone in their bodies. Kate and I were just kids when we got together but I knew even then she was an incredibly special woman. With both Claire and Modesta it has always been the deal from the outset that family comes first. Actually, that was something they both found attractive about me. If a man or woman wants his new partner to meet his exes, then, awkward though it might be at first, it shows how family is his real priority and loyalty is paramount. At least that's how I see it.

*****

I THINK BACK to my upbringing and realise it was my grandma who first taught me about helping people. Although she was often nasty to my mother, I think that was driven by the circumstance they were in. But I suppose no matter how much good any of us do for other people, there is always a time when we don't behave as we would like to. That certainly applies to me. I am aware of my faults and my mistakes and I do try to make certain that I live by kindness and wanting the best for people. That is the driving force behind all my charitable work.

Caudwell Children – which has a huge centre in Stoke – helps children in dire medical need, whatever their illness. Before the pandemic we were helping over 6,000 children a year whose parents don't have the financial ability to help themselves. In some cases, that help completely transforms their lives; in others, it makes their lives more bearable, while for some it can make their dying wishes come true.

My hope for Caudwell Children is that eventually we will help every eligible child in Britain, and in other countries, if I can find like-minded individuals to help me. My work does extend to many other causes, from AIDS in Africa via Elton John's AIDS Foundation, to being the major donor for the Bomber Command Memorial in Green Park, London.

Other major causes I work with are ARK and The Prince's Trust, and in recent years – prompted by family reasons closer to home – I've put a lot of time and money into research and awareness for Lyme Disease and PANS/PANDAS.

I recently received an incredible letter from the research team at Stanford Hospital, one of the leading centres for PANS/PANDAS in the world, saying the money I had given, 'Has been critical to finding the root cause of PANS/PANDAS that will allow us to devise better treatment strategies. This research is key to bringing PANS/PANDAS to national attention as an established disease and is now inspiring research at many centres'. If people ask what makes me happy, it is not walking in to a Michelin-starred restaurant but opening a letter like that.

My message to those who have not yet found philanthropy is that they may well find that it becomes a drug that gives far more pleasure and spiritual satisfaction than the creation of wealth, or the spending of it.

What also really makes me proud is that my passion has become my family's passion and helping others has brought all of us so much closer together.

What drives me on is that there is a world out there in desperate need and there is still so much more I feel I need to do.

ADDENDUM

A CAUDWELL CHILD (AND HER MUM)

By Tilly Griffiths

IN MY FIRST few months at Stanford University, in the heart of sunny California, I got a WhatsApp message from John Caudwell.

'Hi Tilly, I'm in your area. Fancy meeting up for a cup of coffee?'

'There's a Starbucks in my student union,' I replied. 'Can we meet there?'

We did. He cycled the ten miles to Silicon Valley, where Stanford is based, and I made my way the few hundred yards from my room to the Starbucks. Thinking about it now, it probably took us the same amount of time to get there.

But we sat in the sunshine for two or three hours and caught up about our families, life, and my degree course, in Political Science and Communications. Every now and again, John would help me lift my coffee cup to my mouth because he knows that, although I'm a double honours student from Staffordshire in a very prestigious American university, I can't always do simple things, such as lifting a coffee cup to my mouth. I need help with things like that. And ever since I was a baby, John has been in my life to help.

I don't know John Caudwell as an extraordinary businessman who built up a company from nothing to one worth more than a billion pounds. I don't know him as the flamboyant or politically-opinionated man that you might see in the press or on television. I know him as John, the man who changed my life.

To be honest, I've never really thought until now about how I do think of John. I was just four when I first met him, when he invited me, my sister, Candice and my mum and dad to Broughton. I don't even remember John so much then as Rufus because I spent the afternoon racing through rooms with him and Candice. I was in my high-tech, super-nifty wheelchair that had transformed me from a completely immobile, entirely dependent baby into a child who could join in with others, do things for herself and actually have a lot of fun.

I didn't realise it then, but it was John's charity, Caudwell Children, that provided me with the wheelchair that revolutionised my childhood, and gave my family hope for a real future for me. That day in Broughton my mum sat next to John on the settee and cried. I didn't have a clue why. I was having a blast racing round this enormous house and I'd found an amazing new friend in Rufus. I didn't know then, didn't comprehend then, that I had been diagnosed with spinal muscular atrophy and that my muscles were so weak I would never walk or move independently, and that doctors had told my parents I might only have a few years to live. My quality of life had been predicted to be little to non-existent.

Those doctors were right about my muscles but have been proved wrong on every other count. I have been given the most incredible help which hasn't just enabled me to move independently but has also given me strength, confidence, ambition, joy and a desire to push myself further and achieve greater goals. And to help other people like me, because I know the real value of having someone in your corner.

John and the Caudwell Children charity have been as much a

part of my life as my incredible sister, my love of fashion and my disability. They are family. I know his children. Rebekah has come to see me in California, too. You don't think about it as a child, but as an adult I know that I would not be studying at Stanford – and now temporarily (because of Covid-19) – at Magdalen College, Oxford. I would not be planning to move on to study law and to become a human rights lawyer. I would not be sitting talking to a man like John who instead of looking worried and telling me they are not sure it will be possible, says, 'That's great Tilly. You'll be brilliant at that.'

My life isn't particularly easy. You wouldn't believe the amount of stuff I need just for one overnight stay, from a special mattress to breathing equipment to ramps, carers and all sorts of things too long to list. I have been hospitalised innumerable times and seen endless reports on the life expectancy of people with spinal muscular atrophy, but you know what, it's still my life and I'm going to make the best of it.

Maybe something of John's attitude has just become part of who I am. Keep going, push to be your best and never short-change your dreams. I've been skiing, rock climbing, ice-skating and sailing. I haven't done any of those things the way girls without my disability would do them, but I've still done them, still felt the wind in my hair at the top of the Roaches in the Peak District.

When I was at secondary school, my classmates started hanging out together in town and at weekends. I couldn't and I went through a period of feeling isolated and lonely. I didn't have a social life and there was really nothing I could do about it.

I thought about it. I had other things. Since I was eight years old I had been invited to speak at the Caudwell Children Ball, and had the satisfaction of fundraising through public speaking. I had incredible people around me, from my own family to people I had met through

Caudwell Children, and I refused to give into any form of self-pity. It was then that I decided that was just the way things were and instead I would focus on studying hard in my after-school time.

At that time, I was a huge fan of High School Musical and the idea of Stanford came into my mind. I did really well at school, achieving all A-stars, and the plan I made at eleven has become the reality I live in today.

I cannot imagine how my life would have been if it hadn't been for John and Caudwell Children. I really can't. I've been to balls, I've heard amazing people talk, I've written a book and had unbelievable experiences and opportunities thanks to this incredible charity and extraordinary man.

If I am an example of a Caudwell child then I am so very proud to have that honour. It's given me something to live up to and a confidence and a belief that even if I can't lift a cup of coffee it doesn't matter. I know a man who will help me. And next I want to help change the world to become a better place for others living with disability like me.

*****

By Jackie Griffiths

I ALWAYS KNEW there was something wrong with my beautiful baby girl, Tilly. She was sweet and lovely but she didn't hit the same marks as her older sister, Candice. Doctors told me not to worry, until our GP finally also realised that she wasn't right.

Back then, twenty years ago, it took a long time to get a diagnosis. We went to a specialist in Manchester and then months later my husband, Rolf and I, sat in his office where we first heard the words,

'Spinal Muscular Atrophy'. Those words were swiftly followed by a statement, 'This child won't see her second birthday.'

There are few words to describe what happened next. Devastation, blackness, a fall into bottomless despair. A bombardment of bleak and brutal medical appointments. We had no experience of disability. Rolf and I ran a bed-and-breakfast in a small village in Staffordshire. We had no idea what we were going to do. There seemed to be no hope and we had no clue about finding help for our little girl.

I felt, in those first few months after her diagnosis, as if we were living in a dark cave. Then after one hospital visit, a leading paediatric neurologist took one look at Tilly, who I'd propped into a seated position with the help of cushions and said, 'Ahh, she's a Type Two...'

I looked at her blankly, and then said, 'Does that mean we can keep her?'

She smiled and nodded. 'All you need to think of is independent mobility and mainstream education.'

I walked out of there, feeling on cloud nine. A light – as dim as it was – had been switched on for me. I felt we could leave our dark cave. I had a tiny photo frame which I'd bought to give to Rolf with a picture of Tilly. Instead I wrote in it the words, 'We can do this.'

Of course, I didn't know exactly what we were going to do. But I was now focused on finding what I could do to make life easier. There were lots of places and lots of waiting lists. 'Yes, you can have a supportive buggy. We'll add you to the waiting list,' I'd hear. The waiting lists were 14 months and upwards. So I went to local radio stations, who helped me raise money. And then the landlord of a local pub told me about a man called John Caudwell. 'He runs a charity for children. You should get in touch with him...'

Tilly was now two-and-a-half-years-old, but she wasn't really talking. We had to carry her everywhere. She couldn't do anything for herself. In my head I could hear the doctor's advice, 'independent mobility' and, finally, I found a perfect, tiny wheelchair. 'It's £11,500,' I told my husband. He buried his face in his hands, feeling wretched because we simply couldn't afford it.

Finally, I remembered what I'd been told by the landlord and I approached Caudwell Children. They made an appointment to come round and meet Tilly and I spoke with their specialist about the wheelchair. There was no waiting list. Within weeks it was delivered.

It was incredible the difference this wheelchair made. Tilly mastered the controls almost immediately, and soon she was whirring about the house.

She started really engaging, laughing... All of a sudden, the real, fun-loving, clever, incredible Tilly was born. And thanks to the wheelchair she could join her sister at the local nursery school – the first key step in her mainstream education.

John asked if he could meet us. He didn't ask for just me and Tilly, he invited the whole family to his house in Broughton. That made me want to cry because I knew it meant he realised that a disability doesn't just affect a child; it affects every single person in the family – and the extended family. Everyone becomes part of the story.

Of course, we all gasped when we arrived at Broughton. It was nothing like we'd ever known. Amazing cars in the driveway, suits of armour in the hall. But John – sitting on a settee in his living room with his little boy, Rufus – couldn't have seemed more down to earth. The kids immediately started playing and I went and sat with John. He asked me questions no-one had really asked about me, Candice and Rolf, as well as Tilly. I spent an hour crying and telling him things I'd never really told anyone. We also laughed. I felt like I was talking to my big brother.

That wheelchair turned Tilly from a helpless child into a little girl. It's impossible to overplay what a difference that independence made to her. We watched our daughter flower in front of our eyes.

We felt that not only could we do this, but we were going to do this and that we were not alone.

Over the years John and Caudwell Children were there when we needed help; equipment, advice, someone to talk to or the opportunity to help someone else. We have dealt with many great charities over the years but there is a huge difference with John and his charity. He is about family and the charity is all about family. They don't just believe in supporting the child; they support and help rebuild all of you. And for me, personally, John gave me a voice.

He asked me to speak at events and conferences. I was asked to be part of committees and to help advise on various boards, as was Rolf. We felt incredibly valued and really part of something bigger. I'd go from cleaning toilets and changing beds in the B-and-B, to getting into a nice outfit and volunteering in the Caudwell Children offices where I feel I am doing a lot of good.

Candice, who is two years older than Tilly, was always included by John in trips to pantomimes, picnics, balls and events. So many siblings of severely disabled children are overlooked and they struggle with their own issues. Candice was part of the journey and that was never forgotten. That is a real example of dealing with people who really want to understand you as a family and understand how to treat absolutely everyone with dignity and kindness.

We are not, by any means, the only family he has helped. We are just one of thousands whose lives have been transformed. Sometimes I look at John, who gave us – and so many others – his time, his commitment and all the assistance from his charity, and I think, 'Why does he do this?' I know some of what he and his own family are going through with Rufus and how incredibly hard that is, but still he does all this for others. He absolutely doesn't need to but I know he wants to make a difference. And that overwhelms me. He's abseiled down the Shard, cycled thousands of miles to personally raise funds, often matching pound-for-pound any sponsorship. He is inspirational. He makes you feel that everything is possible, and you need that more than anything.

Today, I love giving talks. I feel so confident in what I know and what I have to offer, and I'm able to help other families who are in that darkness we found ourselves in at the beginning of this journey.

A few years ago, I was driving Tilly to sixth form college. We sat in the car and she said to me, 'I think people would imagine that if I was given a magic wand, I would take away my disability. But I am really happy with who I am.'

That was a moment I will remember forever. She has far exceeded any expectation. I have a daughter at Stanford and my eldest daughter, Candice, graduated from Cambridge University. We have a family motto, 'We will all settle, but only for the absolute best'.

It's hard to persuade people to give money to charity – especially in these hard times. There are so many in need and often you might question whether the money you give really does make a difference. But all I can tell anyone is that my family may never have survived without people like John and charity organisations like Caudwell Children.

I close my eyes and remember the darkness, the helplessness and the fear that could have destroyed us. And then I open them and see what we have become with help and assistance from incredible charities. All of us have become our best.

For that I am truly thankful. But I know there are other families out there with seriously-ill children, massively in need of help. I know John's charity and so many other charities need help to change the lives of others.

And I know that by continuing to support these charities in any way we can, it is the only way to make the world a better place.

ACKNOWLEDGEMENTS

In writing this autobiography I am very thankful to Brian Caudwell, Kate Caudwell, Rebekah Caudwell, Libby Caudwell, Rufus Caudwell, Scarlett Caudwell-Burgess, Jacobi Caudwell, Leo, Claire Johnson, Modesta Vzesniauskaite, Louise Gannon, Michele Owen, Claire Powell, Jane Burgess, Tilly Griffiths, Jackie Griffiths, Trudi Beswick, Chris Brereton, Michael McGuinness, Simon Monk, Paul Dove, Rick Cooke, Steve Hanrahan and to all those who have helped and supported me along the way. And my little post-script, William John Caudwell.